D1711473

Sir Philip Sidney

SIR PHILIP SIDNEY
Rebellion in Arcadia

Richard C. McCoy

Rutgers University Press
New Brunswick, New Jersey

Publication of this book was partially supported by a grant from the
American Council of Learned Societies to the Rutgers University Press
in recognition of its contribution to humanistic scholarship. The funds
were provided by the Andrew W. Mellon Foundation and are to be
applied to the publication of first and second books by scholars in the
humanities.

Quotations from *The Poems of Sir Philip Sidney,* edited by William A.
Ringler, Jr., © Oxford University Press 1962, and from *The Countess
of Pembroke's Arcadia* by Sir Philip Sidney, edited by Jean Robertson,
© Oxford University Press 1973, are reprinted by permission of
Oxford University Press.

Library of Congress Cataloging in Publication Data

McCoy, Richard C., 1946–
  Sir Philip Sidney: rebellion in Arcadia.

  Bibliography: p.
  Includes index.
    1. Sidney, Philip, Sir, 1554–1586. 2. Politics
in literature. 3. Poets, English—Early modern,
1500–1700—Biography.
PR2343.M3   821'.3   78–24220
ISBN 0–8135–0869–X

To Marsha and Kate
who waited

Contents

PREFACE

This book is a study of Sir Philip Sidney's major works of literature—*Astrophil and Stella* and the *Old* and *New Arcadia*—and their relationship to Elizabethan politics. The connection may at first glance seem tenuous. The prose works depict a world of pastoral retirement and romantic dalliance, and Astrophil dismisses the concerns of the court's "busie wits" to devote himself to love. Indeed, Sidney probably wrote much of his fiction during his own withdrawal from court. His sister's home at Wilton provided an idyllic escape from the difficulties of his political career. Yet politics still intrude, even in Arcadia. There are occasional topical allusions as well as speculative remarks about the problems of government. More pervasive still is an issue of fundamental importance to Sidney and his contemporaries: the relationship between sovereign and subject. In the *Old* and *New Arcadia*, romantic intrigue leads to a rebellious defiance of political authority. The sonnets' scope is more restricted, but the emphasis is still on sexual politics and the precarious balance of power between lover and beloved. All three works pose a series of deliberately sharpened conflicts between obedient submission to authority and the recalcitrant urges of desire, conflicts that Sidney never subdues or resolves.

Sidney's own difficulties with his sovereign, Queen Elizabeth, are well known, and I have found it appropriate to explore parallels between his heroes' predicaments and his own. Occasionally these parallels are stated in explicitly political terms. In the third book of the *New Arcadia*, Amphialus proclaims the autonomy of the subaltern magistrate, a doctrine of considerable interest to Renaissance aristocrats. Sidney was obviously intrigued with this theory because he was himself a frustrated subaltern, but its transparently subversive nature prompts him to drop the subject almost as soon as it comes up. His hero persists in his defiance of authority, but Amphialus's true motives are shown to be personal and emotional rather than political. This blurring of purpose is typical in Sidney's fiction, as the conflict between sovereign and subject frequently descends to a more covert psychological level. The shift in levels reflects several things: Sidney's ideological uncertainty about the legitimacy of self-assertion and autonomy is reinforced by feelings of guilt and ambivalence. The impact of these feelings on his literature is apparent in the recurrent pattern of contradiction and irresolution.

In order to understand this aspect of Sidney's literature, I have found it necessary to consider certain features of his life and historical situation. I focus primarily on his troublesome relationship with authority, and my analysis deals with its psychological as well as its political implications. This is not a complete biographical study because I do not think Sidney's difficulties are unique to his career; nor is it an attempt at psychoanalysis because I do not try to trace the origins of his difficulties to some specific source in Sidney's infancy. Instead I begin by examining the social and personal predicament of an Elizabethan aristocrat, caught up in a tangle of diminishing feudal power, Renaissance notions of statecraft, a zeal for military glory, courtly dependence and intrigue, and a cult of devotion to a formidable, emasculating queen. Sidney's dilemma is both distinctive and representative, and his fiction depicting the problems of subordination has a vast and vivid significance for his entire age. This significance can only be realized through a straightforwardly biographical approach. The problems with such an approach are obvious: trying to combine literary criticism with speculations in social history and psychoanalysis can spread one's resources rather thin and threaten the integrity of the works. Yet critics who have refused to make such connections have overlooked or rationalized the works' recurrent contradictions and diminished the fiction's scope and vitality. I have found that, as difficult as they are to make, these biographical and psychological connections are essential to an interpretation of Sidney's art.

I begin this study by reviewing the pertinent aspects of Sidney's life and historical context, describing specific problems of his class and political situation. In the second chapter, I consider the essential themes of all Sidney's fiction, and I examine debate as a means of organizing and intensifying thematic tensions. Conflict is more restricted in *Astrophil and Stella,* and this narrowing of focus is the topic of the third chapter. Chapters four and five explore the inconclusive narrative pattern of both versions of *Arcadia,* finding here the same tendency toward irresolution discernible in the debates. The final chapter deals with problems of closure in the revision, where Arcadian intrigue erupts in a war of rebellion. The persistent tensions within the Elizabethan world order are most apparent in the revision's third book, but they can be seen throughout Sidney's fiction. Although he does not succeed in resolving these tensions, his efforts do serve to illuminate them.

I am grateful to all those who read this book in one form or another. Three whose instruction and support were especially valuable were Paul Alpers, Frederick Crews, and Natalie Zemon Davis. Stephen Greenblatt, Daniel Javitch, David Kalstone, and Margaret Ferguson have provided important suggestions and encouragement. I have also greatly appreciated the patience, efficiency, and interest of Margaret Christ, Herbert Mann, and others at Rutgers University Press. One reader has helped with this book through all its various stages, offering detailed criticism and continual support, all the while working on numerous projects of her own: to my wife, Marsha Wagner, I owe the greatest thanks.

ABBREVIATIONS

AS *Astrophil and Stella,* quotations from *The Poems of Sir Philip Sidney.* Ed. William A. Ringler, Jr. 1962; rpt. Oxford: Clarendon, 1967.

CS *Certain Sonnets,* quotations from ibid.

NA *New Arcadia,* quotations from *The Prose Works of Sir Philip Sidney.* Ed. Albert Feuillerat. Vol. 1. 1912; rpt. Cambridge: Cambridge University Press, 1969.

OA *Old Arcadia,* quotations from *The Countess of Pembroke's Arcadia (The Old Arcadia).* Ed. Jean Robertson. Oxford: Clarendon, 1973.

Poems *The Poems of Sir Philip Sidney,* op. cit.

Chapter One

THE HISTORICAL CONTEXT

*S*IR PHILIP SIDNEY was not one of Queen Elizabeth's favorite courtiers. In 1579 their relationship, which had never been good, reached its nadir. The Duke of Alençon, younger brother of the King of France, had renewed his marriage suit, and Elizabeth, for reasons of her own, seemed inclined to respond. Her apparent enthusiasm for the match alarmed many of her subjects. Puritans were particularly horrified by an alliance with the Catholic son of the hated Catherine de Medici. A tract was secretly printed in September, entitled "The Discovery of a Gaping Gulf whereinto England is like to be swallowed by another French marriage, if the Lord forbid not the banns by letting her Majesty see the sin and punishment thereof." The author, John Stubbs, and his printer had their right hands cut off.[1]

Sidney stated his own objections to "Hir Mariage with Monsieur" in a letter written about the same time. In it, he repudiates any criticism of her as "blasphemy," but still he tries to exploit its effects, warning Elizabeth that if "the affectionat have their affections weakened, & the discontented have a gapp to utter their discontentacion I think it will seeme an evill preparative for the patient

1. J. E. Neale, *Queen Elizabeth* 1, pp. 248–249.

I

(I meane your Estate) to a greater siknes."[2] He emphasizes the Queen's dependence on the loyalty of her subjects, showing their love was her "chefe, if not sole, strenght."[3]

Sidney had several motives for writing this letter. He shared in the Protestant distaste for a French alliance, and his aversion was based on the same religious and patriotic convictions. He was also the nephew of Robert Dudley, the Earl of Leicester, once Elizabeth's favored suitor, and a marriage with Alençon threatened both the policies and the influence of the Dudley faction. Robert Dudley may have put Philip up to it, exploiting, in his typical fashion, the latter's high-minded eloquence for his own selfish aims. Leicester's schemes backfired when his year-old secret marriage was revealed to the Queen by Simier, the clever agent of Alençon. She was furious at such hypocrisy and deceit.[4] Sidney's role in these machinations, however naïve, could not have pleased her. His status and the relative discretion of his letter spared him the fate of John Stubbs, but his exertions on behalf of a declining faction did not endear him to his sovereign.

Shortly after this crisis, Sidney quarreled with Edward de Vere, the Earl of Oxford, a favorite of the Queen. A fight over the use of a tennis court had led from insults to a formal challenge; the presence of the Frenchmen responsible for negotiating marriage may have increased Sidney's defiance. The council intervened to prevent a duel and effect a reconciliation, but Sir Philip would not yield. The Queen was asked to speak with him herself, and their exchange

2. "A Discourse of Syr Ph. S. To the Queenes Majesty Touching Hir Marriage with Monsieur," in *The Prose Works of Sir Philip Sidney*, ed. Albert Feuillerat, III, 59, 53. In quoting from Feuillerat's edition (as well as other texts of the period), I have tried to follow his text's spelling and punctuation with two exceptions: I do not italicize proper names, and I use the letter *n* instead of the mark used in the text.

3. Ibid., p. 52.

4. Neale, *Queen Elizabeth*, pp. 251–252.

reveals a great deal about Sidney's character and situation and the peculiar nature of their relationship.

The best account of this episode is offered by Sir Fulke Greville, Sidney's devoted friend and biographer. He tells us how Elizabeth begins by seeking to put Sir Philip in his place, reminding him of "the difference in degree between Earls, and Gentlemen; the respect inferiors ought to their superiors; and the necessity in Princes to maintain their own creations, as degrees descending between the peoples licentiousness, and the anoynted Soveraignty of Crowns."[5] Sidney boldly replies "that place was never intended for privilege to wrong"; yet the defiant thrust of his assertion is muted by a convenient evasion: "witness her self," he says, "who how Soveraign soever she were by Throne, Birth, Education, and Nature; yet was she content to cast her own affections into the same moulds her Subjects did, and govern all her rights by their Laws."[6] According to Sidney, the monarch chooses to submit to the constraints of common law, thus voluntarily restricting royal authority.

Sidney's explanation of the Queen's relationship with her subjects is in one sense correct. Tudor sovereignty was limited in practice and in theory, though the nature and extent of these limits remained rather muddled for some time to come. Yet he is wrong in his assessment of the Queen's attitude toward such claims; she was certainly not "content" to suffer a subject's insistence on his rights. Elizabeth preferred and generally received tribute far more humble than this, and Sidney's attempts at independence would not thrive under her rule. Greville claims to find here an "authentical president [i.e., precedent] to after ages, that howsoever tyrants allow of no scope, stamp, or standard, but their own will; yet with Princes there is a

5. Sir Fulke Greville, *The Life of the Renowned Sir Philip Sidney*, pp. 67–68. I have again made two exceptions to the conventions of the original text: I have used *s* instead of *f* where appropriate, as well as avoiding italics for proper names.

6. Ibid., p. 68.

latitude for subjects to reserve native, & legall freedom, by paying humble tribute in manner, though not in matter, to them.["]7 Yet his analysis is wishfully disingenuous, for the boundaries of such "latitude" could not be defined with any precision, and Sidney failed to establish any sure footing for his "native, & legall freedom."

Greville's own life presents an interesting contrast to Sidney's career. The former was an adroit compromiser and a far more successful politician. Although he praised Sir Philip's "unbounded spirit," Greville chose another course, explaining his decision in this way: "I finding the specious fires of youth to prove far more scorching, then glorious, called my second thoughts to counsell, and in that Map cleerly discerning Action, and Honor, to fly with more wings then one: and that it was sufficient for the plant to grow where his Soveraignes hand had planted it; I found reason to contract my thoughts from those larger, but wandring Horizons, of the world abroad, and bound my prospect within the safe limits of duty, in such home services, as were acceptable to my Soveraigne."8 Greville thus describes his renunciation of foreign military adventure, the attractions of which proved damaging and ultimately fatal to Sidney. Greville's choice of a more peaceful and submissive course was, as he acknowledges, one that both his Queen and the circumstances favored. In explaining his behavior, he speaks more accurately about the extent of the subject's "native, & legall freedom," asking "the judicious Reader, whether there be any latitude left (more then humble obedience) in these nice cases between duty, and selfenesse, in a Soveraignes service?"9 In his own case he makes no fine distinction between matter and manner, nor does he find much "latitude" for maneuver.

The prototype for such successful adaptation was that preeminent

7. Ibid., p. 69.
8. Ibid., p. 149.
9. Ibid., p. 147.

councillor to Elizabeth, Robert Cecil, Lord Burghley. Making his intentions clear from the beginning, he promised the Queen that he would "be a minister of your Majesty's determinations and not of my own, or of others, though they be never so many. . . . And as for any other service, though it were in your Majesty's kitchen or garden, from the bottom of my heart I am ready without respect of estimation, wealth or ease, to do your Majesty's commandment."[10] Burghley's inclinations were reinforced by the political requirements of their situation. The dangers posed to the state by the overmighty subject and chaotic factional strife were still a vivid memory for the subjects of Elizabeth. Political stability demanded this kind of canny obedience.

These virtues were still further confirmed by the beliefs of Renaissance statecraft. According to *The Book of the Courtier,* the exemplary attendant must "devote all his thought and strength of spirit to loving and almost adoring the prince he serves above all else, devoting his every desire and habit and manner to pleasing him."[11] Machiavelli addresses his instructions directly to the prince, explaining the criterion by which a ruler "can come to understand and evaluate his ministers infallibly. When you see that a minister thinks more of himself than of you—that in all activities he is pursuing some purpose of his own—you know that he cannot be a good minister of your affairs, and that you can never put your trust in him. The man who is entrusted with the administration of the state of another should never think of himself but of his prince, and should concern himself with nothing that does not pertain to the prince's interest."[12] The court became the means of enforcing this ethos of submission. As Lawrence Stone points out in *The Crisis of the Aristocracy,* the court became the source of all political and

10. Quoted by A. L. Rowse, *The England of Elizabeth,* p. 276.
11. Baldesar Castiglione, *The Book of the Courtier,* p. 110.
12. Niccolo Machiavelli, *The Prince,* in *The Prince and Discourses,* p. 86.

military appointments and of the allotment of monopolies, displacing the nobility from their feudal base of power.[13] Through this agency of royal control, "once-formidable local potentates were transformed into fawning courtiers and tame state pensionaries."[14] The new code of courtly civility had firm institutional backing, and political success demanded adaptation.

There were, however, other forces at work in Elizabethan politics, and Sidney's career reveals their tense and unsteady interplay. As the quarrel with Oxford shows, aristocratic pride was not entirely suppressed by an ethos of courtly submission. Sidney insists, in his "Defence of the Earl of Leicester," on "the nobility of that blood whereof I am descended," repudiating any slur against the dignity and prerogatives of his family.[15] He had a hot temper, and his mentor and devoted correspondent, Hubert Languet, felt it necessary to warn the younger man to be less irritable, "unless you wish to pass your whole life in quarreling."[16] When Sir Henry Sidney was recalled from Ireland, Philip accused his father's secretary of treachery and threatened him with violence.[17] Stone, who mentions this episode, sees Sidney's anger as part of a larger class phenomenon.[18] In some sense, the violence and recklessness of the aristocracy was an expression of thwarted ambition and frustration with the peculiar constraints imposed by royal hegemony. Often their impulsiveness took the form of personal antagonism toward Burghley's cautious style. As Stone explains, "there grew up a whole new generation of high-spirited young aristocrats in open rebellion against the conservative establishment in general and Lord Burghley in particular. Very

13. Lawrence Stone, *The Crisis of the Aristocracy, 1588–1641*, pp. 217–219.
14. Ibid., p. 183.
15. *Prose,* Feuillerat, III, 66.
16. *The Correspondence of Sir Philip Sidney and Hubert Languet,* trans. Stuart A. Pears, pp. 88–89. I have again substituted *s* for *ſ* where appropriate.
17. Malcolm William Wallace, *The Life of Sir Philip Sidney,* p. 201.
18. Stone, *Aristocracy,* p. 108.

many, like Oxford, Rutland, Southampton, Bedford, and Essex, had been wards of the old man and were reacting violently against his counsels of worldly prudence."[19]

The impetuous bravado and discontent of these men posed a grave threat to Elizabethan doctrines of obedience. The Essex Rebellion of 1601 was the culmination of these tendencies; although it was no more high minded than it was effective, this aristocratic insurgence still had serious political implications. Even Essex, for all his shallow impulsiveness, could still pose a serious ideological challenge to the Queen's sovereignty: "What, cannot Princes err?" he rashly wrote. "Cannot subjects receive wrong? Is an earthly power or authority infinite? Pardon me, pardon me, my good lord, I can never subscribe to these principles."[20] Alarmed by such heretical sentiments, Sir William Knollys warned Essex "that there is no contesting between sovereignty and obedience,"[21] but such prudent truisms did not prevent an outburst of aristocratic defiance. Essex, in fact, saw himself as the heir to Sidney's legacy of daring independence and chivalric heroism; Sidney had bequeathed Essex his best sword, and the latter had married Sidney's widow, Frances Walsingham. Although Essex was more selfish and erratic than Sidney in his defiance of the crown, he still sustained the aristocratic desire for autonomy.

Sidney's genuine religious convictions posed an even greater challenge to the code of obedience. The ultimate supremacy of the prince was sometimes thrown into doubt as the religious conflicts of the age provoked serious differences of policy. Sir Francis Walsingham was a loyal and effective councillor to Elizabeth, but his ardent support for the Protestant cause in Europe often irked her. Sidney, who was Walsingham's son-in-law, describes his own

19. Ibid., p. 265.
20. Robert Lacey, *Robert, Earl of Essex*, p. 213.
21. Ibid., p. 215.

devotion to the cause in a letter to Sir Francis in which he takes a freely critical view of the Queen:

> If her Majesty wear the fowntain I woold fear considring what I daily fynd that we shold wax dry, but she is but a means whom God useth and I know not whether I am deceaved but I am faithfully persuaded that if she shold withdraw her self other springes woold ryse to help this action. For me thinkes I see the great work indeed in hand, against the abusers of the world, wherein it is no greater fault to have confidence in mans power, then it is to hastily to despair of Gods work. I think a wyse and constant man ought never to greev whyle he doth plai as a man mai sai his own part truly though others be out but if him self leav his hold becaws other marrin[ers] will be ydle he will hardli forg[ive] him self his own fault. For me I can not promis of my own cource no nor of the my [   ] becaws I know there is a hyer power that must uphold me or els I shall fall, but certainly I trust, I shall not by other mens wantes be drawn from my self.[22]

His resolution and assurance anticipate the liberating fervor of later Protestants, and faith in "a hyer power" clearly inspires greater self-confidence and independence.

Nevertheless, although Sidney did remain true to himself, the part he played had little political consequence. Circumstances did not allow him the effective autonomy he desired, and his status made his situation even more difficult. Michael Walzer has examined the rebellious impulses of the Protestant aristocracy in his excellent study, *The Revolution of the Saints*. In France, a difference of religion between monarch and nobleman combined with increasing royal power to stir up antagonism between the two parties, but Huguenot radicalism was dampened by the nobles' stake in the status quo.[23] In England the situation was even more confused. As Walzer explains,

22. "Correspondence," LXXXIX, "To Sir Francis Walsingham" (Mar. 24, 1586), in *Prose*, Feuillerat, III, 166–167.
23. Michael Walzer, *The Revolution of the Saints*, pp. 89–90.

"The vision of a Protestant nation presided over by an elite of godly aristocrats waging chivalric warfare for God's glory, born in the mind of a man like Sir Philip Sidney, had no chance of realization in Elizabeth's England."[24] Even if the Queen had been Catholic, Walzer points out, the Protestant nobility lacked "a suitable territorial base or private army" to oppose her.[25]

Walzer glances here at another obstacle to aristocratic success, one that he examines in more detail elsewhere. The mystique of chivalric glory was a persistent anachronism, an oddly volatile element in the Elizabethan world order. For Sidney and his peers, war remained a heroic undertaking, an "occasion for honorable self-display and the public performance of 'fine deeds.' "[26] It could also become, as it did for Sidney, an occasion for splendid self-destruction. In a futile skirmish at Zutphen he sportingly cast off part of his armor and was shot in the thigh. Thus Sidney succumbed to the cult of martial glory and died of his gangrenous wounds. His death capped a career of noble failure. Paradoxically, his pointless martyrdom advanced the Protestant cause far more than his most diligent practical exertions. His dying gestures combined selflessness and self-dramatization, securing him a legendary esteem.

Finally, Sir Philip Sidney's career presents a complex picture. It blends heroic zeal with hapless pathos, dazzling promise, and recurrent defeat. Greville's biography offers melancholy tribute to his friend's high ideals and ambitions, all thwarted by degrading circumstances and conflicts. Sidney must finally be remembered for his "large and sincere resolutions" rather than for any actual accomplishment, for he "never was magistrate, nor possessed of any fit stage for eminence to act upon."[27] Yet he still achieved a singular eminence. His proud conviction and integrity stirred the fascination

24. Ibid., p. 116.
25. Ibid.
26. Ibid., p. 272. Walzer is quoting Castiglione.
27. Greville, *Life,* p. 38.

and respect of his contemporaries. The complexity of his character and career have significance for us as well, because they illuminate the contradictions of his age. Sidney's life reveals the tensions within the Elizabethan world order, showing how the balance between sovereignty and autonomy is complicated by the forces of courtly civility, aristocratic pride, religious conviction, and chivalric zeal.

We have not only his life but his literature as well, and Sidney's writings reflect the complex tensions of the period. He does not simply exemplify these conflicts in the flamboyant manner of Essex; he seeks to give them a comprehensible form. In the *Apology for Poetry*, Sidney envisions an exhilarating autonomy for the mind in literature. Freed of the constraints of circumstance, the "erected wit" aspires to almost transcendent clarity.[28] Yet even here limits intrude on his "large and sincere resolutions." Submission still prompts feelings of frustration, defiance, and painful inadequacy, while self-assertion arouses guilt and confusion. The conflicts of the period prove as intractable for him in literature as they do in life, and his ambivalence and uncertainty prevent him from following his ideas through to any conclusion. Each of Sidney's works reveals some problem of development and closure. Although most readers have been sensitive to these problems, few critics have understood their origins in Sidney's life. I plan to show clearer links between his life and the ambiguous patterns of his fiction. The confused and elliptical ending of the *Old Arcadia* reflects a mixture of sympathy, guilt, and defiance that Sidney could not fully articulate. The unsuccessful heroics of the revision reveal his doubts about autonomy. His sonnets treat the conflict of deference and desire with more control and assurance, but he never achieves a solution to the problem. Obtaining a clearer understanding of each of these works is one reason for reexamining their connections to Sidney's life and period. This un-

28. Sir Philip Sidney, *An Apology for Poetry, or the Defence of Poetry*, p. 101.

derstanding will, in turn, allow a deeper perception of the complexities of Elizabethan culture.

SIDNEY'S CAREER HAD BEGUN AUSPICIOUSLY, suffused with the "great expectation" of noble birth.[29] Ancestral pride was a persistent feature of Sidney's character, nearly boiling over in his defense of Leicester, his uncle.[30] These feelings were instilled early in such advice as his father's "Remember, my son, the noble blood you are descended of by your mother's side; and think that only by virtuous life and good action you may be an ornament to that illustrious family."[31]

For certain aristocrats, seeking a more powerful role for their class, traditional feudal claims were reinforced by new ideas of statesmanship. In France, the more advanced of the Huguenot nobility espoused a theory of subaltern magistrate. Walzer sees this doctrine as "the nearest approach of the French nobility of early modern times to an independent ideological position. It attempts a highly rationalized and legalized view of the rights and duties of the aristocracy, considering its members not as heads of feudal households, but as officers of the realm. Huguenot theory may be considered an unsuccessful effort to transform feudal status into constitutional position."[32] During his travels on the Continent, Sidney met some of these prominent statesmen of the Reformation and found that he shared the self-assurance, religious convictions, and political aspirations of men like Coligny and de Mornay. From Saint Bartholomew's Day until his death, Sidney was fired with enthusiasm for a militant pan-Protestant alliance led by an elite of righteous noblemen.

29. The phrase is from *Astrophil and Stella*, Sonnet 21.
30. See the "Defence of the Earl of Leicester," in *Prose*, Feuillerat, III, 61–71. "I sai that my cheefest honor is to be a Dudlei and truli am glad to have caws to sett foorth the nobility of that blood whereof I am descended" (pp. 65–66).
31. Wallace, *Life*, p. 69.
32. Walzer, *Saints*, pp. 72–73.

For a time, realization of his hopes seemed imminent. In 1577 Sidney was sent on an official mission sponsored by Sir Francis Walsingham to seek formal support for a Protestant alliance from the Germans and the Netherlanders. John Casimir, Count Palatine of the Rhine, and William of Orange committed their forces to this project, and their plans included proposals highly favorable to Sidney: alliances of marriage, territorial possessions, and a high military command were all discussed. The success of these negotiations would have assured fulfillment of Sidney's ideals and ambitions, and he returned to seek full support for the Protestant cause.[33]

Unfortunately, his prospects began to decline at this point and his extraordinary success on the Continent may have been the cause. Greville attributes his difficulties to the envious anxiety of his superiors at court: "So I may well say, that this Gentlemans large, yet uniform disposition was everywhere praised; greater in himself than in the world; yet greater there in fame and honour than many of his superiors; reverenced by forrain Nations in one forme, of his own in another; easily censured, hardly imitated; and therefore no received Standard at home, because his industry, judgement, and affections, perchance seemed too great for the cautious wisdomes of little Monarchies to be safe in."[34] Osborn speculates more specifically that Sidney's preeminence in the Protestant cause may have alarmed the Queen and provoked her disfavor. Both their differences of policy and his alliance with the Dudley faction could prompt more serious opposition once he secured a military and political base in the Netherlands. "He could then," Osborn suggests, "become the

---

33. See James M. Osborn, *Young Philip Sidney 1572–1577:* Coligny, pp. 34, 54–55, 65; Saint Bartholomew, pp. 66–73; the 1577 mission, pp. 448 ff.; marriage proposals, pp. 478–479, 491; the offer of command, p. 499. See also Wallace, *Life:* Coligny, p. 118; Saint Bartholomew, pp. 120–122; the 1577 mission, pp. 173–183; marriage proposals, pp. 184–187; offers of command, p. 198.

34. Greville, *Life,* pp. 39–40.

Dudley candidate for Elizabeth's own throne."[35] Whatever her suspicions of Sidney, the Queen's habitual distaste for war and expenditure caused her to drop the plan for a Protestant league, thus denying Sidney's hopes their best opportunity.

His return to England was beset by still further difficulties. Elizabeth became irritated with his father's conduct as Lord Deputy of Ireland, and she recalled him in 1578. Osborn cites a communique from the Queen to Daniel Rogers in which she makes a testy remark, in reference to Henry Sidney, about foreign conspiracies against her sovereignty over her governors.[36] Osborn's inferences are prudently circumspect, but he implies that the swift decline of the Sidneys' fortunes may have been caused by their involvement in foreign military adventure, among other things. As Essex would demonstrate during his tenure in Ireland, the Queen's hold on her magnates grew tenuous once they left court and acquired the command of large armies, so such distrust was not entirely unjustified.

The next year Sidney wrote his letter opposing her marriage to Alençon and quarreled with one of her favorites. It seems that his standing at court was permanently weakened by these excesses.[37] The collapse of his grand political scheme did not diminish Sidney's energy and resilience, and he contemplated a variety of private projects. Even these were blocked, however, for he was denied permission to join, first, Casimir's army in the Netherlands, later, Sir Francis Drake's voyage to the New World.[38] Fulke Greville joined with his friend in the latter attempt, and he feelingly describes the typical nature of their defeat: "Sir Philip found this, and many other of his large, and sincere resolutions imprisoned within the

35. Osborn, *Young Sidney*, p. 497.
36. Ibid., pp. 496–497.
37. Osborn, *Young Sidney*, pp. 496–500. Cf. Wallace, *Life*, p. 219; the latter feels the damage to Sidney's standing was only temporary.
38. Osborn, *Young Sidney*, pp. 501, 511–512; Wallace, *Life*, pp. 199, 317–319.

pleights of their fortunes, that mixed good, and evill together unequally."[39]

Indeed, near the end of his career, Sidney was frequently distracted from these large resolutions by more cramped and dispiriting concerns. By 1581 he wrote plaintively to Sir Christopher Hatton of his need "to be delyvered oute of this comber of debtes."[40] His "desyre for the beeing busied in a thing of som serviseable experience"[41] had become almost desperate, and he was grateful for a subordinate post in the Ordnance Office. This appointment apparently relieved Sidney of the necessity of accepting more degrading financial remedies. The Queen had offered him the "forfeyture of papistes goodes,"[42] but he was queasy about sharing in this plunder. He wrote to Leicester of his misgivings, complaining that "truly I lyke not their persons and much worse their religions, but I think my fortune very hard that my reward must be built uppon other mens punishmentes."[43] Sidney's next sentence defines the basic nature of his predicament: "Well my Lord yowr Lordeshippe made me a cowrtier do yow thinke of it as seemes best unto yow."[44] Personal ambition and religious conviction, along with changing ideas of civil responsibility and freedom, had inspired Sidney to seek a more authoritative political role. He had wanted to be one of the Reformation's influential statesmen, but the humiliations of debts, unemployment, and royal disfavor made him a reluctant and largely unsuccessful courtier.[45] These roles were essentially irreconcilable, as Roger Howell explains in his biography of Sir Philip: "Sidney knew

39. Greville, *Life,* p. 77.
40. "Correspondence," L, "To Sir Christopher Hatton" (Nov. 13, 1581), in *Prose,* Feuillerat, III, 138.
41. Ibid., LVII, "To Lord Burghley" (Jan. 27, 1582), p. 143.
42. Ibid., LII, "To Sir Christopher Hatton" (Dec. 18, 1581), p. 139.
43. Ibid., LIV, "To the Earl of Leicester" (Dec. 28, 1581), p. 140.
44. Ibid.
45. Sidney's difficulties with the "alternatives of the statesman or the courtier" are discussed by F. J. Levy, "Philip Sidney Reconsidered," p. 11.

that his proper role was to be a courtier and a servant to his Queen and country. It was a lesson impressed on him from his earliest schooling. Yet he knew, too, both from the perusal of the past history of his family and from a glance at the situation of Europe, that such a role was not an easy one to play" because the "heritage of family, religion, and service to sovereign contained elements that were not always compatible."[46]

The problems of the latter role are immediately apparent, even in the most idealized version of life at court. In the *Book of the Courtier*, one character is troubled by the prospect of the "noble flatterer"; it becomes an obvious occupational hazard for one who is urged to love and almost adore "the prince he serves above all else."[47] The reply that "flatterers love neither their prince nor their friends" hardly solves the problem.[48] In actual practice, the contradictions of this role can be still more vividly perceived. That Hubert Languet felt them is clear from his advice to Sir Philip. The older man warns Sidney on the latter's return to England that "one who wishes to live free of scorn in the courts of mighty kings must govern his emotions, swallow many vexations, very carefully avoid all motives of controversy, and cultivate those men in whose hands supreme power lies."[49] He even encourages pretense if it will advance one's intimacy and influence with the powerful. Yet Languet betrays an anxious awareness of the court's dangers in his bitter tirade against Italians:

> But does not most praise in Italy go to those who know how to dissemble, who know how to flatter, and to insinuate themselves into the favor of powerful men in every possible way, and to adapt themselves so well to their moods. . . .

46. Roger Howell, *Sir Philip Sidney*, p. 23.
47. Castiglione, *Courtier*, p. 110.
48. Ibid.
49. Osborn, *Young Sidney*, p. 296.

In fact their spirits are broken by long servitude, and they
happily endure any indignities and insults, as long as they are not
deprived of money and of base pleasures; and they consider themselves excellently treated if the one upon whose nod they hang
looks at them from time to time with, as the poet says, closed lip.
    As for me, I believe that nothing is more harmful to the intel-
lects of free men than these arts, which soften their manly virtue
and prepare their spirits for servility.[50]

The courtier's art had an unsettling way of backfiring. Strategies
designed to allow one to "live free of scorn in the courts of mighty
kings" degraded their practitioners. The ethos of courtly service
degenerated, perhaps inevitably, into the habits of mere servility.
Languet's disgust at such a prospect reveals a profound anxiety
about courtly submission. Citing the reference to the "closed lip" as
evidence of Languet's "strong feelings," Osborn explains that this is
an allusion to Martial's "closed lip" of the courtesan.[51] The latent
pun on courtship conflates political and sexual submission, a con-
flation that was, of course, basic to this ethos from its beginnings.
In Languet's diatribe, both terms become an occasion for distress,
threatening one's freedom and "manly virtue" in every way.

Despite these disturbing contradictions, courtly service remained
one of the few viable roles for the Elizabethan politician. Sidney
had to submit to its rules because there were few practical alternatives. Walzer regards this as an especially painful dilemma for men
like Sidney and his French counterpart, de Mornay: "animated by
a fine sense of personal virtue, they were conditioned at the same
time by a new Calvinist zeal. The court offered no arena for their
idealistic ambitions, yet both were drawn to it as the only center of
political life."[52] Sidney's grandfather was John Dudley, the Duke of

50. Ibid., pp. 208–209.
51. Ibid., p. 209. Osborn cites Charles Levy as the source of this
information.
52. Walzer, *Saints*, p. 241. See also pp. 115–116.

16

Northumberland, England's "kingmaker" and the epitome of the overmighty subject—one who lost in his final gamble for power. If the grandson was not fully tamed by the Elizabethan court, he was certainly thoroughly frustrated.

Denied a position of political influence and galled by the strain of courtly subservience, Sidney aspired to the more traditional role of the heroic warrior. Warfare allowed a more active pursuit of his convictions and policies as well as an opportunity for heroic fulfillment. Yet these seemingly compatible goals contained a contradiction, one exacerbated by the standards of his class. In the sixteenth century the nature of combat was rapidly changing, and its altered technical and strategic aspects rendered a code of personal heroism increasingly anachronistic. In a passage evocative of Sidney's own demise, Stone describes the military causes of the aristocracy's decline:

> As armies grew in size with the domination of the field by the infantry pikemen and as the technical services like pioneers and ordnance increased in importance, war ceased to be an exciting *chevauchée* led by high-spirited young men out for a lark. Now that small-arms had been invented, strength, courage, and skill on horseback were no longer any protection against sudden and ignominious death. War was no fun any more, and the tiltyard at Westminster Palace had to serve as a substitute for the fields of Crécy and Agincourt. A military commander had now to be an expert in logistics, in transport and victualling, in engineering and administration. The nobility were ill-adapted to such a change, which in any case deprived war of most of its aristrocratic glamour.[53]

This change in the nature of warfare is the subject of *Don Quixote,* the period's greatest work of prose fiction. In one of his more lucid moments, Don Quixote laments this change, one he resolutely ignores in his pursuit of adventure:

53. Stone, *Aristocracy,* p. 130.

Blessed were the times which lacked the dreadful fury of those diabolical engines, the artillery, whose inventor I firmly believe is now receiving the reward for his devilish invention in hell; an invention which allows a base and cowardly hand to take the life of a brave knight, in such a way that, without his knowing how or why, when his valiant heart is fullest of furious courage, there comes some random shot—discharged perhaps by a man who fled in terror from the flash the accursed machine made in firing— and puts an end in a moment to the consciousness of one who deserved to enjoy life for many an age. And when I think of that, I am tempted to say that it grieves me to the heart to have adopted this profession of knight errantry in such a detestable age as we now live in. For although no danger frightens me, still it causes me misgivings to think that powder and lead may deprive me of the chance of winning fame and renown by the strength of my arm and the edge of my sword, over all the known earth.[54]

Within this changing context, Sidney's own military career presents a rather complex picture. Certainly he succumbed to the conventional aristocratic enthusiasm for the tournament and duel. He did not, however, approach war as though "out for a lark." His advocacy of war with Spain was motivated by serious policy considerations and religious convictions.[55] Moreover, in his comportment as military governor of Flushing he was scrupulously attentive to technical details: "For instance; how like a Souldier did he behave himself, first in contriving, then in executing the surprise of Axil? where he revived that ancient, and secure discipline of order, & silence in their March; and after their entrance into the town, placed a band of choice souldiers to make a stand in the Marketplace, for securitie to the rest, that were forced to wander up and down by direction of Commanders; and when the service was done,

54. Miguel de Cervantes Saavedra, *The Adventures of Don Quixote,* trans. J. M. Cohen (1950; rpt. New York: Penguin, 1967), p. 344.
55. Osborn, *Young Sidney,* p. 511 passim and Wallace, *Life,* pp. 317–319.

rewarded that obedience of discipline in every one, liberally, out of his own purse."[56] Throughout the Netherlands campaign he repeatedly urged Leicester, his superior, to concern himself with logistical problems and concentrate less, perhaps, on the appearance of his "band . . . of very hansome men."[57] Sidney expressed continual anxiety about their provisions and the overextension of their troops. In a letter to Walsingham, he writes that Elizabeth "need be discouraged with no thing whyle she keepes these principal sea places, nai I think it wear hard to sai whether it wear not better for us to embrace no more but we do still make camps and streight again mar them for want of meanes, and so lose our monei to no purpos."[58] Nevertheless, all these methodical concerns were flaunted in Sidney's final engagement at Zutphen. Tossing off his cuisses, he reverted to a kind of sporting flamboyance and received the fatal wound in the thigh.

The significance of Sidney's death, with its aura of reckless bravado and heroic sacrifice, is hard to assess. Traditionally, these final actions have been regarded as his finest, constituting a kind of martyrdom for a sacred cause. His state funeral in England was an occasion for lavish tribute, and it became, according to F. J. Levy, "a grand show of national unity and purpose."[59] Yet even as he notes the importance of Sidney's death for the Protestant cause, Levy also emphasizes the rather pathetic irony of a life whose major event

56. Greville, *Life,* p. 121.
57. "Correspondence," LXXX, "To the Earl of Leicester" (Feb. 12, 1580), in *Prose,* Feuillerat, III, 160. Sidney is alarmed that Leicester's retinue is "unarmed spending monei and tyme to no purpose." See also ibid., LXXI, "To Lord Burghley" (Dec. 11, 1585), p. 152; LXXVIII, "To the Earl of Leicester: (Feb. 2, 1586), p. 158; and LXXXI, "To the Earl of Leicester" (Feb. 19, 1586), p. 162.
58. Ibid., CVIII, "To Sir Francis Walsingham" (Aug. 14, 1586), p. 179.
59. Levy, "Sidney Reconsidered," p. 15. This edition of *English Literary Renaissance,* a special Sidney issue, contains Thomas Lant's illustrations of the funeral procession.

was its end.[60] Some others have denied the episode at Zutphen even this consequence, maintaining that Elizabeth could either ignore or manipulate the glory of this episode to her own ends.[61] Paul Johnson maintains that the Queen was completely indifferent to Sidney's death. In his account, the Netherlands campaign "brought little glory to English arms. When Sir Philip Sidney was killed in a skirmish outside Zutphen, the political nation went into mourning, and tales of his gallantry and self-sacrifice became instant legend. Elizabeth, being a realist, was not impressed by this pointless incident. A state funeral was held, but she did not attend, and it was left to Walsingham—Leicester, Sidney's godfather, having defaulted—to pay the hero's £6,000 debts."[62] One encounters the same unsentimental realism, and grim prophecy as well, in Languet's warning to Sidney written eight years earlier: "I would not even if I could, weaken or blunt the edge of your spirit, still I must advise you now and then to reflect that young men who rush into danger incautiously almost always meet an inglorious end, and deprive themselves of the power of serving their country; for a man who falls at an early age cannot have done much for his country."[63] His death reflects the contradictions of his life in its combination of chivalric splendor and noble pathos with reckless futility and defeat.

Sidney's literature allows a greater sense of his accomplishment. He says in An Apology for Poetry that literature, for him, was an "unelected vocation,"[64] but as the Apology makes clear, he brings the same enthusiasm, intelligence, and energy to this new undertaking that he brings to his political career. He also retains many of the same concerns, for the problematic issues of his life emerge as central themes in his writings.

60. Ibid. See also Howell, Sidney, p. 5.
61. Richard A. Lanham, "Sidney: The Ornament of His Age," p. 338.
62. Paul Johnson, Elizabeth I, p. 273.
63. Languet, Pears, p. 137.
64. Sidney, Apology, p. 95.

The clearest example of this connection is his first literary venture, *The Lady of May*. This was a masque presented before Queen Elizabeth at Wanstead during the Earl of Leicester's entertainments. The masque required the Queen to make a marriage choice in a contest between a forester and a shepherd who respectively personify virile activism and cautious inertia. Sidney makes the best case for the exuberant forester, Therion, a case that may have had specific topical purposes. Some have suggested a reference to Elizabeth's own marriage question—certainly an issue of concern for Sidney and the Leicester faction at this time and one that would prompt a more direct address to the Queen the next year, when Sidney would write the letter opposing her marriage to Alençon.[65] William Ringler, while questioning the relevance of the French marriage problem, suggests a possible allusion to military aid for the Netherlands.[66] Sidney was also quite eager for a more active, less cautious foreign policy, and the masque could reflect these desires. If Elizabeth was at all sensitive to these possibilities, her choice of the shepherd, Espilus, the May Lady's other suitor, may have been prompted by a clear recognition of her persistent disagreements with Sidney.[67]

In both versions of the *Arcadia*, the political issues are less immediately topical. Romantic intrigue has broader political consequences and more generalized implications as Sidney examines the social constraints on individual impulse, problems of royal misgovernment and rebellion, and the difficult balance between autonomy and obedience. The plot of both versions culminates in political upheaval, either in confrontation with stern patriarchal authority or in open war of rebellion. Only in *Astrophil and Stella* are these political implications muted and is the focus restricted to the amatory con-

---

65. Robert Kimbrough and Philip Murphy, "The Helmingham Hall Manuscript of Sidney's *The Lady of May*," pp. 104–106.

66. "Commentary," in *The Poems of Sir Philip Sidney*, ed. William A. Ringler, Jr., p. 362.

67. Kimbrough and Murphy, "Helmingham Hall Manuscript," p. 105.

test. Desire is still thwarted and the conflict is intense, but tensions are contained. Sidney's sonnets impart a much greater sense of control and composure than his other major works.

There is yet another overlap between Sidney's career and his art. In his literature, he adheres to the same blend of practical and idealistic objectives as he did in politics. Greville gives us an excellent account of these goals: "his end was not writing, even while he wrote; nor his knowledge moulded for tables, or schooles; but both his wit, and understanding bent upon his heart, to make himself and others, not in words or opinion, but in life, and action, good and great."[68] In its concern with "life, and action," the fiction is intended as a guide to proper conduct. Greville's remarks on the "Arcadian romantics" are particularly pertinent: "his end in them was not vanishing pleasures alone, but morall Images, and Examples, (as directing threds) to guide every man through the confused Labyrinth of his own desires and life."[69] He praises their narrative complexity: "In which traverses (I know) his purpose was to limn out such exact pictures, of every posture in the minde, that any man being forced, in the straines of this life, to pass through any straights, or latitudes of good, or ill fortune, might (as in a glasse) see how to set a good countenance upon all the discountenances of adversitie, and a stay upon the exorbitant smilings of chance."[70] The achievement of equanimity and integrity in the midst of life's overwhelming complexity is the objective. By following the heroes' exploits and responses to various narrative contingencies, the reader might also learn how to attain perspective and poise. "Read the Countesse of Pembrookes Arcadia," writes Gabriel Harvey, "a gallant Legendary full of pleasurable accidents and proffitable discourses; . . . He that will looue, let him learne to looue of him that will teach him to

68. Greville, *Life*, p. 18.
69. Ibid., p. 223.
70. Ibid., p. 16.

Liue, and furnish him with many pithy and effectuall instructions."[71] Sidney would teach us how to live. The death of Charles I presents the most famous application of these "proffitable . . . instructions"; for Milton, it was infamous. The King is said to have recited one of Pamela's lofty speeches as a prayer in his captivity so that he too might "set a good countenance upon all the discountenance of adversitie."

Many readers feel that the practical concerns of Sidney's writings become more specifically political. In his concentration on conflicts with authority, he raises basic questions about the traditional relationship between subject and sovereign. If he does not actively encourage resistance to royal misgovernment, Sidney still portrays in vivid detail the blatant fallibility of earthly rulers. In this respect, Sidney can be seen to provide "pithy and effectual instructions" to rebellious subjects as well as royal martyrs. F. J. Levy emphasizes the importance of Sidney's intellectual contribution to the opponents of Charles I: "in their frustration at being denied employment, Sidney and his associates forced themselves to examine critically the monarchy which had abandoned them; they turned for inspiration to Tacitus and to Machiavelli, and thus initiated that realistic appraisal of government which led to the 'politic history' of the early seventeenth century and, ultimately, to the revolution."[72] Christopher Hill has examined this kind of contribution more comprehensively in his *Intellectual Origins of the English Revolution*. While the lines of influence are not as clear or direct as Levy seems to suggest, many of the same connections are made between the monarchy's sixteenth-century victims and its seventeenth-century persecutors. Hill shows how the alienation of many aspiring, serious politicians, like Bacon and Ralegh, led them to think critically of the state, and how enforced retirement allowed them opportunity to expand on their dis-

---

71. Gabriel Harvey, "Pierce's Supererogation," p. 263.
72. Levy, "Sidney Reconsidered," p. 18.

contents; their difficulties with the sovereign only increased their subsequent prestige.[73]

Sidney's writings, in this view, serve as a kind of outlet for Sidney's political interests, compensating for the frustrations and failures of the active life. Problems that proved insurmountable in his career he confronts on a more intellectual plane in his fiction, and at this level, he acquires a new speculative freedom. He is bound, as he says in the *Apology*, by "no law but wit"; in poetry's sovereign domain, one can "range, only reined with learned discretion, into the divine consideration of what may be and should be."[74] In an excellent essay on the *Apology*, Margaret W. Ferguson points out that it was written shortly after the letter opposing the Queen's marriage and argues that it too was addressed to an authority who was as "ungrateful" for Sidney's eloquence as Plato was for poetry's eloquence in general; Sidney complains that "idle England" has "grown so hard a stepmother" that poets cannot "flourish," and he appeals to sovereign as well as critical authority to become "our patron and not our adversary."[75] Ferguson concludes that "the text's complex meditation on the master-servant relation must be read in light of what historians have taught us about the 'crisis of the aristocracy' in Sidney's age. Sidney, like many members of his class, had little money and was dependent on the Queen for all of his 'great expectations.' When he asserts that 'Poets should be makers of themselves and not takers of others' he is expressing a social as well as literary protest against the facts of his life."[76] Yet even in poetry Sidney cannot escape "the facts of his life," and Ferguson maintains that, in the *Apology*, Sidney attempts to come to terms with the limits on his ambitions.

One of the more fundamental obstacles is acknowledged in the

73. Christopher Hill, *Intellectual Origins of the English Revolution*, p. 287.
74. Sidney, *Apology*, p. 102.
75. Margaret W. Ferguson, "Sidney's *Defence of Poetry*."
76. Ibid.

Apology, where Sidney acknowledges the constraints imposed by "our infected will" upon the freedom of the "erected wit."[77] Sidney apparently saw these limitations with a new, poignant clarity from his deathbed, where according to Greville, "he then discovered, not onely the imperfection, but vanitie of these shadowes, how daintily soever limned: as seeing that even beauty it self, in all earthly complexions, was more apt to allure men to evill, than to fashion any goodness in them. And from this ground, in that memorable testament of this, he bequeathed no other legacie, but the fire, to this unpolished Embrio."[78] Although Greville could not bear to destroy these "delicate (though inferior) Pictures" of Sidney's own virtues, he concedes their imperfection, maintaining a firm distinction between "that excellent intended patterne" of his art and its "unperfected shape."[79] In his early enthusiasm for his new avocation, Sidney had seen poetry as one of man's highest attainments. The "erected wit" achieves its exhilarating autonomy through a kind of imaginative liberation, and Sidney's striking trope conveys the transcendence of poetic insight. "Only the poet," he proudly declares, "disdaining to be tied to any such subjection, lifted up with the vigour of his own invention, doth grow in effect into another nature."[80] Yet as Greville points out, the defects of human nature still intrude upon this inventive freedom, corrupting "even beauty it self"; thus even in literature, Sidney's "unbounded spirit" was still subject to earthly constraints.[81]

Sidney's life and circumstances present him with obstacles that, though less cosmic, also hinder him in his literary objectives. Again, the *Lady of May* provides the clearest illustration of these circumstan-

77. Sidney, *Apology,* p. 101.
78. Greville, *Life,* pp. 16–17.
79. Ibid., pp. 223–224. Cf. Sidney's idea of the "fore-conceit of the work" in Sidney, *Apology,* p. 101.
80. Sidney, *Apology,* p. 100.
81. Greville, *Life,* pp. 16–17.

tial constraints. Sidney's anticipated conclusion, in which the forester Therion triumphed, would have fulfilled both dramatic and political expectations. The final song of Silvanus, god of foresters, has idle Pan defeated by active Hercules.[82] Unfortunately, this happy ending was thwarted by the Queen's choice of Espilus. Life and its problems intrude directly on Sidney's art, in the person of his most formidable opponent.

In Sidney's other works the intrusion is less overt and dramatic, but it still occurs. Even when he retired from court, escaping its immediate pressures, Sidney could not escape its inner, ideological inhibitions. In his fictive exploration of the problems of sovereignty, obedience, and autonomy, he was blocked in his thinking. His major poetry and prose all present some conflict with authority, a clash between individual impulse and social order, between freedom and submission. Yet in nearly every instance, these struggles culminate in an impasse, their implications and consequences never fully clarified. Sidney could not follow his defiant feelings and ideas through to completion. He was afflicted by that same "stop in the mind" Christopher Hill sees hindering thinkers more radical than Sidney; until the civil war, opponents of the crown could not mount an effective challenge to its authority or conceive a true share in sovereignty.[83] In Sidney's literature, the result of such inhibitions is a pattern of evasion and obscurity. All the major works are marked by inconclusive development, thematic contradictions, and problems of closure.

There is still another ambiguity in these fictive conflicts with authority. Though they have political implications, these struggles are romantic and psychological in their origins. They are caused by feelings of love, feelings that are uncontrollable and irresistible. Sidney's characters find the tyranny of their own emotions as

<hr>

82. "The Lady of May," in *Prose*, Feuillerat, II, 217.
83. Christopher Hill, *The Century of Revolution, 1603–1714*, p. 63.

menacing as the intervention of authority, and they have difficulty negotiating a responsible and autonomous course. The conflicts that result are prompted by a sudden eruption of impulse rather than by serious differences of policy. Moreover, this emotional willfulness does not lead to effective action or resistance; rather, the frustrations of unrequited love and chivalric misadventure prevail in most of Sidney's works. His protagonists' principal characteristic is a kind of heroic pathos in which they are defeated by their own impulses and exertions.

This peculiar combination of heroism and pathos undoubtedly derives from the conventions of Renaissance love poetry and chivalric romance. Sidney examines the movements of the will in the psychological and narrative terms of contemporary literature. Desire is first expressed in love, then chastened and contained by moral constraints and social circumstances. Sidney still charges this drama with a peculiar intensity, for there is something more at stake than fulfillment in love. Even in the more purely amatory realm of *Astrophil and Stella,* a keen perception of sexual politics is apparent, for power and autonomy remain concerns in all of Sidney's love stories. Yet the conflict remains on a rather generalized and basic psychological level, achieving specifically political expression less frequently. For Sidney, individual willfulness is essentially arbitrary and impulsive rather than systematic and disciplined; it is more a matter of "selfnesse" than a principled assertion of rights. This attitude determines the treatment of autonomy in his fiction and poetry. As well as reflecting certain literary conventions of his culture, this willfulness also reveals contradictory aspects of the aristocratic ethos, for assertion remains somewhat romantic and individualistic. The archaic code of honor and chivalric glory and the genuinely impetuous elements are hard to reconcile with the systematic, rationalizing demands of policy. In the quarrel with Oxford and the doomed charge at Zutphen, political or tactical concerns seem secondary or irrelevant.

SIR PHILIP SIDNEY

THE IMPACT OF THESE AMBIGUITIES on Sidney's creative efforts poses serious problems of assessment. The historical restrictions on his political ambitions are fairly clear. In his excellent biography of Greville, Ronald Rebholz describes Sidney's and Greville's situation with lucid precision, explaining that there were

> few opportunities for a courtier to act, as an individual or member of a group, in some decisive way that enabled him to feel he had served the kingdom of God in England or on the continent. Even a man of Philip Sidney's talents and courage found scant latitude for heroic Christian action amidst the complexities of Elizabethan government, the limits set on foreign policy by lack of treasure, the corruption of entrenched bureaucrats, the self-serving actions of other courtiers, the conflict between factions, and the mixture of shrewdness and indecision that was the Queen. Sidney became the pattern of chivalry only by dying. Alive, he had to be satisfied with bold and unavailing criticism of the government."[84]

Here is a clear but compassionate sense of the limits on Sidney's "large and sincere resolutions."

Yet turning to the criticism of Sidney's literature, one finds almost no sense of human or historical limitations. It is generally assumed that in his fiction Sidney obtains the sense of mastery and ordered comprehension denied him in life. For traditional critics, this achievement is based on a harmonious synthesis of orthodox Renaissance values. Petrarchan acceptance, Neoplatonic hierarchy, and Christian heroism are all components of an inclusive doctrinal order in this scheme; and courtly, political, and religious service turn out to be mutually supportive virtues. For Richard Young, the tensions of *Astrophil and Stella* are resolved by submission to Petrarchan tradition, and urgent individual impulses are subdued by a "ritual purgation."[85] Walter Davis treats the composite *Arcadia* of 1593 as

84. Ronald A. Rebholz, *The Life of Sir Fulke Greville*, pp. xxiii–xxiv.
85. Richard B. Young, "English Petrarke: A Study of Sidney's *Astrophel and Stella*," p. 81.

a profoundly religious work whose story traces the platonic "perfection of the hero through love" and exalts the values of Christian patience and contemplation.[86]

More interesting are the critics who acknowledge the persistence of conflict in Sidney's literature. "Sidney seemed instinctively to feel," Stephen Greenblatt explains, "that for the world he wished to portray, there could be no unified, pure form with a single style, a uniform set of characters, and a fixed perspective."[87] He consciously "exposes the instability and uncertainty of human judgment," for, amid the general concern for order and stability, "Sidney as artist is more a connoisseur of doubt."[88] Similarly, Richard Lanham argues for a more complex and sophisticated notion of didactic purpose. In his view the *Arcadia* does not aim to inculcate the conventional wisdom and "good old truths" of the age.[89] Dialectic predominates over synthesis, demanding a more alert and flexible response from the reader, something approaching negative capability. Sidney becomes an advocate of ambiguity, maintaining an artistic independence from the special pleading of rhetoricians and moralists. Lanham finds that, with Sidney, the "genuinely persuasive part of his work states the paradox, not its solution. Sidney clearly saw this as an artist, if he did not always admit to it as a man. . . . For Sidney knew that though the rhetorician can never admit to doubt, the poet—if he is wise—will never pretend to certainty."[90]

In this approach, however, contradictions are conceded only to be rationalized and reconciled within a more contemporary orthodoxy. Conflicts are smoothly translated into the familiar values of paradox, irony, and ambiguity. Even ambivalence is sanitized of all troubling implications as it becomes a synonym for open-mindedness. Sidney's

86. Walter R. Davis, "A Map of Arcadia," pp. 67–68.
87. Stephen J. Greenblatt, "Sidney's *Arcadia* and the Mixed Mode," p. 271.
88. Ibid., p. 274.
89. Richard A. Lanham, "The Old *Arcadia*," p. 331.
90. Ibid., pp. 330–331.

"ambivalences and ironies" are lumped together by Elizabeth Dipple into one creative state of mind.[91] Dipple uses these terms with strange abandon. In another article, she endows Sidney with "creative literary hysteria."[92] Lanham also remarks on a "fundamental ambivalence in attitude" in the *Old Arcadia,* but the transition from ambivalence to ambiguity is naturally assumed.[93] With things thus seen from all sides, narrative order and control are maintained. Whether the work's conflicts are contained by harmonious synthesis or dialectical irony, both interpretations lead to the same sense of omniscient comprehension.

There is at work here a certain eagerness to make a virtue of necessity. Critics like Lanham are determined to find lucid order in labyrinthine complexity and insight—even wisdom in uncertainty. "It is the juxtaposition of a rhetorical language moving in one direction and a plot constantly moving in another which gives us our main clue to Sidney's final intention. . . . It seems almost willful misinterpretation to think Sidney unaware of this."[94] Yet his interpretation of these enigmatic clues is no less willful or arbitrary in its assumptions. Having made his inferential leap, Lanham can make excellent sense of Sidney's "persistent ironic shorthand" and "indirect comment"; he can even find ironies in those utterances "passed on by a tongue-in-cheek narrator without comment."[95]

In his treatment of the various ambiguities in Sidney's work, Lanham, like many others, essentially follows the procedures established by William Empson. In *Seven Types of Ambiguity,* Empson declares with disarming bluntness that "any contradiction is likely to have some sensible interpretations; and if you think of interpretations which are not sensible, it puts the blame on you. . . . Since it

91. Elizabeth Dipple, " 'Unjust Justice' in the *Old Arcadia,*" p. 86.
92. Elizabeth Dipple, "Harmony and Pastoral in the *Old Arcadia,*" p. 328.
93. Lanham, "Old *Arcadia,*" p. 194.
94. Ibid., p. 373.
95. Ibid., pp. 323, 355, 322.

is the business of the reader to extract the meanings useful to him and ignore the meanings he thinks foolish, it is evident that contra-diction is a powerful literary weapon."[96] Empson also freely ac-knowledges his preference for harmonious resolution, arguing that "the contradiction must somehow form a larger unity if the final effect is to be satisfying." If the ambiguities are not explicitly re-solved, "the onus of reconciliation can be laid very heavily on the receiving end."[97] Empson assigns these critical responsibilities with a certain self-conscious irony and ambiguity of his own. Nevertheless, his tone has not prevented an unreflective, even dogmatic, applica-tion of these ideas in the criticism of the last forty years.

There is, of course, nothing wrong with a desire for "sensible in-terpretations," inasmuch as the point of all interpretation is to make sense of something. Rather, the problem involves an interpretive focus that is too rationalistic and narrow. This approach to ambigu-ity encourages an irrational faith in the artist as omnipotent creator whose creations are fully conscious and self-contained. Empson's insistence on "sensible interpretations" can lead, paradoxically, to mystification. In John Danby's criticism, this tendency reaches the level of religious conviction as he assures us that Sidney "is so con-sciously the intellectual moralizer of his material that in any case where we might suspect discrepancy, it is wise to bear in mind the possibility that we have missed his plan. What might seem his con-fusion might be our obtuseness."[98] The critic sounds like Pamela speaking of God's providence, as every contradiction is imputed to conscious plan and the wisdom of genius. This lays the "onus of reconciliation" quite heavily on the reader, who is exhorted to a kind of appreciative solemnity as any suspicion of "discrepancy" or "confusion" is stilled.

96. William Empson, *Seven Types of Ambiguity,* p. 197.
97. Ibid., p. 193, n. 1.
98. John F. Danby, *Poets on Fortune's Hill,* p. 57.

In dealing with the ambiguities of Sidney's works, this interpretive approach, with its rationalistic bias, preference for resolution, and insistence on artistic omniscience, leads to serious distortions. It requires that contradictions be either ignored or rationalized and that Sidney's creative mastery be grossly overestimated. Yet Sidney's fiction contains conflicts and uncertainties not intelligible on their own terms, and his control of these is tenuous and problematic. A determination to treat these difficulties as signs of genius only conceals their true significance. To discover this significance, one must see Sidney's literature in its historical context; this connection is essential to a more inclusive and realistic understanding of his fiction's ambiguities and a clarification of their sources and meaning, their depth and complexity.

A consistently historical and biographical approach will also correct other critical errors. Often the belief in Sidney's literary perfection is linked to a romantic and fairly vaporous conception of his life. Danby argues that Sidney's creative powers derive from a fantastically lofty social status: "The man placed as Sidney was is in a sense free. . . . In such poetry the state has withered away. The result is the disinterestedness, directness, and sincerity—the essential truthfulness" of social and poetic mastery.[99] Danby is preoccupied here with the degrading effects of patronage on those of less exalted status; and because, for him, patronage is the only problem, Sidney's exemption from it allows a preternatural freedom. Danby's is a very partial and rather dazed view of Sidney and his class, a view that ignores all the limitations and difficulties of the aristocracy's predicament. His incongruous allusion to Marx makes these sentiments no less fanciful.

Such inflated claims for Sidney's achievement and autonomy have inspired an inevitable, if rather infrequent, reaction. Ben Jonson was one of the first to take a somewhat skeptical attitude toward this

99. Ibid., p. 32.

legendary figure. His cryptic statement about Sir Philip's pimples seems intended to deflate later notions, such as Shelley's, of a "spirit without spot."[100] Richard Lanham's recent attacks on Sidney indulge in more fulsome antagonism. His curious shifts in attitude reflect many of the problems of recent Sidney criticism. In his study of the *Old Arcadia*, Lanham established his aversion to " 'extrinsic' " criticism when he insisted that Sidney's purpose "can reasonably be inferred from the text. We need not flee to biography."[101] His examination certainly does follow the text, but his conclusions involve an abrupt flight to biography, deriving all sorts of thematic and textual implications from a single biographical event: "It seems plausible that Sidney, lacerated as he was by his passion for Penelope Devereux, should seek the solace of a rehearsal of his problem and an explanation for it, in writing the Old *Arcadia*. (I hardly see how we can avoid concluding that Sidney was fully in love with her when he wrote the Old *Arcadia*, whatever final dating may be decided upon.) Marriage was for him, I have no doubt, the just and proper solution for such an infatuation."[102]

In a later article on *Astrophil and Stella*, Lanham sees the sonnets as an even more transparent vehicle for these same concerns, and his assessment of Sidney's motives takes an abusive turn. His respect for Sidney's poetic intelligence has drastically diminished, and he announces this with imposing sonority: "I, and I seem to be alone in this, do not find the heart into which Sidney looks one of any extraordinary richness. His themes are few, his scale hardly vast."[103] Lanham accuses Sidney of a glib, self-serving rhetoric of which the single-minded purpose, the seduction of Penelope Devereux, precludes all complexity of thought. Lanham compares Sidney's sonnets

100. Ben Jonson, "Conversations with William Drummond of Hawthornden," in *Works*, 1, pp. 138–139.
101. Lanham, "Old *Arcadia*," p. 197.
102. Ibid., p. 375.
103. Richard A. Lanham, *"Astrophil and Stella,"* p. 104.

with Shakespeare's, and this becomes a basis for contrast between the latter's "more capacious soul" and the "young, fiery, adolescent" urgency and shallowness of Sidney.[104]

Lanham examines the biography more directly in an article mockingly entitled "Sidney: The Ornament of his Age." In it Lanham enumerates all Sidney's failures and frustrations and holds him personally responsible for them; "adolescent naïveté," "aristocratic pride," and quixotically "rigid idealism" are among the charges he levels.[105] Sidney personifies, according to Lanham, "a chivalric ideal irrelevant to the world of affairs," whose ornamental attractions were exploited by more adroit political operators to advance their own purposes.[106]

Lanham's view of Sidney is, in the end, rather confusing. He begins by renouncing biographical speculation, but the repressed returns with a vengeance. In Lanham's later view, Sidney's career is ruined by an abundance of personal deficiencies. Either his art is overwhelmed by the shallow "adolescent" concerns of his life, or it achieves an irrelevant, and presumably ornamental, transcendence. The latter alternative is taken up in the biographical account, in which Lanham displays a patronizing contempt for Sidney's fiction, arguing that "only in religion—or in literature—can a life of unrelieved idealism be comfortably lived."[107] Having once praised Sidney's writings for their tough-minded appreciation of life's uncertainties, Lanham now dismisses them as a vehicle for purest wish fulfillment. Lanham's notion of religion and literature as realms of comforting illusions betrays some surprisingly philistine assumptions. Moreover, his view of Sidney's life lacks any historical perspective. Sidney's failures are genuine, but they do not result from naïve

104. Ibid.
105. Lanham, "Sidney," pp. 327, 333.
106. Ibid., p. 329 passim.
107. Ibid., p. 332.

idealism or capricious arrogance; in other words, his failings are not simply personal.

A new understanding of Sidney's life and art is essential for several reasons. It will allow full recognition of the various contradictions in his fiction, in all their intensity, as well as a more satisfactory account of their significance. A knowledge of their origins in his own situation should allow both a more sympathetic understanding of his predicament and a greater realism, for one can appreciate the actual obstacles to his success in both his artistic and political undertakings. An understanding of the difficulties and risks and limited alternatives should discourage facile abuse. On the other hand, such knowledge will certainly hinder the hagiographic tendencies of most Sidney criticism, which oversimplifies the assessment of his literature as well as his life. Such overestimation is ultimately a disservice, for the human and historical significance of his conflicts is diminished by such easy solutions.

A more consistent and inclusive interpretation can make the essential connections between Sidney's life and art in a straightforward and responsible way. I hope to clarify the problematic contradictions and complexities as I examine each text, moving beyond rationalizations and impressionistic value judgments to a clearer understanding of Sidney's achievement. Placing his achievement in the context of the English Renaissance should amplify our appreciation of Sidney and his times, dispelling any notion of his ornamental irrelevance to the period's essential issues.

Chapter Two

THE PATTERN OF CONFLICT:
DISPUTATION AND IMPASSE

IN THE FALL OF 1579, Sir Philip Sidney wrote his first version of the *Arcadia,* dedicating it to his sister Mary, the Countess of Pembroke. It was written during his residence at Wilton, the rural estate of Mary's husband, for the entertainment of the Countess and her friends, "being done," as Sidney says in his dedication to his sister, "in loose sheets of paper, most of it in your presence, the rest by sheets sent unto you as fast as they were done."[1] He deems it an "idle work," a mere "trifle, and that triflingly handled," concluding with this self-deprecating appeal: "Read it then at your idle times, and

---

1. *The Countess of Pembroke's Arcadia* (*The Old Arcadia*), ed. Jean Robertson, p. 3. The *Old Arcadia* is hereafter cited in the text by the notation *OA* followed by the page number and, when the reference is to the poetry, the line number, e.g., *OA,* 340.12. Feuillerat's edition of the *New Arcadia,* which is in the first volume of *The Prose Works of Sir Philip Sidney,* is hereafter cited with the notation *NA* followed by the page number, then the line number if any. I have chosen to follow Robertson's spelling of "Euarchus" rather than "Evarchus." For both sides of this controversy, see Franklin B. Williams' review of her edition of the *Old Arcadia* in *Renaissance Quarterly,* 27 (1974), 237–242, and Robertson's reply in *Renaissance Quarterly,* 28 (1975), 298–299. The *Old* and *New Arcadia* have many things in common, and I treat them both, to some extent, as a sustained undertaking. When I am discussing both together, I refer to them inclusively; when it is important to distinguish between them, I use the traditional nomenclature of *Old* and *New.*

the follies your good judgement will find in it, blame not, but laugh at. And so, looking for no better stuff than, as in a haberdasher's shop, glasses or feathers, you will continue to love the writer who doth exceedingly love you, and most heartily prays you may long live to be a principal ornament to the family of the Sidneys" (*OA*, 3). He thus presents his first major work with the charming *sprezzatura* expected of an accomplished courtier.

Sidney himself seems to have had fun with this playfully intricate story. He brings his tale of romantic intrigue and disguise to a desperately complicated climax and then cuts through these complexities with an abrupt, deus ex machina conclusion. Thus he displays an enthusiasm, typical of the late sixteenth century, for the *favola intreccio* or " 'knotted' fable," whose potentially tragic difficulties are resolved by a comic ending.[2] Two princes, Pyrocles and Musidorus, fall in love with the two daughters of Basilius, the errant ruler of Arcadia. Troubled by a strange oracle, the Arcadian king has chosen a life of rustic solitude and forbidden his daughters to marry. The heroes disguise themselves as an Amazon and a shepherd in order secretly to woo their ladies, but although they succeed in their romantic endeavors, their schemes lead to political catastrophe. By the end, the king is apparently dead, his wife and daughters are disgraced, Arcadia is racked by the threat of anarchy and rebellion, and the princes are on trial for their lives. Sidney gives the catastrophe one more twist by bringing in the father of Pyrocles to pass judgment on their crimes; when their true identity is revealed, the old man's stern principles still force him to condemn his son and his ward to death. The sudden revival of Basilius averts this disaster and assures a conventional happy ending. This witty romantic comedy undoubtedly amused its audience at Wilton, and its elegant pastoral eclogues provided a lyrical idealization of their pleasant surroundings.

2. See Giovanni Battista Guarini's praise of this type of plot in his preface to the 1602 edition of *Il Pastor Fido*, p. 177.

For Sidney, the work must have been an engaging diversion from the previous year's battles of faction and policy. Yet his political preoccupations persist in more generalized form, for the duke's follies and the heroes' disobedience inevitably have social implications. Self-assertion and filial autonomy are opposed by the arbitrary whims and paternal severity of royal authority—opposed, that is, until the last moment, when they are magnanimously indulged. These are, of course, the traditional themes of romance literature from Heliodorus to Guarini. In Sidney's fiction, these same themes achieve an intriguing complexity and intensity that can best be explained by their relevance to his life and situation. This happens because the work's crucial issues do not remain simply romantic or fictive; they become political and even biographical, and in some instances historically specific.

Many readers have noted a resemblance between the duke's abdication of responsibility and passive yielding to fate and Elizabeth's vacillations. Basilius has a good counselor named Philanax who urges a course of activism and constancy, but such advice has no impact on rulers like Basilius. Later, when Basilius falls in love with the Amazon, Pyrocles, the Arcadians become alarmed by their ruler's odd conduct. Rumors of their king's seduction by a foreigner provide a pretext for revolt. William Zeeveld sees in this a persistent concern with the French marriage and its ramifications in England. The Arcadians rebel at "the prospect of a stranger's possessing their secrets, draining the treasury, conquering the country without opposition; and, if necessary, they, too, would have taken the government into their own hands rather than leave their prince to foreigners."[3] All these grievances and threats were, as Zeeveld points out, enumerated in the hapless John Stubbs's "Gaping Gulf."

Although the references to foreign dangers are altered in the revi-

3. W. Gordon Zeeveld, "The Uprising of the Commons in Sidney's *Arcadia*," p. 216.

sion, the rebellion persists and even expands in scope and detail. In the *New Arcadia*, the princely Amphialus participates openly in the rebellion against Basilius, invoking the Huguenot doctrine of the subaltern magistracy to justify his defiance. William Briggs emphasizes the importance and legitimacy of this doctrine for Sidney (while conceding that this "particular application" is wrong), and he draws intriguing parallels between James VI and Amphialus and between Mary Stuart and the evil Cecropia.[4] His interpretation is disputed by Irving Ribner, who insists that Sidney condemns all rebellion "in unmistakable terms" and affirms the necessity, in the *Old Arcadia's* trial scenes, of absolute obedience; Sidney does this because he shares the "great fear" of all Tudor Englishmen: a "return to the chaos and horror of the fifteenth century when one powerful noble after another had taken arms against the king."[5] Ernest William Talbert takes the middle ground in this argument, emphasizing the importance of more moderate political theories. Sidney was acquainted, according to Talbert, with the radical doctrines of Hotman, de Mornay, and others, and, given his position, it is not surprising that he "considered subalterns . . . a necessary feature of a commonweal."[6] Nevertheless, his ideas on this topic derive less from a rebellious antagonism toward the monarchy than from conventional English notions of the "mixed state"; the writings of John Ponet, Sir Thomas Smith, and Richard Hooker were more influential than the radical concepts of the Huguenots: "Although Sidney's attitude toward rule may seem confusing at times, it is essentially orthodox," Talbert concludes.[7] This moderation allows Sidney to present in the *Arcadia* "a treatment of political commonplaces . . . which is more complicated, more realistic, more conducive to ironies than that represented by any Elizabethan world-picture of a musically

4. William D. Briggs, "Political Ideas in Sidney's *Arcadia*," pp. 150, 139.
5. Irving Ribner, "Sir Philip Sidney on Civil Insurrection," p. 262, n. 21.
6. Ernest William Talbert, *The Problem of Order*, p. 105.
7. Ibid., p. 92.

simple order and degree," allowing its readers to argue "for conclusions both orthodox and rebellious."[8] This is shrewd and, in several respects, accurate, although Talbert fails, as many others do, to explain precisely how these ironies are sustained. Nevertheless, the problem with each of these interpretations is the same: Briggs, Ribner, and Talbert all impute a kind of ideological clarity to Sidney's writing which it does not have. The political implications of the *Old* and *New Arcadia* often acquire a striking historical and theoretical specificity, and the books' relevance to his own career is often apparent. Yet nothing is resolved in clear political terms because the issue of rebellion is never fully confronted.

Sidney's youthful heroes persist in their defiance of authority, and their defiance is neither condemned nor justified; it is instead rather ambiguously indulged. This indulgence is encouraged by certain narrative inconsistencies. In the *Old Arcadia,* the terms of their sentence shift abruptly with the revival of Basilius, and the original charges of "ravishment" are ignored. The fate of self-assertion and insubordination is obscured by the conclusion. Similarly, the original Huguenot justification for the rebellion of Amphialus is abandoned as the war continues. Because Amphialus too is in love with one of Basilius's daughters, his motives for disobedience are personal and erotic. The political pretext is a mere ruse, inspired by his evil mother; and his innocent passivity and romantic anguish increase one's sympathy and forestall censure. As I suggested earlier, Sidney does not sustain his heroes' willfulness in any systematic way. The grounds for self-assertion constantly shift in his fictions from the straightforward claims of political expression to the more ambiguous impulses of personal desire. The battle between autonomy and submission is never resolved. Sidney could impose neither a sternly conservative nor an explicitly radical solution, for neither one would fit his fiction or his life. Nor could he work out a moderately

8. Ibid., p. 117.

balanced relationship between sovereign and subordinate. Instead the conflict simply persists in both versions of *Arcadia* in a palpably unsettling and unconscious fashion. Sidney covertly resists the dominance of authority and the dangers of a stable settlement; though he could not finally win it, he kept the conflict going.

In the *Old Arcadia,* the social harmony of the opening scene is swiftly dissipated by the caprice of authority. "Arcadia," Sidney tells us, "among all the provinces of Greece was ever had in singular reputation, partly for the sweetness of the air and other natural benefits, but principally for the moderate and well tempered minds of the people. . . . In this place some time there dwelled a mighty duke named Basilius, a prince of sufficient skill to govern so quiet a country where the good minds of the former princes had set down good laws, and the well bringing up of the people did serve as a most sure bond to keep them" (*OA,* 4). Arcadia is a place of extraordinary stability, but this pastoral calm is jeopardized when Basilius renounces his responsibilities. The trouble begins when the duke first feels the anxieties of old age. He grows "desirous to know the certainty of things to come, wherein," the narrator adds, "there is nothing so certain as our continual uncertainty" (*OA,* 5). To satisfy his desire, Basilius consults the Delphic oracle, but the cryptic prophecies cause him even greater confusion and dread. Still, the ominous tone is clear enough, and the duke decides on a curious and, of course, futile stratagem: abdication of his throne and pastoral retirement. "And so for himself, being so cruelly menaced by fortune, he would draw himself out of her way by this loneliness, which he thought was the surest mean to avoid her blows" (*OA,* 6). When he discloses his intentions to Philanax and assigns to the latter the responsibility for the government of Arcadia, the counselor opposes his ruler's action and their debate begins.

Philanax proposes that "wisdom and virtue be the only destinies appointed to man to follow." These are "guides" that " cannot fail," pointing "so direct a way of proceeding as prosperity must necessarily ensue" and precluding the need for such devious evasions as the duke adopts (*OA*, 7). Basilius responds by emphasizing the problem of accommodation to fortune, questioning the soundness of Philanax's simplistic inflexibility: "and would you, then, . . . that in change of fortune I shall not change my determination, as we do our apparel according to the air, and as the ship doth her course with the wind?" (*OA*, 9). Philanax elaborates on his original advice only slightly. He still maintains that "a constant virtue, well settled, [is] little subject unto it [i.e., change]"; "in great necessity" would he allow for alteration, and this must be moderate and "well proportioned" (*OA*, 9). Their debate concludes with epigrammatic symmetry: Basilius's pliancy is opposed by his counselor's insistence on steadfast rigor. " 'Yet the reeds stand with yielding,' said the duke. 'And so are they but reeds, most worthy Prince,' said Philanax, 'but the rocks stand still and are rocks' " (*OA*, 9).

The basic issues are defined with stark clarity. Pastoral withdrawal is opposed by political responsibility; passive relaxation, by unflinching rigor. The most important aspect of this conflict involves the problem of constancy and change. Constancy is the principal virtue in the *Arcadia,* a condition of moral balance and sanity to which all the characters aspire. At the same time, its ethical primacy coincides with the predominance of change. As in many other works of the period, mutability is a central thematic and narrative concern. The tension between constancy and change is one source of the work's extraordinary complexity.

In this context, constancy is defined as the basis of the sovereign's authority and responsibility. Tudor theorists considered *iustitia immobilis* the essential virtue of the monarch.[9] Philanax invokes this principle, urging his sovereign, "Let your subjects have you in their eyes, let them see the benefits of your justice daily more and more; and so must they needs rather like of present sureties than uncertain

---

9. Elizabeth Dipple, " 'Unjust Justice' in the *Old Arcadia*," p. 90.

changes" (*OA*, 7–8). Ensuing developments will vindicate this demand for royal constancy. As a result of Basilius's negligence, the entire country is engulfed in chaotic change. Moreover, the restoration of order requires the intervention of Euarchus, the sovereign epitome of "unmoveable" justice.

Initially, the conflict seems clear-cut, for Basilius flagrantly violates his responsibilities. Sidney presents him as a weak, self-indulgent, negligent ruler and father, and the case against him is confirmed by his subsequent behavior. At the same time, there are aspects of Philanax's behavior that qualify one's acceptance of him. His response to uncertainty is tinged with arrogance, and there is something too absolute in his assertion of man's self-sufficiency. Although his convictions make Philanax an effective governor, they can also carry him to ruthless excess. The long-range implications of his position are no less disturbing than the results of Basilius's choice. At the trial, Philanax becomes a self-righteous, vengeful monster, thwarted only when fortune discloses forces beyond the scope of man's "wisdom and virtue." In the opening debate the troublesome aspects of his ethical presumptions and notions of sovereignty remain an undertone; yet his claims can still make one uneasy, amplifying one's appreciation of human uncertainty. The conflict has a more equivocal tone than one might initially presume.

The opening debate provides a dramatic point of departure, for it defines the implications of Basilius's choice with cogency and force. This is a first in a series of formal arguments encountered throughout both versions of the *Arcadia*. Debate is one of Sidney's favorite narrative devices, as Richard Lanham has recognized, and others have noted its general influence on literature of the period.[10] Disputation had, of course, sources outside of literature and a broad cultural pur-

10. Richard A. Lanham, "The Old *Arcadia*," p. 328. See also G. K. Hunter, *John Lyly*, pp. 44–45, 118 ff.; Rosemond Tuve, *Elizabethan and Metaphysical Imagery*, pp. 206–207; Hardin Craig, *The Enchanted Glass*, p. 150.

pose as well. It was a basic pedagogical technique of Tudor schools, and Sidney, who learned it there, was apparently very skilled at it.[11] In addition to training persuasive orators, it was supposed to enable students to see all sides of a question. Controversy thus became the means of discovering the truth. It is celebrated accordingly by Milton, whose enthusiasm for "the struggle of contrarieties" was prompted by this lofty aim.[12] "Where there is much desire to learn," he writes, "there of necessity will be much arguing."[13]

Richard Lanham has remarked on Sidney's "fondness for dialectic," and he traces its influence from the debates, to the complex "double plot," down to Sidney's syntax with its "balanced and antithetical" phrases.[14] This type of sentence is, in fact, the basic unit of wit at this period, revealing its formal structures on their smallest scale. Two opposing points of view are held up for scrutiny in clear and careful balance. Wit's various components are displayed and fully anatomized in Lyly's *Euphues*. Its basic meaning is simply "native intelligence," but its stylistic principles give it a special purpose in the Renaissance. It becomes a means of negotiating conflict and sustaining graceful poise, and it acquires its connotations of intellectual agility, verbal grace, and a playful detachment and humor.[15] In his excellent study of Lyly, G. K. Hunter concludes that wit is the ability to make "complex valuations of different kinds of worldly experience. The ease with which a man moves among these comparative valuations may be measured by his capacity to play them off one against the other."[16] For Sidney, wit also serves this broad

11. James M. Osborn, *Young Philip Sidney, 1572–1577*, p. 23.
12. John Milton, *The Reason of Church Government Urged Against Prelaty*, in *Complete Poems and Major Prose*, p. 662.
13. Ibid., *Areopagitica*, p. 743.
14. Lanham, "Old *Arcadia*," pp. 327, 204, 399, 345.
15. See T. S. Eliot, "Andrew Marvell," in *Selected Essays*, pp. 292–304; and F. R. Leavis, "The Line of Wit," in *Revaluation*, pp. 10–41.
16. Hunter, *Lyly*, p. 10.

expository purpose, and debate and antithesis are the stylistic means to this end. Disputation defines relationships among the characters, illuminates and advances the action, and clarifies thematic concerns.

At the same time, there are signs of another, more contradictory purpose. The first dispute introduces a jarring note of conflict into a setting of peaceful harmony; despite the stylized manner, the tone of antagonism often becomes quite harsh. More significantly, the debate is not resolved. Different contestants engage in the same argument over and over without reaching any settlement. The persistence of certain crucial issues, the intransigence of the conflict, and the pattern of its development distinguish Sidney's disputes from the raillery and wit play of other Elizabethan writers.

The ambivalent tone of the first argument increases as one's sympathy for the victims of change increases. Philisides is a victim who elicits considerable sympathy. One of those "stranger shepherds" whose melancholy brought him to retire to Arcadia, he has the singular advantage of representing his author in debate, and a certain favoritism is shown him from his first appearance; William Ringler calls him "Sidney's fictionalized self-portrait."[17] Unlike Basilius, he incurs no reproach for pastoral retirement. Philisides' motivation, as well as his identity, elicits one's sympathy, for its sources are romantic: he was securely virtuous until "love . . . diverted this course of tranquillity" and reduced him to "this change, much in state but more in mind" (*OA*, 335).

Philisides' crisis occurs in a dream-vision in which the judgment of Paris is reenacted. Diana and Venus appear to him as a pair of bickering crones, but they are attended by a beautiful nymph, Mira. Asked to settle their "discord" by assigning precedence to one, Philisides chooses Mira. The goddesses must bestow their respective gifts upon the winner, but they vengefully make Mira's reward a curse on Philisides:

17. *The Poems of Sir Philip Sidney,* ed. William A. Ringler, Jr., p. 418.

'Yet thou shalt not go free,' quoth Venus, 'such a fire
Her beauty kindle shall within thy foolish mind
That thou full oft shalt wish thy judging eyes were blind.'
'Nay then' Diana, said, 'the chasteness I will give
In ashes of despair, though burnt, shall make thee live.'

(OA, 340.12–16)

The synthesis of beauty and chastity leads to oxymoronic anguish, and the contest's "settlement" has ominously discordant implications. When this poem is transferred to Amphialus in the *New Arcadia*, the allusion to Paris acquires a more sinister significance, for his desires provoke an epic struggle. Philisides' belligerence is restricted to his debate with Geron, but his altered condition still entangles him in conflict with others.

Geron provokes Philisides' wrath by urging the younger man to "let sorrows go" (*OA*, 72.4). When he fails to cheer Philisides up, Geron turns to more serious problems:

Yet sure an end to each thing time doth give,
Though woes now live, at length thy woes must die.
Then virtue try, if she can work in thee
That which we see in many time hath wrought,
And weakest hearts to constant temper brought.

(OA, 72.14–18)

He proposes an end to Philisides' impassioned suffering, an end that is both a termination and a resolution. This could be achieved by willful exertion or by the passage of time or both, and the crucial outcome would be the restoration of constancy.

Philisides repudiates this solution, replying caustically, "Time shall in one my life and sorrows end, / And me perchance your constant temper lend" (*OA*, 72.22–23). His response has several implications. For one thing, his predicament is so dramatically grave that death is the only deliverance. At the same time, he dismisses Geron's "constant temper" as enfeebled stolidity, subtly suggesting the hypocrisy of old men who make a virtue of decrepitude. Finally, he betrays an odd ambivalence toward the work's central virtue: in this context, constancy becomes moribund quiescence, imposed rather than chosen. Geron has proposed time as one means of achieving stability, but its effects on the old man are hardly edifying. "This 'live-dead man in this old dungeon flung" (*OA*, 74.18) provokes only disgust.

The effects of virtue seem no less menacing, and Geron's hortatory belligerence confirms Philisides' fears; constancy is indeed a form of imprisonment here: "Rebel, rebel, in golden fetters bind / This tyrant love; or rather do suppress / Those rebel thoughts which are thy slaves by kind" (*OA*, 73.13–15). Geron's bullying diminishes his moral authority, and the argument becomes a pugnacious contest of wills. No conclusion is reached, as the controversy ends in a draw.

The same issues are argued in the "skirmish betwixt Reason and Passion" (*OA*, 135), and the argument develops along similar lines. This pastoral exercise, the first in the second eclogues, takes the form of a choral dialogue between the two sets of shepherds. Their exchange reenacts the "rude tumult of the Phagonians," the rebels whose chaotic assault upon the royal family concluded Book II. In this masquelike entertainment, rebellion is internalized, and mental and political conflict are connected. Reason's stance is immediately imperious: "Thou rebel vile, come, to thy master yield" (*OA*, 135.13). Passion, however, defiantly resists: "No tyrant, no; mine, mine shall be the field" (*OA*, 135.15). Passion's grievance involves the loss of freedom as well as rule, and this is the basis of the charge of tyranny.

> *Reason.* Can Reason then a tyrant counted be?
> *Passion.* If Reason will that Passions be not free.
> *R.* But Reason will that Reason govern most.
> *P.* And Passion will that Passion rule the roast.
>
> (*OA*, 135.16–19)

47

Sidney's irony undercuts the ordinarily unassailable "rationality" of Reason's claims. The truism begins to sound like narrow, tautological self-interest. The next two lines draw out the point, showing that Reason is no less willful than will: "*R.* Your will is will; but Reason reason is. / *P.* Will hath his will when Reason's will doth miss" (*OA*, 135.20–21). With Reason's efforts to establish special privilege consistently defeated, the conventional humanist hierarchy is supplanted by a terse, antithetic equivalence. Typically, Sidney makes orthodoxy problematic.

Once subordination is ruled out, any relationship becomes extremely difficult. Reason insists on sovereignty, but Passion's demands for equality are undiminished: "*R.* By nature you to Reason faith have sworn. / *P.* Not so, but fellowlike together born" (*OA*, 135.24–25). Their difficulty only increases when Reason resorts to exasperated bullying: "Weakness you are, dare you with our strength fight?" (*OA*, 136.7). Passion's clever exploitation of this weakness which "weak'neth all your might" (*OA*, 136.8) turns this assault to an advantage.

Somewhat chastened, Reason becomes willing to compromise: "But yet our strife sure peace in end doth breed" (*OA*, 136.13). The hope expressed is more modest than previous assertions, but it is still consistent with rational principles. One is reminded of the purposes of dialogue, as the promise of synthesis is invoked. The skirmish seems to enact this goal choreographically when both factions approach, "and, instead of fighting, embrace one another" (*OA*, 136). Still, the dispute must be resolved discursively, and while Reason renews its demands in more conciliatory tones ("We are too strong; but Reason seeks not blood" [*OA*, 136.17]), Passion requires more convincing assurances: "*R.* Yet Passion, yield at length to Reason's stroke. / *P.* What shall we win by taking Reason's yoke? / *R.* The joys you have shall be made permanent" (*OA*, 136.21–23).

This promise of permanence is the compromise offered by George Chapman in his continuation of *Hero and Leander*. There he insists on the ceremonial regulation of passion, because only by a stable synthesis of virtue and passion can love be "so order'd that it still excites desire"; without this, Chapman argues there is only sensual waste.[18] The yearning to see pleasure reconciled to virtue is a central theme of Renaissance literature, one inspiring pointed irony and skepticism as well as beatific harmonies. Sidney's writing could sustain such lofty hopes; his description of Urania in the *New Arcadia* is proof of that. Here, however, Sidney insists on the fundamental opposition of reason and passion. Their conflicting demands are irreconcilable and compromise is spurious. As soon as Reason proposes a future settlement, the dialogue founders on the problem of now and then; the attitudes toward time are completely inconsistent. Passion's response to this proposal is characteristic, affirming its conventional allegiance to the moment: "We now have peace, your peace we do not need" (*OA*, 136.14). Yet fear of the future, more than pleasures of the present, drives Sidney's passionate shepherds. The promise of permanent joys forces contemplation of the long view, and this provokes characteristic apprehensions: "But so we shall with grief learn to repent" (*OA*, 136.24) Reason's exultant non sequitur confirms the fearful disparity of values: "Repent indeed, but that shall be your bliss" (*OA*, 136.25) Passion cannot be accomodated in this scheme; it can only be extinguished. Conflict persists, as the dialogue moves toward the inevitable impasse.

The last couplet seems to offer a way out of this: "*R. P.* Then let us both to heav'nly rules give place, Which Passions kill, and Reason do deface" (*OA*, 136.29–30). Transcendent authority is invoked, for final settlement requires heavenly intervention. Throughout, debate has served to expose Reason's aggression, and the rule of Reason is thus discredited and forestalled. At the debate's end, a crucial shift occurs in which the last word is assigned to celestial authority. In part, this solution reflects the lingering

18. George Chapman in Christopher Marlowe, *Plays and Poems,* p. 396.

tradition of *contemptus mundi,* encountered in the concluding poems of Sidney's *Certain Sonnets:* "For vertue hath this better lesson taught, / Within my selfe to seeke my onelie hire: / Desiring nought but how to kill desire."[19] Yet the appeal also serves more immediate, practical purposes, for it thwarts the oppressive presumptions of worldly power. The same purpose is obtained by John Milton in his famous defense of controversy, when he concedes conclusive judgment only to "the angel's ministry at the end of mortal things."[20] Thus, there is all the time in the world for conflict and no bishop or king can put a stop to it. This crucial ideological maneuver has origins early in the Reformation, for it was an important part of Martin Luther's attack on paternal and ecclesiastical authority. In Erik Erikson's insightful explanation, Luther justified this attack by shifting "the whole matter of obedience and disavowal to a higher, and historically significant plane."[21]

While this shift in allegiance allowed considerable room for maneuver, there were also problems. Erikson also emphasizes the psychological risks of this strategy for Luther: "One may say that by radically transferring the desperation of his filial position into the human condition vis-à-vis God, and by insisting, as it were, on a cosmic test case, he forced himself either to find a new avenue toward faith or to fail."[22] Political conflict with authority, what J. E. Neale calls the "art of opposition," was extremely difficult for men accustomed to submission.[23] It was some time before Englishmen could attain the clear-minded, revolutionary assurance of someone like Milton, and the old habits were still never fully lost. Guilt and fear (feelings that the awesome remoteness of their deity could

---

19. *Certain Sonnets,* 31, in *Poems,* Ringler, p. 161. All further references are cited by the sonnet number (e.g., *CS* 31) in the text.

20. Milton, *Areopagitica,* in *Poems and Prose,* p. 747.

21. Erik H. Erikson, *Young Man Luther,* p. 94.

22. Ibid., p. 157.

23. J. E. Neale, *Elizabeth I and Her Parliaments* 1584–1601, p. 436.

hardly allay) persisted. Sidney's final couplet betrays obvious anxiety, for "heav'nly rules" impose a settlement even less benign than Reason's. Peace is achieved not by reconciliation but rather by mutual annihilation, "which Passions kill, and Reason do deface." The brief glimpse of the hereafter reveals only the cold stasis of death—the "stark and dead congealment" that debate was intended to prevent.[24]

As a consequence, the "skirmish" moves nimbly on to yet another conclusion, returning from this grimly neat *sententia* to the murky contradictions of the plot: "Then embraced they one another, and came to the duke who framed his praises of them according to Cleophila's liking" (*OA,* 136). The pastoral exercise finally ceases with a conventional gesture, one whose ironies radiate in several directions. The performance is, as I have already suggested, a kind of masque in its combination of allegory, debate, and choreography. As in the *Lady of May,* the dispute also moves out into its audience, and it requires some response from its royal spectator, the "figure whose function it is to arbitrate."[25] Basilius cannot make a clear assessment, for, taken in by the hero's Amazon disguise, he has fallen foolishly in love with Pyrocles-Cleophila. In some sense, this scene affords another instance of Basilius's irresponsibility, because he shirks even this simple, ceremonial duty. Still, his response, however muddled, constitutes a choice, one determined by his own passions and his infatuation with the disguised hero. This is really the final settlement, one whose moral laxity and confusion is suffused with a prejudicial sympathy for Pyrocles. It is a covert victory for passion. Such laxity is, in fact, crucial to sympathy. As Boulon says elsewhere in the second eclogues, "Self-guilty folk [are] most prone to feel compassion" (*OA,* 150.23).

The general pattern of the "skirmish betwixt Reason and Passion

24. Milton, *Aeropagitica,* in *Poems and Prose,* p. 747.
25. Stephen Orgel, *The Jonsonian Masque,* p. 21.

is profoundly ambiguous. The conflict is first intensified rather than moderated, culminating in persistent opposition. A conclusive settlement, conceived in grimly punitive terms, is then threatened from above and deftly evaded. Antagonism and judgment finally dissolve in confusion, and all is forgotten and forgiven by a lax and indulgent authority. The *Old Arcadia*'s final scenes are thus prefigured in this dialogue in which the work's basic conflicts are enacted and the solution's contradictory elements are set forth. In the *Old Arcadia*, the erotic and political intrigue culminates in chaos, with Basilius apparently dead midway through the fourth book. The onset of these disastrous events is announced by the invocation of "everlasting justice," which uses "ourselves to be the punishers of our faults, and . . . our own actions the beginning of our chastisement" (*OA*, 265). When Euarchus, whose devotion to justice is preeminent, intervenes in these events, a conclusive settlement is imposed, and it is, of course, ruthlessly punitive. This judgment is then dramatically reversed by the resurrection of Basilius, who recalls the oracle that predicted all this and assumes "all had fallen out by the highest providence" (*OA*, 416). Euarchus's assessment is effectively blocked by this shift to a higher providential level of perception. Once this is achieved, it becomes clear that Sidney has returned the narrative to the muddled understanding of Basilius. Transcendence is relinquished and evasive irony takes its place. Sidney calls attention only to Basilius's ignorance of his wife, yet there are just as many problems with his acquittal of the heroes. They are still guilty of seducing his daughters, a crime whose treasonous implications Euarchus cited in his condemnation of them. Moreover, they had even contemplated armed resistance to the ruler (*OA*, 173). Sexual and political assertion is finally neither accommodated nor punished in this conclusion; it is simply obscured. Sidney's solution has a kind of hectic and intriguing instability, readily perceived by many critics but not very well explained. I think it derives not only from the conclusion's obvious contradictions but also from a suspicion, shared

by Sidney and his readers, that much of what he is up to here is not really legitimate. Ambivalent about subjective impulse and mistrustful of its ultimate vindication, he must fall back on the approval of authority for support.

The problematic nature of this solution is still clearer in the heroes' protracted disputation. Pyrocles falls in love early in the *Old Arcadia,* and the effects are notable immediately. Musidorus tells his friend "that since our late coming into this country I have marked in you, I will not say an alteration, but a relenting, truly, and slacking of the main career you had so notably begun and almost performed" (*OA*, 13). Formerly inclined "to seek the familiarity of excellent men in learning and soldiery," Pyrocles is now accused of letting his "mind fall asleep" (*OA*, 13) and seeking out "solitariness, the sly enemy that doth most separate a man from well doing" (*OA*, 14). Musidorus's main point is the same as Philanax's: "A mind well trained and long exercised in virtue, my sweet and worthy cousin, doth not easily change any course it once undertakes but upon well grounded and well weighed causes. . . . Even the very countenance and behaviour of such a man doth show forth images of the same constancy by maintaining the right harmony betwixt it and the inward good"; for such a man, adherence to the "well chosen course in virtue" comes naturally (*OA*, 13).

Pyrocles defends his behavior in highly evocative terms:

And yet, under the leave of your better judgement, I must needs say thus much, my dear cousin, that I find not myself wholly to be condemned because I do not with a continual vehemency follow those knowledges which you call the bettering of my mind; for both the mind itself must, like other things, sometimes be unbent, or else it will be either weakened or broken, and these knowledges, as they are of good use, so are they not all the mind may stretch itself unto. Who knows whether I feed not my mind with higher thoughts? Truly, as I know not all the particularities, so yet see I the bounds of all those knowledges; but the workings of the mind,

53

I find, much more infinite than can be led unto by the eye or imagined by any that distract their thoughts without themselves.

(OA, 14)

Once again, yielding pliancy is opposed to inflexible vehemence, recalling the final terms of Basilius and Philanax. Pyrocles insists on the need for relaxation from the masculine pursuits urged on him by Musidorus. His praise of contemplation only provokes the suspicions of Musidorus, who thinks this "is but a glorious title to idleness" and believes in the supremacy of the active life (*OA*, 16).

In his discussion of the *Arcadia,* Neil Rudenstine calls attention to Sidney's correspondence with Hubert Languet, noting its preoccupation with these same topics.[26] Writing to Languet, Sidney describes political tension in the same terms Pyrocles uses to convey mental strain: "In your letters I fancy I see a picture of the age in which we live: an age that resembles a bow too long bent, it must be unstrung or it will break."[27] Elsewhere Sidney expresses a yearning for withdrawal from action, for relaxation and a "refreshing of the mind."[28] Languet is alarmed and anxious at the persistence of his desire to drop out: "I am especially sorry to hear you say that you are weary of the life to which I have no doubt God has called you, and desire to fly from the light of your court and betake yourself to the privacy of secluded places to escape the tempest of affairs by which statesmen are generally harrassed."[29] Later, in response to Sidney's long retirement at Wilton, during which time he completed the *Old Arcadia,* Languet writes to Sidney that their friends on the Continent are worried "that the sweetness of your lengthened retirements may somewhat relax the vigorous energy with which you

---

26. Neil L. Rudenstine, *Sidney's Poetic Development,* pp. 16–22 passim.
27. *The Correspondence of Sir Philip Sidney and Hubert Languet,* trans. Stuart A. Pears, p. 36.
28. Ibid., p. 65.
29. Ibid., p. 155.

used to rise to noble undertakings, and a love of ease, which you once despised, creep by degrees over your spirit."[30]

It is illuminating to analyze the stance Sidney assumes in his letters, as it is clearly designed to provoke such urgent and importunate moralizing:

> And my mind itself, if it was ever active in any thing, is now beginning, by reason of my indolent ease, imperceptibly to lose its strength, and to relax without any reluctance. For to what purpose should our thoughts be directed to various kinds of knowledge, unless room be afforded for putting it into practice, so that public advantage may be the result, which in a corrupt age we cannot hope for? . . . But the mind itself, you will say, that particle of the divine mind, is cultivated in this manner. This indeed, if we allow it to be the case, is a very great advantage: but let us see whether we are not giving a beautiful but false appearance to our splendid errors. For while the mind is thus, as it were, drawn out of itself, it cannot turn its powers inward for thorough self-examination; to which employment no labour that men can undertake, is in any way to be compared. Do you not see that I am cleverly playing the stoic? yea and I shal be a cynic too, unless you reclaim me. Wherefore, if you please, prepare yourself to attack me. I have now pointed out the field of battle, and I openly declare war against you.[31]

All of Pyrocles' symptoms are discernible here: the helpless lapse into "indolent ease," the loss of strength and breakdown of discipline, the withdrawal and introversion, and the provocative challenge to authority. In the *Arcadia* these are caused by love, whereas in the letter, the motive is noticeably absent. The sources of Sidney's odd malaise are more generalized and diffuse, acquiring their focus only through paternalistic reproach. His expectation of Languet's disapproval is the clearest part of this passage, and Sidney turns all

30. Ibid., p. 183.
31. Ibid., pp. 143–144.

his energy and attention to it. This doting father substitute is simultaneously provoked and placated by the subtle combination of contradictory poses. The playful tone of this exchange and the choice of a benevolent surrogate preclude any serious risk. For all his querulous reproaches, very few of them in earnest, Languet remains tenderly solicitous. Their relationship sustains and even thrives on a surprising amount of aggressive banter.

Sidney may have found his father's admonitions less playfully indulgent. In an interesting book called *The Elizabethan Prodigals,* Richard Helgerson cites Sir Henry Sidney's letter to young Philip as an example of stern paternal moralism: " 'Remember, my son,' Sir Henry writes, 'the noble blood you are descended of by your mother's side; and think that only by virtuous life and good action you may be an ornament to that illustrious family. Otherwise, through vice and sloth, you may be counted *labes generis,* one of the greatest curses that can happen to man.' In signing himself, 'Your loving father, so long as you live in the fear of God,' Sir Henry further intimates that any falling away from the straight path of virtue will cost Philip his father's affection as well as the respect of his family."[32] Helgerson finds in such sententiousness the point of departure for a great deal of Elizabethan fiction, including Sidney's own: "story after story begins in the same way—with a scene of moral admonition. . . . Invariably, the young man (it is always a young man) to whom the admonition is addressed goes out and does exactly what he has been told not to do. And, just as invariably, he suffers for what he does."[33] Helgerson's book deals with the theme of the prodigal son in Elizabethan fiction, a prodigal whose defiance is ambivalent and guilt ridden, leading to repentance rather than liberation.[34] Still, the longing for freedom persists.

32. Richard Helgerson, *The Elizabethan Prodigals,* p. 22.
33. Ibid., p. 1.
34. Ibid., p. 13.

This yearning for some respite from the stringencies of submission and self-control becomes a concern for other young aristocrats of the period. The many wards of Lord Burghley often chafed under the restrictive tutelage of this preeminent father substitute. In 1586 Henry Wriothesley, the young Earl of Southampton, was assigned a Latin theme on the topic, "The arduous studies of youth are agreeable relaxations in old age." He wrote this earnest appeal in response: "Yet young men may, with justice, relax their minds and give themselves up to enjoyment. But let them then beware of excess and be mindful of modesty. Cicero, however, says (in his speech in defence of M. Caelius) 'Let some allowance be made for a person's years, let youth be allowed greater freedom, let not everything be denied to the passions, let not that severe and unbending reason always prevail, let desire and pleasure sometimes triumph over reason.' "[35] The tone is less witty than Sidney's, but the desire is the same: both young men want some sort of license from the constraints of Geron. Their frustrations give rise to erratic and contradictory feelings. A longing for sybaritic languor and a zeal for deeds of war suffuse several of Sidney's letters. "The situation was such," Rudenstine tells us, "that Languet, in the single long letter of October 22, 1578, could reproach Sidney both for rushing into battle against the will of his sovereign and also for trying to 'escape the tempest of affairs' by haunting 'the privacy of secluded places.' "[36] Southampton's early career gives even more dramatic, if less articulate, expression to sensual and rebellious passions, a career nearly ended by his role in the Essex conspiracy. That abortive event shows how the psychological pressures on the Elizabethan aristocracy could have dire political consequences.

In his prose and poetry, Sidney gives rein to these same feelings

35. Quoted by G. P. V. Akrigg, *Shakespeare and the Earl of Southampton,* pp. 29–30.
36. Rudenstine, *Poetic Development,* p. 14.

and makes the same attack on authority as he does in his correspondence. Rudenstine perceptively notes that the "war" Sidney declares on Languet is the central conflict in the *Arcadia,* and he says that Sidney "arranges matters in such a way that his heroes emerge from it as slightly battered but essentially unblemished victors."[37] This is indeed the same struggle, and Sidney is certainly adept at compelling his readers' indulgence, but the nature of this "victory" is ultimately rather ambiguous. The heroes' belligerence blends aggression and pathos, bluntness and evasion in the same fashion as Sidney's attacks on Languet. The humor of this contest is finally enigmatic, and its conclusion reflects unconscious ambivalence more than careful evaluative arrangement. This ambivalence about liberty is discernible in the antic poses of Sidney's letter and in the development of the disputation: it becomes even more acute in the debate's second half.

Musidorus is horrified when love is disclosed as the cause of Pyrocles' "transformation," and he delivers an exhaustive formal reproof. He begins by invoking "your old father," on whose behalf he must rebuke this errant son. He establishes his authority as a father substitute. This figure's importance for Sidney is clear in the correspondence, where the role is eagerly assumed by Languet: "To offend *me* is of little consequence, but reflect how grievously you would be sinning against your excellent Father, who has placed all his hopes in you, and who . . . expects to see the full harvest of all those virtues, which your character promises so largely to produce."[38]

Musidorus forthrightly declares the moral doctrine informing his censure: "Remember (for I know you know it) that, if we will be men, the reasonable part of our soul is to have absolute commandment, against which if any sensual weakness arise, we are to yield all our sound forces to the overthrowing of so unnatural a rebellion;

37. Ibid., p. 46.
38. *Languet,* Pears, p. 2.

wherein how can we want courage, since we are to deal against so weak an adversary that in itself is nothing but weakness?" (*OA*, 19). Musidorus affirms the basic humanist tenet of will's subordination to wit. His metaphor of legitimate government threatened by rebellious forces employs the conventional trope for self-control, one that also serves to recall the *Arcadia*'s political values. The good prince and heroic knight govern their impulses the same way they govern their subjects and soldiers. He asserts the *Arcadia*'s moral hierarchy and heroic ethos with brisk and authoritative clarity.

The second half of Musidorus's speech undercuts the dignity of his opening statement. His blustering denunciation of love and women makes him sound like the conventional *alazon*: "But this bastard love (for, indeed, the name of love is unworthily applied to so hateful a humour as it is, engendered betwixt lust and idleness) . . . is nothing but a certain base weakness, which some gentle fools call a gentle heart" (*OA*, 19–20). He concludes by warning, "this effeminate love of a woman doth so womanize a man" that even greater indignities than his Amazon disguise are in store for Pyrocles (*OA*, 20).

As a proponent of reason and self-control, Musidorus assumes a familiar stance. He expounds unimpeachable principles, but as the argument proceeds, arrogance and aggression erode his authority. By contrast, Pyrocles is meticulously deferential in his own defense. He chivalrously acquits women of his friend's charges and proceeds to an elaborate, Neoplatonic exposition of love's value: "notable men have attributed unto it," he contends, invoking the proper authorities, "the highest power of the mind" (*OA*, 22). His defense proceeds disjunctively, generating a sequence of definitions and divisions between essence, effect, and accident; and it concludes thus: "And in that heavenly love, since there are two parts (the one, the love itself; the other, the excellency of the thing loved), I (not able at the first leap to frame both in myself) do now, like a diligent workman, make ready the chief instrument and first part of that

great work, which is love itself. Which, when I have a while prac-
tised in this sort, then you shall see me turn it to greater matters"
(*OA*, 22).

Pyrocles presents himself as a romantic ingenue, preoccupied with
a laborious rehearsal of his own part. The tone of this speech is that
of an assiduous student, earnestly and self-consciously going through
required rhetorical paces. There is a marked correspondence between
the style and substance of his defense, both suggesting submission to
an exacting discipline. The stance is characteristic of Sidney's heroes,
and it is an essential aspect of Astrophil's persona. He is the victim,
in Sonnets 4 and 10, of amusingly pedantic personifications of
"Vertue" and "Reason," whereas he describes himself in Sonnet 19
as a tender "Scholler" writing under Love's stern tutelage; ordered
by this teacher to "bend hitherward your wit," he expands copiously
on the theme assigned.[39] In the disputation, Pyrocles' pose also recalls debate's origins in the schoolroom, suggesting submission to the
demands of the master. The tone of deference and dependence is
combined with scrupulous adherence to the rules. Sidney's protagonists tend to establish, by their rhetoric, a passive relationship with
authority, defending themselves against an outburst of punitive
wrath by constraining their impulses.

This submission is not the only feature of their style, nor is it
definitive. Pyrocles concludes his high-minded oration by blurting
out that no one should think that "because I wear a woman's
apparel, I will be the more womanish; since, I assure you, for all
my apparel, there is nothing I desire more than fully to prove myself
a man in this enterprise" (*OA*, 22–23). His point is to allay any
doubts of his virility that may be occasioned by his effeminate dis-

---

39. *Astrophil and Stella,* 19, in *Poems,* Ringler, p. 174. All further references to *Astrophil and Stella* are cited by the sonnet number (e.g., *AS* 19) in
the text. Line numbers are indicated in the longer poems (e.g., *AS* ii.1–4,
meaning Song ii, lines 1–4). I have tried to follow Ringler's spelling and
punctuation, except that I have not italicized proper names.

guise, doubts to which Musidorus has already alluded. One critic regards this conclusion as a bawdy joke of Sidney's meant to subvert the exalted Neoplatonism that preceded by exposing it as specious rationalization.[40] From this perspective, the conclusion can be seen to work in the same way as the last lines of many of the sonnets. The forceful impact of the conclusions of *AS* 25 ("for I do burne in love") or *AS* 71 (" 'But ah,' Desire still cries, 'give me some food' ") is brilliantly prepared for in the highly schematic and restrained thirteen lines preceding. Indeed, this stylistic trait has led many to regard Sidney as the most virile of the English sonneteers, the robust exploder of Petrarchan and Neoplatonic cant and the aggressive exponent of the potency of sexual desire.

The rhetoric also works in another way, however, reflecting more ambivalent impulses. In each of these instances, Sidney's protagonist calls attention to his capacity and desire for sexual assertion, while the ingratiating wit and slight tone of pathos allay the fear that he might do something about it. *AS* 71 is an excellent example of this sort of equivocation. The last line's urgent and demanding tone seems at first rather alarming, but the auditor is presumably relieved by the plaintiveness of the "ah" and "cries." In fact, Desire emerges as a vulnerable infant crying for simple oral gratification. Behind this personification is the explicit embodiment of Desire as a baby crying for pap in *CS* 6.

Sidney's stylistic strategy, in which he climaxes a lengthy schematic passage of anguished restraint and deference with an outburst of energy, suggests several contradictory motives. The rhetoric is alternately passive and aggressive, defensive and impulsive. His protagonists conceal and then dramatically reveal their capacity for self-assertion. Pyrocles' speech is like his disguise, which is another means of deviously evading the strictures of authority. His sexual objectives are advanced only by concealing his virility from the father. In

40. Peter Alan Lindenbaum, "The Anti-pastoral Pastoral," pp. 57–58.

Sidney's *Arcadia* the status of male potency—and of political potency—are precarious, and their expression is circumspect and cautious.

Musidorus renews his attack with another reference to Pyrocles' "old careful father" and urges his friend "(who is now upon the point of falling or rising), to purge your head of this vile infection" (*OA*, 24). His aggression culminates with the threat of rejection: "Otherwise, give me leave rather in absence to bewail your mishap than to bide the continual pang of seeing your danger with mine eyes" (*OA*, 24). This is the pivotal moment of the disputation ("the point of falling or rising"), and Pyrocles initially appears to be falling. He starts to cry, lamenting, "If you seek the victory, take it; and if you list, triumph. Have you all the reason of the world, and with me remain all the imperfections" (*OA*, 24). Following this total capitulation, a swift reversal is effected by Pyrocles' plaintive emphasis of his total vulnerability: "I am sick, and sick to the death. I am prisoner; neither is there any redress but by her to whom I am slave. Now, if you list, leave him that loves you in the highest degree; but remember ever to carry this with you: that you abandon your friend in his greatest need" (*OA*, 24). He wallows in his pathos, groveling before this harsh judge and gradually shifting to a reproach of such pitiless cruelty:

> And herewith, the deep wound of his love being rubbed afresh with this new unkindness, began, as it were, to bleed again, in such sort that he was unable to bear it any longer; but, gushing out abundance of tears and crossing his arms over his woeful heart, he sank down to the ground. Which sudden trance went so to the heart of Musidorus, that falling down by him, and kissing the weeping eyes of his friend, he besought him not to make account of his speech which, if it had been over vehement, yet was it to be borne withal, because it came out of a love much more vehement; that he had never thought fancy could have received so deep a wound, but now finding in him the force of it, he would no further contrary it, but employ all his service to medicine it in

such sort as the nature of it required. But even this kindness made Pyrocles the more melt in the former unkindness, which his man-like tears well showed, with a silent look upon Musidorus, as who should say, 'and is it possible that Musidorus should threaten to leave me?' And this strook Musidorus's mind and senses so dumb, too, that for grief not being able to say anything, they rested with their eyes placed one upon another, in such sort as might well paint out the true passion of unkindness, which is never aright but betwixt them that most dearly love.

(*OA*, 24–25)

I quote this passage in its entirety because it is the culmination of Sidney's defensive strategy. The argument's conclusion is frantically emotional, and the gushing effulgence of tears, combined with the excited rubbing, swooning, sinking, and kissing, all suggest something like sexual climax. Just as it reaches its most threatening intensity, the punitive wrath of Musidorus provokes a kind of masochistic release. Pyrocles concludes his abject admission of guilt by completely collapsing. His breakdown is consistent with his shame and passivity, and it reflects a profound vulnerability to paternal censure. At the same time, he can covertly attack this judgmental father substitute, forcing the latter to feel responsible for all this pain and degradation. The victory Musidorus had achieved in debate is completely subverted by Pyrocles' passive aggression; struck dumb in his "mind and senses," Musidorus cannot even speak.

Musidorus is now under the coyly diffident control of Pyrocles, who commands that "you continue to love me, and look upon my imperfections with more affection than judgement" (*OA*, 26). The pattern of the other conflict, the "skirmish betwixt Reason and Passion," prevails here, the contradictions between sympathy and judgment achieving a kind of frantic intensity. Here, the bid for sympathy becomes more flagrantly coercive as the threat of punishment increases. Pyrocles' vulnerability and pathos paradoxically allow him to command directly the suspension of judgment. There is, I think, a striking resemblance between his demand and Sidney's address to his sister in the dedication of the *Old Arcadia*. The same equivocal appeal is made for the entire creation, an appeal advanced in the playful terms of *sprezzatura*. Sidney dismisses it as an "idle work" and a child with "deformities," and he pleads his sister's indulgence and "protection" for "a great offender" (*OA*, 3). By threatening "to cast out in some desert of forgetfulness this child which I am loath to father," Sidney mockingly identifies himself with those "cruel fathers among the Greeks" (*OA*, 3). His witty deprecation imparts a droll and different charm to his pleas for mercy. Commenting on this same appeal to the reader, Helgerson remarks on its coercive aspects: "Pardon the book he asks, for the sake of its author. . . . But the *Arcadia* makes of sympathy a trap. By his confident insinuation that they, knowing at first hand the power of love will understand, and understanding will pity, and pitying will forgive, the narrator manipulates his readers into sharing the guilt and the awareness of guilt that characterizes Pyrocles, Musidorus, and Sidney himself."[41]

Sidney is ultimately more interested in sympathy and indulgence than in anything else—a sympathy that can sometimes prevent clear assessment. One's affection for the heroes and their author is an essential precondition, defining one's response to their activities. One's affection still cannot spare Sidney's heroes from punitive abuse. Their pain is caused by their own anguished scruples as well as by the moralizing wrath of authority. While this may increase sympathy for them and scorn for their opponents, one also detects in their suffering an uneasiness, an uncertain blend of the needs for punishment and for forgiveness. Sidney's conflicting emotions are reflected in a tendency to apologize for his characters, his literary efforts, even the whole of poetry. Frederick Crews finds such apologetic impulses common for many authors: "Among the countless

41. Helgerson, *Prodigals,* p. 136.

possibilities for literary exchange, one relationship seems frequent enough to merit special emphasis. An author often places his reader in the role of parent and begs his absolution. By revealing what has been on his mind, mixing oblique confession with a reassertion of commitment to decency and reality and beauty, and by involving the reader in everything he discloses, the author claims the right to be accepted as he is."[42] Yet Sidney's appeals for compassion and forgiveness are generally graceful and assured, and his favoritism is amusingly subtle. When Musidorus helps Pyrocles with his Amazon costume, the narrator drolly asks the reader's collaboration in this disguise: "thus did Pyrocles become Cleophila—which name for a time hereafter I will use, for I myself feel such compassion of his passion that I find even part of his fear lest his name should be uttered before fit time for it; which you, fair ladies that vouchsafe to read this, I doubt not will account excusable" (*OA*, 27). Wit and *sprezzatura* banish any trace of guilt, while laughter precludes "blame." Regarded humorously, the heroes' transgressions become mere "follies," harmless and endearing.

The triumph of Pyrocles is still rather ambiguous, as the remainder of Book I shows. Sidney's hero wants to be regarded by those in authority "with more affection than judgement," and Pyrocles certainly arouses an abundance of affection. Both parents fall in love with him immediately, Gynecia having seen through his disguise while Basilius continues to be deluded by it. They dote on Pyrocles "like a father and mother to a beloved child" (*OA*, 49), and their infatuation affords considerable amusement. The description of Basilius's ardor suggests another source of pleasure, more affecting than laughter: "Whoever saw a man to whom a beloved child long lost did, unlooked for, return might easily figure unto his fancy the very fashion of Basilius's countenance—so far had love become his master" (*OA*, 36). This brief scene derives much of its

42. Frederick Crews, ed. *Psychoanalysis and Literary Process*, p. 23.

power from its wishful inversion of the parable of the prodigal son. This lost child actually had been banished by the father, because of his sex, but the child benevolently alters his sexual status, forgives the punitive father, and returns ("unlooked for") to the delight of the older man. The analogy presents the son as the passive object of paternal love and the active subject of a rescue fantasy.

Basilius's passion also allows the pleasures of revenge. Pyrocles-Cleophila defies paternal strictures against withdrawal and self-absorption, and he asserts with imposing authority his independence from all such strictures. He looks upon Basilius "with a grave majesty" and declares, "I seek no better warrant . . . than mine own conscience, nor no greater pleasure than mine own contentation" (*OA*, 35). Basilius persists in the conventional admonitions—"Yet virtue seeks to satisfy others" (*OA*, 35)—but these are discredited here by his blatant and fatuous hypocrisy. The older man is, of course, equally guilty of sexual passion and withdrawal into passivity. Indeed, he is condemned more severely for these same impulses, serving as a scapegoat for the younger men. What is allowed to the son is denied to the father, an informing principle—originating in Oedipal hostility—in many stories with the *senex amans* as their comic butt.

Yet the consequences of parental affection are increasingly troublesome. Not only is Pyrocles hampered in his wooing of Philoclea, but he also finds her parents' desires oppressive in themselves. Basilius's attentions are, for the most part, ridiculous, but Gynecia's are more sinister. Her passion exemplifies the most disturbing and violent effects of love. In her lust for the son, "she would stir up terrible tragedies rather than fail of her intent" (*OA*, 96). Oedipal fears are clearly one source of the dread engendered by this ferocious mother figure. She is the seductive mother, luring innocent filial victims into catastrophic entanglement. Gynecia brings the Oedipal nightmare close to fulfillment, for the son will stand accused of conspiracy with her against the sovereign father. In the shifting patterns of family romance, parental affection proves as dangerous as parental wrath.

The apparent triumph of Pyrocles has, then, rather dubious results, for the fondness of authority proves curiously volatile. The ephemeral nature of the father's humiliation is also clear from ensuing developments. Musidorus's continued mortification illustrates this reversal. He succumbs to the same romantic "metamorphosis" for which he chastened Pyrocles, and the latter now gloats over his friend's lapse, reminding him of his arrogant self-righteousness: " 'Why, how now, dear cousin,' said she, 'you that were even now so high in the pulpit against love, are you now become so mean an auditor? Remember that love is a passion, and that a worthy man's reason must ever have the masterhood' " (*OA*, 42). This is a gratifying revenge against the censorious father figure, and Musidorus is reduced to "falling down prostrate" and crying " 'I recant!' " (*OA*, 42).

After a little more jocular banter, Pyrocles' "friendly heart felt a great impression of pity" (*OA*, 43), and he begins to see the lamentable aspects of his friend's defeat. In the *New Arcadia*, Musidorus expands on the nature of his fall with effects that are both frightening and demoralizing:

> But alas, well have I found, that Love to a yeelding hart is a king; but to a resisting, is a tyrant. The more with arguments I shaked the stake, which he had planted in the grounde of my harte, the deeper still it sanke into it. But what meane I to speake of the causes of my love, which is as impossible to describe, as to measure the backside of heaven? Let this word suffice, I love.
>
> (*NA*, 115)

The conventional trope of Cupid and his arrows is used to harrowing effect. The god of love attains a fearful enormity as a "tyrant" crushing any resistance. The slender arrows become a huge stake driven painfully deep in "the grounde of my harte." The entire

67

scene reminds one of the torture of Amoret by Busyrane in Book III of *The Faerie Queene,* both in its emblematic separation of the heart from the subject and in the image of an excruciating wound; there is also a possibility that Musidorus is tied to the stake, making sense of his efforts to shake it.

Musidorus's defeat recalls the equivocal pattern of the "skirmish betwixt Reason and Passion." The oppressive dominance of Reason's forces is thwarted by the triumph of a superior power. Dominance from above is still inescapable in the *Arcadia,* and its effects are never benign. Love is, characteristically, an aggressive tyrant who allows no escape from abject submission; for those who would resist, degradation is more forceful. Once they suffer the same fate, the fraternal identification of Pyrocles and Musidorus is renewed. The latter's autonomy and control were based on his assumption of the paternal role, one whose risks and difficulties his humiliation illustrates. Now both are alike in their submissive vulnerability. The defeat of this surrogate simply exposes his presumptuous unworthiness: paternal authority remains constant, invincible in its shifting manifestations. Sidney's attitude toward it remains ambivalent, an attitude reflected in the postures of his heroes. The passive "yielding" of Pyrocles provokes feelings of shame and degradation, but Musidorus's "continual vehemency" is no match for these awesome larger forces. The heroes oscillate between humiliating submission and helplessly defiant assertion, futile variants in a constantly redundant pattern. Arcadia provides no refuge from this painful and oppressive conflict with authority.

Chapter Three

Astrophil and Stella:
"ALL SELFNESSE HE FORBEARES"

S INCE IT FIRST APPEARED, *Astrophil and Stella* has stirred biographical speculation. The links between the poems and the facts of Sidney's life have proved confusing for many readers, and some have sought to minimize the connection.[1] The principal resemblance is unavoidably obvious, however, for as William Ringler, the sonnets' recent editor, points out, "Sidney went out of his way to identify himself as Astrophil and Stella as Lady Rich."[2] Lady Rich was the former Penelope Devereux, sister to Essex, and the charge of several of Philip's close relations. She was presented at court in January 1581, the same month that Sidney returned from his rustication. On New Year's Day he had presented a "whip garnished with small diamonds" to the Queen as a token of his deference to her judgment in the Anjou marriage question.[3] Penelope was engaged that spring to Lord Rich and married him in November. For his part, Sidney was extremely active in the affairs of court and Parliament, and he participated in several tournaments. It seems that he fell in love with the young lady shortly after her marriage and remained troubled by

1. See Jack Stillinger, "The Biographical Problem of *Astrophel and Stella*," p. 626, and Robert Kimbrough, *Sir Philip Sidney*, pp. 121–123.

2. *The Poems of Sir Philip Sidney*, ed. William A. Ringler, Jr., p. xliv.

3. Ibid., p. 440.

this adulterous preoccupation until his death, when he mentioned his concern to an attending chaplain.[4]

Astrophil and Stella was begun in 1582, and it developed into one of the most coherent sonnet sequences in English. Sidney deals with recent events and characters from his life, but he imposes a clear dramatic structure. *Astrophil and Stella* is not a documentary record of an affair, nor is it a "versified diary."[5] In fact, the rather remarkable feature of the sequence, as Ringler points out, is the numerous biographical omissions:

> When we compare the known facts of Sidney's life during the years 1581–2 with the sonnets and songs of *Astrophil and Stella,* we are immediately struck with how much of his biography he left out of his poem. He tells us nothing about the disappointment of his hopes in being superseded as the Earl of Leicester's heir, nothing about his trip to Antwerp, nothing about his dominating interest in politics and international affairs—his friendship with the exiled Earl of Angus and the Portuguese pretender Don Antonio, and, most significant, nothing about his activities in opposition to the proposed marriage of the Duke of Anjou with the Queen.[6]

In short, no aspect of his political career intrudes, a surprising exclusion for a man of Sidney's ambitions. In *AS* 30, for example, the details of public affairs are carefully enumerated only to be renounced as matters indifferent to one in love:

> If French can yet three parts in one agree;
> What now the Dutch in their full diets boast;
> How Holland hearts, now so good townes be lost,
> Trust in the shade of pleasing Orange tree;

4. Jean Robertson, "Sir Philip Sidney and Lady Penelope Rich," pp. 296–297.
5. *Poems,* Ringler, p. xliv.
6. Ibid., p. 447.

> How Ulster likes of that same golden bit,
>> Wherewith my father once made it halfe tame;
>> If in the Scottishe Court be weltring yet;
> These questions busie wits to me do frame;
>> I, cumbred with good maners, answer do,
>> But know now how, for still I thinke of you.
>>> (*AS* 30)

Like other heroes of Elizabethan sonnets, Astrophil banishes all other concerns in his love for Stella. Love becomes, in J. W. Lever's apt phrase, "the supreme and inalienable individual experience,"[7] diminishing all other values and dismissing rival claims. John Donne pushes the lover's prerogative to its celestial limits in his songs and sonnets, scorning other interests as trivial distractions. The belligerence that accompanies this erotic *contemptus mundi* is another connection between Sidney and Donne. The latter's "Canonization" begins with a tone of contentious riposte frequently assumed by Astrophil, but Donne moves beyond the conflicts and equivocations of the earlier poetry to an irreproachable sanctimony, brazenly fusing the carnal and platonic. Sidney is distinctive both in his insistence on their split and in his emphasis on the troubling aspects of sexual desire. In his excellent study of Sidney's poetry, David Kalstone finds a persistent and "sharply defined concern for the corrosive effects of love upon the heroic life."[8]

Yet, while the virtue of love may be less absolute for Sidney, it still represents a profoundly absorbing experience. All the major thematic concerns of his other works are organized and contained within the bounds of this poetic courtship. This restriction of focus gives this work a clarifying force, the impact of which is well described by Theodore Spencer: "Who Stella was, and whether or not Sidney as a man felt a genuine passion for her, are puzzling questions, but

7. J. W. Lever, *The Elizabethan Love Sonnet*, p. 141.
8. David Kalstone, *Sidney's Poetry*, p. 106.

not worth much conjecture. All that matters is that she was a symbol around which were mustered a set of important emotions, emotions which were multiplied and intensified, sometimes perhaps even induced by Sidney's desire to express them."[9] *Astrophil and Stella* not only depicts the vicissitudes of courtship and sexual desire; it also allows Sidney his clearest expression of other crucial issues. Romantic intrigue reveals the clash between autonomy and submission in a more clearly focused narrative, freed of all the troubling connections and details of Sidney's political career.

As I have shown, these connections are more explicit in his other works, and the conflict becomes more unwieldy. The larger narrative scope of the *Arcadia* allows Sidney to include more of his immediate concerns, and both versions expand to their own artistic detriment. Their problematic complexity subverts Sidney's control of his material. *Astrophil and Stella* presents a more restricted drama from which Sidney omits "the full range of his interests and activities, but only [writes] about those directly connected with his love for Stella. His emotion may or may not have been recollected in tranquillity, but he was obviously in full command of himself and of his materials while he was writing. Everything in his poem is focused on his relations with Stella; everything in his experience during those months which did not directly relate to his central theme he ruthlessly excluded. Therefore, though the substance of his poem was autobiographical, mere fact was made subservient to the requirements of art."[10] It is this "ruthless exclusion" that makes *Astrophil and Stella* such a successful sequence. Sidney deals with the problem of control and autonomy in purely romantic terms. The politics here are exclusively sexual, and he examines them with a clarity, humor, and assurance lacking in the other works.

The political aspect of love is immediately apparent in all of

9. Theodore Spencer, "The Poetry of Sir Philip Sidney," p. 270.
10. *Poems,* Ringler, p. 447.

Sidney's writing. "But alas," Musidorus sighs, "well have I found, that Love to a yeelding hart is a king; but to a resisting, is a tyrant" (*NA*, 115). The metaphor has several sources, some psychological and some historical. The Freudian explanation of love's contradictions is certainly pertinent here. In his excellent study of Freud's thought, Philip Rieff says that "by 'nature' (that is, originally) love is authoritarian; sexuality—like liberty—is a later achievement, always in danger of being overwhelmed by our deeper inclinations toward submissiveness and domination."[11] In the *Allegory of Love*, C. S. Lewis sees a similar evolution in consciousness occurring historically, in the medieval emergence of courtly love. Lewis formulates his own "law of transference which determined that all the emotion stored in the vassal's relation to his *seigneur* should attach itself to the new kind of love" for women.[12] "The lover is always abject. Obedience to his lady's lightest wish, however whimsical, and silent acquiescence in her rebukes, however unjust, are the only virtues he dares to claim. There is a service of love closely modelled on the service which a feudal vassal owes to his lord. The lover is the lady's 'man.' He addresses her as *midons*, which etymologically represents not 'my lady' but 'my lord.' The whole attitude has been rightly described as 'a feudalisation of love.'"[13]

Court poetry and court culture sustained these ambiguities in a highly self-conscious fashion, combining sexual impulse and submission with a refined erotic sensibility. The political aspect of love became even more explicit with various challenges to the code of courtly love. In the sixteenth century, a rebellious note sounds with sharp clarity, as Sir Thomas Wyatt rails against the constraints and indignities of erotic vassalage. His particular predicament also re-

11. Philip Rieff, *Freud: The Mind of the Moralist,* p. 175.
12. C. S. Lewis, *The Allegory of Love,* p. 18.
13. Ibid., p. 2.

veals disturbing links between sexual and court politics. Sidney's heroes follow this tradition of "amorous insubordination."[14] Astrophil is grieved and enraged by love's assaults on his integrity. Typically, the insurgence of desire is experienced as a loss of control. Before he succumbs to its tyrannous assaults, Musidorus warns Pyrocles that, "if we will be men, the reasonable part of our soul is to have absolute commandment, against which if any sensual weakness arise, we are to yield all our sound forces to the overthrowing of so unnatural a rebellion" (*OA*, 19). Too rigid in its initial presumptions, this brittle self-government is easily subverted, and the heroes languish helplessly. They are now vulnerable to the intervention of various authority figures, and their autonomy is further threatened. It is a predicament the erotic and psychological aspects of which Sidney handles with finesse in his love poetry, for, in *Astrophil and Stella,* he keeps its troublesome political implications nicely generalized.

The problem of control comes up immediately, in the first sonnet, with an account of Astrophil's difficulties. He begins this enterprise with splendid confidence, but his mood quickly changes:

> Loving in truth, and faine in verse my love to show,
>> That the deare She might take some pleasure of my paine:
>> Pleasure might cause her reade, reading might make her know,
>> Knowledge might pitie winne, and pitie grace obtaine,
> I sought fit words to paint the blackest face of woe,
>> Studying inventions fine, her wits to entertaine:
>> Oft turning others' leaves, to see if thence would flow
>> Some fresh and fruitfull showers upon my sunne-burn'd braine.
> But words came halting forth, wanting Invention's stay,

14. Louis B. Salomon, *The Rebellious Lover in English Poetry,* p. 1.

Invention, Nature's child, fled step-dame Studie's
blowes,
And others' feete still seem'd but strangers in my way.
Thus great with child to speake, and helplesse in my throwes,
Biting my trewand pen, beating my selfe for spite,
'Foole,' said my Muse to me, 'looke in thy heart and
write.'

(*AS* 1)

The octet offers a statement of poetic purpose. The traditional objectives of instruction, "knowledge," and delight ("pleasure") combine with a more urgently affective goal. Poetic *energia*, "inwardly working a stirre to the mynde," could move Stella to some affirmative, reciprocal response.[15] Thus, "knowledge might pitie winne, and pitie grace obtaine." His procedures begin to fail when he embarks on an assiduous study of the works of others. Instead of culminating in creative expression, this imitative study leads to the parched sterility of a "sunne-burn'd braine." Astrophil's difficulties are attributable to the kind of imitation Sidney condemns in the *Apology*: poetry that sounds as though it were written by "men that had rather read lover's writings (and so caught up certain swelling phrases . . .) . . . than that in truth they feel those passions, which easily (as I think) may be betrayed by that same forcibleness or *energia*."[16]

Astrophil's problem is hardly a dearth of passion. On the contrary, his affections are dangerously boxed in as a result of his fruitless methodology, and their force is felt through the building pressures of frustration. This force is baffled by a series of suspended climaxes, the first two in the two quatrains and the third in the first tercet.[17]

15. George Puttenham quoted by Ringler, in *Poems*, p. 459.
16. Sir Philip Sidney, *An Apology for Poetry, or The Defence of Poetry,* pp. 137–138.
17. See Robert L. Montgomery's analysis of this sonnet in *Symmetry and Sense,* p. 84.

The results of the first two are merely conditional, and the third ends in failure. Instead of the "fresh and fruitfull showers" anticipated in the second quatrain, the result is stumbling and anguished agitation. The smooth, orderly discipline of the octet leads to frustration and blockage, breaking down altogether in the sestet.

This breakdown becomes a kind of comic rout as the imagery takes a lively, antic turn: "Invention, Nature's child, fled step-dame Studie's blowes." The poem shifts from the confident erudition of humanism to the clumsy flight of a truant schoolboy. By the end, Astrophil has regressed even further as he is caught in the throes of childbirth. In this final climax, the movements are still more anguished and agitated and their purpose increasingly desperate. Only with the outburst of the last line is some sort of resolution obtained: " 'Foole,' said my Muse to me, 'looke in thy heart and write.' "

The final line is not a plea for heartfelt sincerity or spontaneity; as several critics have shown, the heart as a shrine for the beloved's image and the proper source of invention is a conventional Petrarchan conceit. Neil Rudenstine thus argues that "Astrophel's primary goal remains an objective one: not self-exploration and self-expression as ends in themselves, but the expression of personal feeling for the purposes of rhetorical persuasion."[18] Yet this ignores the affective impact of the sestet and its final line, which allows an assertive outburst of feeling. David Kalstone is more responsive to this aspect when he points out that "the substance of the line is entirely conventional. But the manner of its presentation is not: the violence and release of tension with which the poet is advised to look at Stella's image marks Sidney's version as quite special."[19]

The release from tension felt in this final line is almost palpable, but the resolution is ambiguous. Astrophil had started by submitting

18. Neil L. Rudenstine, *Sidney's Poetic Development,* p. 200.
19. Kalstone, *Poetry,* pp. 126–127.

to a program of poetic study, but its constraints prove oppressive and frustrating. The sestet traces the breakdown and escape from this other-directed discipline, but Astrophil still cannot express himself. The final command offers a sense of release from frustration and uncorks the flow of "fresh and fruitfull showers," but it does so by imposing a simpler, more emphatic discipline. The sonnet traces a diminishing circular movement away from and back to control by others, a pattern typical in *Astrophil and Stella*.

The tone in the second sonnet is somewhat edgier and more belligerent, though many of the issues are the same:

> Not at first sight, nor with a dribbed shot
>> Love gave the wound, which while I breathe will bleed:
>> But knowne worth did in mine of time proceed,
>> Till by degrees it had full conquest got.
> I saw and liked, I liked but loved not,
>> I loved, but straight did not what Love decreed:
>> At length to Love's decrees, I forc'd, agreed,
>> Yet with repining at so partiall lot.
> Now even that footstep of lost libertie
>> Is gone, and now like slave-borne Muscovite,
>> I call it praise to suffer Tyrannie;
> And now employ the remnant of my wit,
>> To make my selfe beleeve, that all is well,
>> While with a feeling skill I paint my hell.
>
> (*AS* 2)

The poem describes the process of falling in love as a gradual submission to "Tyrannie." Astrophil resists erotic vassalage, and submission is by no means automatic, proceeding by slow degrees. Indeed, Astrophil insists on maintaining the processes of choice while he mourns his lost liberty. Sidney echoes Wyatt here, recalling the latter's testy dignity and pathos. Even as he finds himself caught in love's snare, Wyatt insists that "it was my choyse, yt was no chaunce."[20] Astrophil's resistance is sustained throughout, despite its hopelessness, and the bitter conclusion offers no release from tension.

When others intervene, this tension can become explosive. Just as Philisides is pestered by the stereotypical Geron, so is Astrophil troubled by moralizing elders. Amusing personifications of Reason and Virtue urge Astrophil to cease his amorous follies in *AS* 4 and 10, and well-intentioned "friends" remind him of his public duties in *AS* 14 and 21. Their ineffectual *remedia amoris* only exacerbate his afflictions and are brusquely dismissed. In *AS* 14, this meddlesome solicitude becomes the most grievous persecution:

> Alas have I not paine enough my friend,
>> Upon whose breast a fiercer Gripe doth tire
>> Then did on him who first stale downe the fire,
>> While Love on me doth all his quiver spend,
> But with your Rubarb words yow must contend
>> To grieve me worse, in saying that Desire
>> Doth plunge my wel-form'd soule even in the mire
>> Of sinfull thoughts, which do in ruine end?
>
> (*AS* 14)

Astrophil presents himself as a combination of Prometheus and Saint Sebastian. Even as he undergoes excruciating torture at the hands of Love, his friend "must contend / To grieve me worse, in saying that Desire / Doth plunge my wel-form'd soule even in the "mire." Astrophil's predicament is embodied by a striking metaphorical antithesis: the soul hovers between the purity and order of good "form" and a slide into the "mire." The latter image suggests not only the filth of "sinful thoughts" but a loss of shape and structure. Yet, despite this connotation of looseness, the "mire" is also a place where one may be stuck or held fast as in a bog. Astrophil flees from one trap to another, out of the "mire" into Love's "fiercer

---

20. Sir Thomas Wyatt, *Collected Poems*, p. 111.

Gripe," all holding him fast. Astrophil's reply clarifies the significance of this antithesis:

> If that be sinne which doth the maners frame,
>> Well staid with truth in word and faith of deed,
>> Readie of wit and fearing nought but shame:
> If that be sinne which in fixt hearts doth breed
>> A loathing of all loose unchastitie,
>> Then love is sinne, and let me sinfull be.
>
> (AS 14)

Love, he claims, imposes as much rigorous good form as his friend might wish; it frames and holds his "wel-form'd soule" within good "maners" and rigid bonds. Rather than leading to "loose unchastitie," Love enforces "fixt hearts" among its adherents. The verbs, participles, and adjectives sustain the figurative opposition between the loose flow of impurity and the tight frame of love's discipline. They impart a certain subtlety to the otherwise heavy irony of the last line.

Behind Astrophil's posturing, there are more ambiguous ironies that undercut his declamatory triumph. Astrophil escapes his friend's moralistic abuse by insisting with real conviction on his virtue, yet he ends up submitting to the more ruthless discipline of Love. The pain of submission, lamented so dramatically at the sonnet's beginning, is obscured by the flurry of self-righteous assertion at the end. Yet for all his defiant bluster, Astrophil never establishes his autonomy. The odd circular movement of the opening sonnet is repeated here. One set of rules is escaped only to be supplanted by more restrictive regulations, and subordination is inescapable. In *AS* 14, Astrophil literally makes a virtue of this necessity. Thus, in the terms of the poem's latent metaphor, the velvet glove of good manners is drawn over authority's "fiercer Gripe."

In *AS* 18, Astrophil is more humble as he submits to "Reason's audite."

With what sharpe checkes I in my selfe am shent,
    When into Reason's audite I do go:
    And by just counts my selfe a banckrout know
    Of all those goods, which heav'n to me hath lent:
Unable quite to pay even Nature's rent,
    Which unto it by birthright I do ow:
    And which is worse, no good excuse can show,
    But that my wealth I have most idly spent.
My youth doth waste, my knowledge brings forth toyes,
    My wit doth strive those passions to defend,
    Which for reward spoile it with vaine annoyes.
I see my course to lose my selfe doth bend:
    I see and yet no greater sorow take,
    Then that I lose no more for Stella's sake.

                                   (*AS* 18)

The poem combines the parables of the talents and the prodigal son, and each loss is dolefully itemized with no excuse offered. Wealth, youth, skills, knowledge, and ultimately the self are all sacrificed, and yet Astrophil's only regret is "that I lose no more for Stella's sake." The final line has a surprising double meaning: Astrophil is sorry that he has nothing better to lose for Stella as well as nothing left. All the goods relinquished are mere trifles compared to Stella's worth. The careful enumeration of "Reason's audite" makes this sudden devaluation jarring, and the poem forges a paradoxical link between orderly assessment, sacrificial largesse, and casual *sprezzatura*.

The poem's impact again derives, as it did in *AS* 14, from Sidney's inspired use of terms of action. In his analysis of *AS* 18, Robert Montgomery offers a perceptive account of this quality: "the imagery itself may create a living world because it can suggest human action, not by explanation, but by offering a background of movement, gesture, and sensation. Sonnet 18 has an energy which may be explained partly by vocal tonalities and the kind of flexible structure of discourse we have already noted, but mainly by the fact that the

imagery is driven towards physical movement."[21] Sidney often reinforces this impression of movement by visualizing it, describing even
a minor gesture as something literally seen; thus it is actualized and
its importance increased. "A series of strong verbs," Montgomery
explains, "suggestive of physical movement and energy, accompany
the logical development of the trope: 'shent,' 'waste,' 'brings forth,'
'strive,' 'defend,' 'spoile,' 'bend.' These are in no sense remarkable;
they are commonplace, unobtrusive words, but Sidney concentrates
them toward the movement of emotional crisis just before the group-
ing controlled by the repeated 'I see.' "[22] This highly visual sense of
movement in *Astrophil and Stella* is a source of its animation and
vitality. It also imparts a sharp perception of tension and conflict as
passions are visualized in concrete actions.

One of the actions that deserves special attention is *bending*,
appearing as it does in several contexts. "I see my course to lose my
selfe doth bend," Astrophil tells us in *AS* 18. Here it implies a devia-
tion and decline from the straightforward "course" previously adhered to. In the next sonnet, bending is imposed twice, once in the
first line and again in the last.

> On Cupid's bow how are my heart-strings bent,
>> That see my wracke, and yet embrace the same?
>> When most I glorie, then I feele most shame:
>> I willing run, yet while I run, repent.
> My best wits still their owne disgrace invent:
>> My verie inke turnes straight to Stella's name;
>> And yet my words, as them my pen doth frame,
>> Avise themselves that they are vainely spent.
> For though she passe all things, yet what is all
>> That unto me, who fare like him that both
>> Lookes to the skies, and in a ditch doth fall?

21. Montgomery, *Symmetry and Sense,* p. 89.
22. Ibid., p. 90.

O let me prop my mind, yet in his growth
And not in Nature for best fruits unfit:
'Scholler,' saith Love, 'bend hitherward your wit.'

(*AS* 19)

The trope of the bow uses the imagery for clever effect: Astrophil's
heartstrings are tied on Cupid's weapon, thus embracing, and causing, their own destruction. On closer inspection, the imagery makes
less sense because the strings of a bow should be pulled taut and
straight. Yet the sense of painful strain is still forcefully conveyed.
The line recalls a familiar image, used in both the correspondence
and the *Arcadia,* a parallel first noted by Rudenstine.[23] In all three
contexts, the image is one of tension that requires release: "a bow
too long bent . . . ," Sidney writes to Languet, "must be unstrung
or it will break."[24]

In the next two lines, Astrophil's ambivalence is enacted in painful, halting movements: "When most I glorie, then I feele most
shame: / I willing run, yet while I run, repent." These are like the
crippled flights of Pyrocles, who "was like a horse, desirous to runne,
and miserable spurred, but so short rainde, as he cannot stirre
forward." (*NA*, 95). For Astrophil, forward movement is hobbled
by shame and repentance, and he stumbles helplessly in his quest
for the celestial Stella: "For though she passe all things, yet what
is all / That unto me, who fare like him that both / Lookes to the
skies, and in a ditch doth fall?" The bathos of the star gazer who
falls in the ditch recalls in witty and poignant fashion the basic
human dilemma set forth in the *Apology:* "our erected wit maketh
us know what perfection is, and yet our infected will keepeth us from
reaching unto it."[25] The poem's activities are all painfully con-

23. Rudenstine, *Poetic Development,* p. 18.
24. *The Correspondence of Sir Philip Sidney and Hubert Languet,* ed.
Stuart A. Pears, p. 36.
25. Sidney, *Apology,* p. 101.

stricted, pulled back and forth, upward and downward by Astrophil's guilt and misgivings.

In the sestet's second half, the mind is pliable, tender, and youthful; and it requires some support: "O let me prop my mind, yet in his growth / And not in Nature for best fruits unfit." The image has other echoes, recalling the advice of Roger Ascham in *The Scholemaster:* "if will, and witte" are corrupted, Ascham warns, "surelie it is hard with ientleness, but unpossible with seuere crueltie, to call them back to good frame againe. For, where the one, perchance maie bend it, the other shall surelie break it."[26] Young spirits may be injured by too much severity, so Ascham makes a case for more flexible discipline. *The Scholemaster* reflects contemporary shifts in the conception of authority and obedience, shifts discernible in Sidney's writing as well. There are still important differences in their approaches. For Sidney, bending and breaking seem to have the same destructive results: the mind must be "unbent," the bow unstrung, to release them from strain.

Yet despite this yearning for release, it does not occur. Instead discipline is imposed on the young "Scholler," Astrophil, by a magistral personification of Love. Astrophil had pleaded for some edifying "prop" or frame for his delicate mind, whose pliancy and "fruits" evoke an image of a vine. Love comes to his aid, but this brings Astrophil back to where he started. The prop must resemble "Cupid's bow" around which he must bend himself again. The poem's movement is again circular. Perhaps the peremptory final line reflects a rueful and ironic appreciation of pedagogy's subtler pressures. Ascham, after all, sought to bend a student's will and wit less from simple lenience than a desire for increased control. Sidney's hapless "Scholler" discovers that bending is only a more effective means of subjugation. In any case, there is no escaping from this bending submission.

26. Roger Ascham, *The Scholemaster,* in *English Works,* pp. 200–201.

The middle section of *Astrophil and Stella* focuses more directly on Astrophil's increasingly urgent desires. A decision seems to have been made as attention shifts from equivocation and argument to their cause. Nevertheless, a more direct focus on love and passion brings Astrophil no closer to a resolution. Desire is assigned a kind of reified primacy in these middle poems, and the tone is alternately flippant, even cavalier, and anguished. The first attitude is assumed in *AS* 52, in which the strife between Virtue and Love is resolved by a facetious variant on Solomon's wisdom: "Let Vertue have that Stella's selfe," but Astrophil and his ally, Love, will take the body. The joking is less irreverently brash in *AS* 25, but the point is the same:

> The wisest scholler of the wight most wise
>   By Phoebus' doome, with sugred sentence sayes,
>   That Vertue, if it once met with our eyes,
>   Strange flames of Love it in our soules would raise;
>
> (*AS* 25)

The language of platonic ardor is satirically desublimated when Astrophil exclaims in the final line that "I do burne in love."

Astrophil can also be serious in his assertion of desire. The superior virtue of love is affirmed against its detractors in *AS* 31. Astrophil finds a doleful companion in the moon, which also affords him a celestial vantage point far from the arrogant jibes of court "beauties." The sestet consists of a series of melancholy questions concerning love's afflictions:

> Then ev'n of fellowship, ô Moone, tell me
>   Is constant Love deem'd there but want of wit?
>   Are Beauties there as proud as here they be?
> Do they above love to be lov'd, and yet
>   Those Lovers scorne whom that Love doth possesse?
>   Do they call Vertue there ungratefulnesse?
>
> (*AS* 31)

The combination of lyric pathos and reproach for courtly "Vertue" represents an affecting vindication of the "Lover's case." Sidney depicts the same predicament in Song xi toward the end of the sequence, and he elicits the same strong sympathies for the hero's feelings.

Astrophil becomes still more assertive when debate is resumed in *AS* 56. This time he argues with "Patience," whose "leaden counsels" prove tedious. Astrophil demands reciprocity and fair treatment: "No Patience, if thou wilt my good, then make / Her come, and heare with patience my desire, / And then with patience bid me beare my fire" (*AS* 56). The same demand is made in *AS* 64 in a more earnest and direct fashion. Rather than sparring with personified abstractions, Astrophil here refutes Stella herself in fond but deliberate terms:

> No more, my deare, no more these counsels trie,
>> O give my passions leave to run their race:
>> Let Fortune lay on me her worst disgrace,
>> Let folke orecharg'd with braine against me crie,
> Let clouds bedimme my face, breake in mine eye,
>> Let me no steps but of lost labour trace,
>> Let all the earth with scorne recount my case,
>> But do not will me from my Love to flie.
> I do not envie Aristotle's wit,
>> Nor do aspire to Caesar's bleeding fame,
>> Nor ought do care, though some above me sit,
> Nor hope, nor wishe another course to frame,
>> But that which once may win thy cruell hart:
>> Thou art my Wit, and thou my Vertue art.
>
> (*AS* 64)

Her admonitions are swiftly dismissed; his claims on her affections, established. The mortifications invoked prove him Love's willing martyr. Moreover, like Pyrocles who withdraws from the company of all "excellent men in learning and soldiery" (*OA*, 13), Astrophil

renounces traditional male distinctions and professes indifference
to "Aristotle's wit" and "Caesar's bleeding fame." Nor does he
"care, though some above me sit" because all his ambition, wit,
and virtue are contained in Stella. It is one of his best performances,
overwhelming her reproofs with a stunning self-justification.

Two other poems in this middle section are among the most
seriously probing in the entire cycle. *AS* 61 and 62 explore the
fundamental contradictions of love and the self, clarifying certain
irreconcilable conflicts. The lover is fundamentally ambivalent in
his relationship with the beloved because his feelings involve both
self-assertion and self-denial. For Astrophil, these emotional contradictions prove agonizing. Earlier in the sequence, in *AS* 27, he had
denied the suspicions of other courtiers who assumed "that only I /
Fawne on my self," while confessing to "one worse fault, Ambition.
. . . / That makes me oft my best friends overpasse, / Unseene, un-
heard, while thought to highest place / Bends all his powers, even
unto Stella's grace" (*AS* 27). The place of the self in this equivocal
blend of bending and aspiration is left uncertain. In *AS* 61, Stella
forces the issue by demanding a rejection of "all selfnesse." Sidney
seems to have invented this splendid word, which covers a whole
range of troublesome feelings.[27]

> Oft with true sighes, oft with uncalled teares,
>> Now with slow words, now with dumbe eloquence
>> I Stella's eyes assayll, invade her eares;
>> But this at last is her sweet breath'd defence:
> That who indeed infelt affection beares,
>> So captives to his Saint both soule and sence,
>> That wholly hers, all selfnesse he forbeares,
>> Thence his desires he learnes, his live's course thence.
> Now since her chast mind hates this love in me,
>> With chastned mind, I straight must shew that she
>> Shall quickly me from what she hates remove.

27. Mona Wilson quoted by Ringler, in *Poems,* p. 478.

O Doctor Cupid, thou for me reply,
  Driv'n else to graunt by Angel's sophistrie,
  That I love not, without I leave to love.

(AS 61)

The paradoxical conclusion exposes the contradictions of her "so-phistrie" with its own conundrum: he will not love without leaving off or ceasing to love. The other possibility, that he will not love without leave or permission, is, for Astrophil, no less paradoxical than the first. Musidorus, whose speech in the *Arcadia* this echoes, elaborates on the impossibility of fulfilling such a command: "I find my love shalbe proved no love, without I leve to love, being too unfit a vessell in whom so high thoughts should be engraved. Yet since the Love I beare you, hath so joyned it self to the best part of my life, as the one cannot depart, but that th'other will follow, before I seeke to obey you in making my last passage, let me know which is my unworthines, either of mind, estate, or both?" (*NA*, 158). In one sense the heroes' predicaments differ. Pamela might respect "high" amorous sentiments, but she regards Dorus in his shepherd's disguise as an "unfitt vessell." By contrast, Stella's "chast mind hates this love in me," recalling Christ's hatred of the sin and not the sinner. Both heroes are alike though in their insistence on the inseparable integrity of their feelings and identity. "Selfnesse" cannot be split off from the self or, for those who deem it so, the sin from the sinner, without jeopardizing the lover's authenticity and even his life. The requirements of the courtly code, which "so captives to his Saint both soule and sence," demand an impossible self-division and suppression. The system denies fulfillment or reciprocity.

In *AS* 62, such demands are explicitly criticized. When Astrophil accuses Stella of being "unkind," he means that her attitude is both ungenerous and unnatural. He refutes her insistence on chaste love with another paradox: "Alas, if this the only mettall be / Of Love, new-coind to helpe my beggery, / Deare, love me not, that you may love me more" (*AS* 62).

Astrophil's insistent self-justification seems to be having some effect, and the mood begins to change in *AS* 66 and 67 with the promise of "Hope." In the next, he dismisses Stella's efforts "to quench in me the noble fire," and he contemplates her exertions with cool pleasure, thinking "what paradise of joy / It is, so faire a Vertue to enjoy." Stella finally relents in *AS* 69, submitting to his desires on one condition:

> For Stella hath with words where faith doth shine,
>> Of her high heart giv'n me the monarchie:
> I, I, ô I may say, that she is mine.
>> And though she give but thus conditionly
>> This realme of blisse, while vertuous course I take,
>> No kings be crown'd, but they some covenants make.
>>
>> (*AS* 69)

Their relationship is formulated in the hierarchical terms of sovereignty and subjection. Astrophil is elated at the sudden reversal of their positions. Before, in sonnets like *AS* 29 and 36, 40 and 42, he mourned his own enslavement and her tyranny; he considers rebellion in *AS* 47, but his resolve collapses as soon as she appears. In *AS* 69, their relationship abruptly changes, and Astrophil exults in his swift triumph. His cynical disregard for "covenants" is entirely appropriate, for the balance of power is such that no true compromise is possible. Sovereignty is absolute, unbound by any genuine conditions, and Astrophil enjoys it very briefly. In order to enforce the "vertuous course" she stipulates, Stella must simply resume control, and she does so almost immediately.

After a few more moments of silent elation in *AS* 70, Astrophil finds himself at a disadvantage, for Stella again demands the eradication of desire. Astrophil still insists on the inseparability of desire from self:

88

Who will in fairest booke of Nature know,
    How Vertue may best lodg'd in beautie be,
    Let him but learne of Love to reade in thee,
    Stella, those faire lines, which true goodnesse show.
There shall he find all vices' overthrow,
    Not by rude force, but sweetest soveraigntie
    Of reason, from whose light those night-birds flie;
    That inward sunne in thine eyes shineth so.
And not content to be Perfection's heire
    Thy selfe, doest strive all minds that way to move,
    Who marke in thee what is in thee most faire.
So while thy beautie drawes the heart to love,
    As fast thy Vertue bends that love to good:
    "But ah," Desire still cries, "give me some food."

                            (*AS* 71)

The bookish metaphor introduces a subtle hint of pedantry into the otherwise splendid declaration of the octet. Stella's "faire lines" represent an edifying, and rather tendentious, order. In the sestet the coercive aspects become more apparent as Stella strives to uplift her admirers. "And not content to be Perfection's heire. . . ," Stella "doest strive all minds that way to move." Astrophil is once again the victim of a disciplinary design, aimed at imposing the "sweetest soveraigntie / Of reason," as his beloved seeks to bend his impulses into their proper shape. The final line, one of Sidney's most forceful and deliberate non sequiturs, provides the only escape from the ruthless encroachments of Virtue. Desire, although it can bring about an impasse and thwart Virtue's objectives, is still too helpless to achieve its own ends. The final assertion is plaintive and passive; the characterization, infantile. Desire is a helpless babe crying for food, whose innocuous yearnings recall those proclaimed in *CS* 6:

Sleepe Babie mine, Desire, nurse Beautie singeth:
Thy cries, ô Babie, set mine head on aking:
The Babe cries "way, thy love doth keepe me waking."

Lully, lully, my babe, hope cradle bringeth
Unto my children alway good rest taking:
The Babe cries "way, thy love doth keepe me waking."

Since babie mine, from me thy watching springeth,
Sleepe then a litle, pap content is making:
The babe cries "nay, for that abide I waking."

(*CS* 6)

AS 72 adopts a tone of easy and familiar intimacy in its address
to Desire. Stella requires Astrophil to renounce his truest friend and
choose more virtuous associates. "Service and Honor," "feare to
offend," and "care" are recommended. The deferential nature of all
these virtues is clearly a significant link; even the more sublime
attitudes, such as "faith" and "wonder with delight," impose humility. Desire must be banished because it prevents such ready submission, "because thou wouldst have all." It is too voracious and
self-aggrandizing in its demands, for all its pathos. The clinging inseparability of Astrophil's desire from all his other feelings makes
banishment impossible, and this indissoluble bond provokes the final
lament. In this scheme, self-assertion is impossible, and desire is
constrained by guilt, ambivalence, and restrictions imposed from
above.

Astrophil achieves a temporary respite from this quandary in the
poems extending from Song ii to Song viii. Song ii begins with
Astrophil suddenly positioned above his sleeping mistress, plotting
to teach her a lesson:

Have I caught my heav'nly jewell,
Teaching sleepe most faire to be?
Now will I teach her that she,
When she wakes, is too too cruell.

(*AS* ii.1–4)

The poem somewhat luridly emphasizes her being offguard:

> See the hand which waking gardeth,
> Sleeping, grants a free resort:
> Now will I invade the fort;
> Cowards Love with losse rewardeth.
>
> But ô foole, thinke of the danger,
> Of her just and high disdaine:
> Nor will I alas refraine,
> Love feares nothing else but anger.
>
> (*AS* ii.13–20)

Astrophil is hindered from raping her, apparently, only by his fear of her wrath. The complex inhibitions of earlier poems are supplanted here by rather simplistic calculations. Even her anger does not prevent him from stealing a kiss and regretting subsequently that he did not steal more. *AS* 73 returns to this situation, playfully trivializing Stella's indignation by making it a more piquant stimulus to his desires.

AS 75 is a rather sophomorically scandalous poem in which Astrophil exalts Edward IV as his hero. Sidney and his readers were well acquainted with the disreputable character of this king, whom the *Mirror for Magistrates* condemned for his "surfeting and untemperate life," a life "greatly given to fleshely wantonnesse."[28] Praise for this man who chose to "lose his Crowne, rather then faile his love" displays a somewhat heavy frivolity. A more genuinely amusing poem is the next one, *AS* 76, which again desublimates the platonist's sacred fires in very witty fashion.

> She comes, and streight therewith her shining twins
> do move
> Their rayes to me, who in her tedious absence lay
> Benighted in cold wo, but now appears my day,
> The onely light of joy, the onely warmth of Love.

28. Quoted by Ringler, in *Poems*, p. 481.

She comes with light and warmth, which like Aurora
    prove
  Of gentle force, so that mine eyes dare gladly play
  With such a rosie morne, whose beames most
    freshly gay
  Scortch not, but onely do darke chilling sprites
    remove.
But lo, while I do speake, it groweth noone with me,
  Her flamie glistring lights increase with time and
    place;
  My heart cries "ah," it burnes, mine eyes now
    dazled be:
No wind, no shade can coole, what helpe then in my
    case,
  But with short breath, long lookes, staid feet and
    walking hed,
  Pray that my sunne go downe with meeker beames
    to bed.

(*AS* 76)

Stella's eyes, like the sun, dispel "cold wo" from her lover's heart, so that "now appeares my day, / The onely light of joy, the onely warmth of Love." All is "rosie morne" in the octet, but in the sestet all this sweetness and light get out of hand as things heat up too quickly. Sidney offers a very droll, lively parody of conventional praise, literally animating his beloved's attributes with irrepressible *energia*. The result is one of the funniest poems in the sequence.

The third song presents an interesting hiatus in the midst of this segment's sexual dalliance. The astonishing power of love and beauty is the subject, and Astrophil marvels at their effects on the stones and trees, birds and beasts of Grecian myth. The feats of Orpheus and Amphion are alluded to, and love is said to move animals to strange acts of heroism. Stella combines all these effects, and Astrophil is enthralled by the beauty of her appearance and her song. This solemn celebration of her miraculous powers affords a rare contemplative moment in the sequence.

The poem concludes with an odd paradoxical compliment. The continued immobility of the "birds, beasts, stones and trees" in the final stanza is simply proof of deeper love. "Know, that small Love is quicke, and great Love doth amaze." The lively, facile, active response belies feelings that are shallow; "great Love" overwhelms and immobilizes those who genuinely feel it. If animals and objects are thus overwhelmed, what wonder then that men "with reason armed" are similarly "charmed."

The poem finally betrays a peculiar mistrust of poetry's effects. In some ways, its conclusion recalls the contrast of *AS* 54, where "Dumb Swannes, not chatring Pies do Lovers prove." At several points in *Astrophil and Stella* (*AS* 6, 15, 28, 70, and 90), Sidney criticizes the glib fluency of other poet-lovers, and he argues with no less fluency for the virtues of simplicity and silence. Both the ironic and highly conventional aspects of this pose have been pointed out by many critics. Poetic eloquence generally thrives under such attacks. In Song iii, however, the implied criticism goes deeper, beyond the problem of sincerity, to more basic issues. In his depreciation of "quicke Love," Sidney seems to disparage *energia* itself, the lively "stir to the mind" that poetry provokes. Indeed, the miraculous moving power of Orpheus and Amphion is their essential qualification as poets: "as Amphion was said to move stones with his Poetry, to build Thebes, and Orpheus to be listened to by beasts."[29] Yet here the responsive mobility their poetry arouses is deemed inferior to the rapt fixity Stella inspires.

On one level the conclusion of Song iii is simply a clever, complimentary rationalization, yet it has a deeper significance indicated by parallels with *AS* 38, another instance of brief, visionary transcendence:

> This night while sleepe begins with heavy wings
> To hatch mine eyes, and that unbitted thought

29. Sidney, *Apology*, p. 96.

93

Doth fall to stray, and my chiefe powres are brought
  To leave the scepter of all subject things,
The first that straight my fancie's error brings
  Unto my mind, is Stella's image, wrought
  By Love's owne selfe, but with so curious drought,
  That she, me thinks, not onely shines but sings.
I start, looke, hearke, but what in closde up sence
  Was held, in opend sense it flies away,
  Leaving me nought but wailing eloquence:
I, seeing better sights in sight's decay,
  Cald it anew, and wooed sleepe againe:
  But him her host that unkind guest had slaine.

[(*AS* 38)

Here too, Stella "not onely shines but sings." Astrophil attains this happy vision when his thoughts are "unbitted" by sleep, and the cramped and painful vacillations of his waking hours are suspended for a time. The freedom of his mind in sleep is not unlike that achieved in poetry, for Astrophil finds that "my chiefe powres are brought / To leave the scepter of all subject things." In the *Apology*, Sidney distinguishes between fields that have "the works of Nature for his principal object, without which they could not consist, and on which they so depend" and poetry, which disdains "to be tied to any such subjection."[30] Yet the phrase "fancie's error" raises doubts about the legitimacy of this dream-vision before it even begins; once started, the dream cannot be held. "Astrophel is completely incapable of sustaining it," says Rudenstine of this visionary lapse; "It arouses his desire, and his effort to possess the vision quickly dispels it."[31]

Astrophil's failure reveals inherent ambiguities in this imaginative vision of perfection. In his analysis of the third song, Richard Young cites some pertinent remarks of Ficino: "beauty pertains only to the

30. Ibid., pp. 99–100.
31. Rudenstine, *Poetic Development*, p. 234.

mind, sight and hearing. Love, therefore, is limited to these three, but desire which rises from the other senses is called, not love, but lust or madness."[32] *AS* 38 reveals the surprising vulnerability of these senses to the most disruptive desires. The singing, shining, and disembodied image of Stella certainly appeals to these higher faculties, yet her beauty provokes simple lusts as the image turns into a seductive succubus. Once again, the rarefied aspirations of Neoplatonism are undercut.

The dream-vision of Philisides in the *Old Arcadia* reveals similar contradictions. Its prelude is an innocent, peaceful slumber:

> Free all my powers were from those captiving snares,
> Which heav'nly purest gifts defile in muddy cares.
> Ne could my soul itself accuse of such a fault
> As tender conscience might with furious pangs assault.
>
> (*OA*, 335.29–32)

The verse is replete with paradox and guilt. Conscience is both "tender and "furious," its fury springing from its tenderness, and the soul coils back on itself in tight, reflexive harshness. The greatest contradiction involves the source and nature of this vision. Presumably, "those captiving snares" are the subject of "defile," and "heav'nly purest gifts" are the object. The syntax allows, however, and even encourages, an inversion, suggesting that such heavenly sights may infect the viewer with "muddy cares." This disturbing prospect seems confirmed by the consequences of Philisides' vision. This glimpse of his beloved's perfection, however platonically exalted, is the occasion of his fall. The mind is "made of heav'nly stuff" and it is freed from "fleshly bondage" in sleep (*OA*, 336.10–11), but it still remains captive to the flesh and its desires.

These problems do not arise in *The Apology for Poetry*. There, the "erected wit" is freed from the "clayey lodgings" and "dungeon

32. Richard B. Young, "English Petrarke," p. 70.

of the body" by poetic imagination, and the mind ascends "to as high a perfection as our degenerate souls . . . can be capable of."[33] The virtue of poetry consists in this freedom from "subjection" to the limits of sense and fact. Poetry also derives power from its appeal to the emotions, for it can arouse both an active and a contemplative appreciation of its ideals, moving men to desire to do good: "And that moving is of a higher degree than teaching, it may by this appear, that it is well nigh the cause and the effect of teaching. For who will be taught, if he be not moved with desire to be taught? and what so much good doth that teaching bring forth . . . as that it moveth one to do that which it doth teach?"[34] Only once, in a rather cryptic and offhand fashion, does Sidney explicitly concede any difficulties with this scheme, difficulties that arise from the choice of subject. When mundane things are idealized, the poet might finally "make the too much loved earth more lovely."[35]

Sidney's poetry reveals a much deeper distrust of the imagination, a distrust fairly typical in the Renaissance. Greville summarizes the case against the imagination in *A Treatise on Human Learning:*

> So must th'imagination from the sense
> Be misinformed, while our affections cast
> False shapes, and formes on their intelligence,
> And to keepe out true intromissions thence
>   Abstracts the imagination, or distasts
>   With images preoccupately plac'd.
>
> Hence our desires, fears, hopes, love, hate, and sorrow
> In fancy make us heare, feele, see impressions,
> Such as out of our sense they doe not borrow,
> And are the efficient cause, the true progression
>   Of sleeping visions, idle phantasmes waking,
>   Life, dreams; and knowledge, apparitions making[36]

33. Sidney, *Apology,* p. 104.
34. Ibid., p. 112.
35. Ibid., p. 100.
36. Sir Fulke Greville, *Poems and Dramas,* p. 157.

Although Sidney's explicit speculations are much more positive, his poetry shows the mind's vulnerability to corrupting "affections." Astrophil's predicament dramatically shows a conflicted relationship between "erected wit" and "infected will." In fact, the fusion of affect and perception in poetic vision always seems to weight the conflict in favor of desire. Astrophil is undone, in a sense, by *energia*, by his own hyperactive responsiveness. In *AS* 38 his beloved's perfections move him too strongly and his emotional reactions ("I start, looke, hearke") are literally too "quicke." The poetry is too lively to contain its own effects, and desire disrupts the dream: the satisfactions promised in the *Apology* are frustrated by the conflicts of the poetry.

Despite his depreciation of "quicke Love," Astrophil is hyperkinetic in the poems immediately following the third song. In *AS* 84 and 85, he is riding to meet her for a secret assignation. This is the peak of narrative activity in the sequence following Stella's "conditional" surrender. The first of these poems carries to nearly absurd lengths his zeal for racing about:

> Highway since you my chiefe Pernassus be,
>> And that my Muse to some eares not unsweet,
>> Tempers her words to trampling horses feet,
>> More oft then to a chamber melodie;
> Now blessed you, beare onward blessed me
>> To her, where I my heart safeliest shall meet.
>> My Muse and I must you of dutie greet
>> With thankes and wishes, wishing thankfully.
>
> (*AS* 84)

In the sestet, blessings are showered on the road whose comparison with Parnassus links poetry with some rather dubious aspirations. The highway's inspirational virtue consists in its providing both a means for their rendezvous and an occasion for thinking about it.

In *AS* 85 Astrophil's sense of urgency and excitement increases still further when he spots the house:

I see the house, my heart thy selfe containe,
 Beware full sailes drowne not thy tottring barge:
 Least joy, by Nature apt sprites to enlarge,
 Thee to thy wracke beyond thy limits straine.
Nor do like Lords, whose weake confused braine,
 Not pointing to fit folkes each undercharge,
 While everie office themselves will discharge,
 With doing all, leave nothing done but paine.
But give apt servants their due place, let eyes
 See Beautie's totall summe summ'd in her face:
 Let eares heare speech, which wit to wonder ties,
Let breath sucke up those sweetes, let armes embrace
 The globe of weale, lips Love's indentures make:
 Thou but of all the kingly Tribute take.

          (*AS* 85)

The language resembles that of Troilus in its fear of strain beyond
limits. Emotion threatens to overwhelm him amid the confusion
and anxiety of his headlong rush. The sestet depicts a labored effort
to regain self-control. Mastery still proves a precarious achievement.
Various tasks are methodically parceled out to the senses, and while
the pleasures anticipated are kingly, their enjoyment requires rigid
discipline and care. Only thus can composure be restored.

 Song iv brings these events to consummation:

    Onely joy, now here you are,
    Fit to heare and ease my care:
    Let my whispering voyce obtaine,
    Sweete reward for sharpest paine:
    Take me to thee, and thee to me.
    "No, no, no, no, my Deare, let be."

          (*AS* iv.1–5)

Sexual urgency increases with Astrophil's whispering pleas, and the
carpe diem theme is given point by the jostling rhythms:

This small light the Moone bestowes,
Serves thy beames but to disclose,
So to raise my hap more hie;
Feare not else, none can us spie:
Take me to thee, and thee to me.
"No, no, no, no, my Deare, let be."

That you heard was but a Mouse,
Dumbe sleepe holdeth all the house:
Yet a sleepe, me thinkes they say,
Yong folkes, take time while you may:
Take me to thee, and thee to me.
"No, no, no, no, my Deare, let be."

Niggard Time threats, if we misse
This large offer of our blisse,
Long stay ere he graunt the same:
Sweet then, while each thing doth frame:
Take me to thee, and thee to me.
"No, no, no, no, my Deare, let be."

(*AS* iv.19–36)

For all its dramatic immediacy, the scene here is still very generalized and conventional. The protracted courtship of Astrophil and Stella culminates in a kind of jolly Chaucerian fabliaux. The dramatic personalities of each character are here transformed to caricature: with Astrophil, all voluble, charming insistence; with Stella, redundant denial. Sexual frustration had complicated the lineaments of character, but now they are generalized and simplified by satisfaction. The joke, of course, is that Stella's denial finally turns into assent, Astrophil having forced this from her with a combination of petulant threat, sly double entendre, and simple attrition.

Sweet alas, why strive you thus?
Concord better fitteth us:
Leave to Mars the force of hands,

99

Your power in your beautie stands:
Take me to thee, and thee to me.
"No, no, no, no, my Deare, let be."

Wo to me, and do you sweare
Me to hate? But I forbeare,
Cursed be my destines all,
That brought me so high to fall:
Soone with my death I will please thee.
"No, no, no, no, my Deare, let be."

(*AS* iv.43–54)

The consequences and significance of this reversal are still not clear, and some critics have imposed a decorum and distance on Song iv more restrictive than it calls for. Kalstone sees the "sweet flowers on fine bed too" as an invitation to pastoral pleasures;[37] Ringler lumps Songs iv and xi together, placing Astrophil outside Stella's window in each of them.[38] Whatever figurative associations the flowers may bring to this scene, the "fine bed" is at its center; and if any further evidence is required that Astrophil is inside Stella's bedroom, the embrace of the penultimate stanza—"Leave to Mars the force of hands"—seems to provide it. The closeness of the scene and mood suggest that the conclusion's ellipsis is prompted by decorum of another, more courtly sort—protection of a lady's reputation.

Nevertheless, there is still no change or development in their relationship. The tone of witty evasion and the lack of any follow-up prevent that. What could have been the dramatic climax of the entire sequence is muted by a blend of levity and inconsequence. Stella's capitulation is decorously passed over, and her surrender has no profound significance. Their relationship never moves beyond a simple test of wills, and Astrophil obtains no other satisfaction than this momentary triumph.

37. Kalstone, *Poetry*, p. 176.
38. *Poems*, Ringler, p. xlv.

Astrophil and Stella

His triumph is indeed brief. In *AS* 86, the sequence lapses abruptly into quarrelsome disappointment and guilt:

> Alas, whence came this change of lookes? If I
> Have chang'd desert, let mine owne conscience be
> A still felt plague, to selfe condemning me:
> Let wo gripe on my heart, shame loade mine eye.
>
> (*AS* 86)

Once more the balance of power shifts back to Stella. His conscience and her reproaches make Astrophil her "slave," swiftly plunging him to "hell." The belligerence of Song v is transparent bluster, becoming meekly plaintive in the final stanza, and Stella's praises are lovingly proclaimed in the sixth and seventh songs.

Song viii is the first in a series of alternative endings; in it the evanescent pleasures of their affair are conclusively renounced. Pastoral retirement and the past tense soften the pain of relinquishment. The song puts an end to the conflict of wills. Tranquillity and reconciliation prevail in this small pastoral world, and erotic antagonisms are subdued, for a time. The poetry gracefully allows the two lovers to have it both ways. While Astrophil's advances are repelled, Stella's denial is subtly inverted to imply its opposite:

> There his hands in their speech, faine
> Would have made tongue's language plaine;
> But her hands his hands repelling,
> Gave repulse all grace excelling.
>
> Then she spake; her speech was such,
> As not eares but hart did tuch:
> While such wise she love denied,
> As yet love she signified.
>
> (*AS* viii.65–72)

Even if her speech does not signify the more direct assent of Song iv, it still offers sublime affirmation. Promising him the first place in her heart, Stella swears that "All my blisse in thee I lay; / If thou love, my love content thee, / For all love, all faith is meant thee" (*AS* viii.89–91).

Unfortunately, the lovers are blocked from consummation by "Tyran honour," but their mutual submission to this higher tyranny dispels their earlier inequality. Previously, Astrophil had been Stella's slave, but now they are reconciled through shared thralldom. Their bond is reaffirmed in *AS* 87, where it is said that Stella suffers as much as he does under "iron lawes of duty." Their mutual frustration affords the only possible union.

Song viii provides a resolution that is attractive and dramatically satisfying, reconciling several fundamental conflicts, but the seqence does not stop here. Instead the poems continue for another long stretch, disrupting this mood of equanimity and reverting to old problems. In Song x, Astrophil seeks solace in meditation on Stella's charms, but the result is entirely devoid of Petrarch's contemplative reverence.

> Thought therefore I will send thee,
> > To take up the place for me;
> > Long I will not after tary,
> > There unseene thou maist be bold,
> > Those faire wonders to behold,
> > Which in them my hopes do cary.
>
> Thought see thou no place forbeare,
> > Enter bravely every where,
> > Seaze on all to her belonging;
> > But if thou wouldst garded be,
> > Fearing her beames, take with thee
> > Strength of liking, rage of longing.
> > > (*AS* x.13–24)

The exertions of the "erected wit" are lurid and aggressively dissolute. These fantasies of ravishment are followed by image of yielding lips, "opening rubies, pearles deviding" (*AS* x.30). In this erotic revery, Astrophil is restored to his "most Princely power. . . "

> When I blessed shall devower,
> With my greedy licorous sences,
> Beauty, musicke, sweetnesse, love
> While she doth against me prove
> Her strong darts, but weake defences.

> Thinke, thinke of those dalyings,
> When with Dovelike murmurings,
> With glad moning passed anguish,
> We change eyes, and hart for hart,
> Each to other do imparte,
> Joying till joy make us languish.
>
> (*AS* x.31–42)

All these voluptuous fantasies end, however, in swooning delirium. Such license clearly makes Astrophil uneasy:

> O my thought my thoughts surcease,
> Thy delights my woes increase,
> My life melts with too much thinking;
> Thinke no more but die in me,
> Till thou shalt revived be,
> At her lips my Nectar drinking.
>
> (*AS* x.43–48)

He is disappointed that these pleasures were merely fanciful and yearns for a genuine kiss. Yet there is also a fear of "melting" dissolution in the midst of unrestrained indulgence as old fears of "loose unchastitie" are revived. The tenth song moves beyond the conflicts and hesitating preliminaries to explicit fulfillment of desire. The evanescent vision of Stella glimpsed in *AS* 38 is forcefully held and fully developed through embrace to sated ecstasy. And yet the poem is undone by its own libertine excesses leading to melancholy distress.

The agonized self-reproach and exaggerated guilt of the next poem, *AS* 93, are a natural sequel to Song x:

> I have (live I and know this) harmed thee,
> Tho worlds quite me, shall I my selfe forgive?
> Only with paines my paines thus eased be,
> That all thy hurts in my hart's wracke I reede;
> I cry thy sighs; my deere, thy teares I bleede.
>
> (*AS* 93)

AS 93 through 99 all concern themselves with night, sadness, and isolation. In *AS* 94, Astrophil is nearly stupefied by sorrow:

> Griefe find the words, for thou hast made my braine
> So darke with misty vapors, which arise
> From out thy heavy mould, that inbent eyes
> Can scarce discerne the shape of mine owne paine.
>
> (*AS* 94)

He simply chooses to dwell in darkness in *AS* 99. For a time, Stella continues to share in his pain and affliction, and their empathy is portrayed in AS 100 through 103, but all this changes in the eleventh song:

> "Who is it that this darke night,
> Underneath my window playneth?"
> It is one who from thy sight
> Being (ah) exild, disdayneth
> Every other vulgar light.
>
> "Why alas, and are you he?
> Be not yet those fancies changed?"
> Deere when you find change in me,
> Though from me you be estranged,
> Let my chaunge to ruine be.
>
> (*AS* xi.1–10)

Astrophil's fidelity is indeed unshakable, and Stella, who is now eager to be rid of him, prescribes the conventional *remedia amoris:* "well in absence this will dy," and "time will these thoughts remove." She lumps "reason's purest light" with the distractions of "new beauties," cynically presuming that either one or both will be effective in shaking off his irksome constancy. Astrophil, however, is not so capriciously changeable. Stella finally becomes exasperated and brusquely dismisses him:

> "Peace, I thinke that some give eare:
> Come no more, least I get anger."
> Blisse, I will my blisse forbeare,
> Fearing (sweete) you to endanger,
> But my soule shall harbour there.
>
> "Well, be gone, be gone I say,
> Lest that Argus eyes perceive you."
> O unjustest fortune's sway,
> Which can make me thus to leave you,
> And from lowts to run away.
>
> (*AS* xi.36–45)

The eleventh song and the sonnet before it, *AS* 104, stand together as a vindication of Astrophil's love. The "envious wits" of the court mock him for his hapless devotion. They exult in their gossip, "and puffing prove that I / Do Stella love," but Astrophil flings this discovery back in their faces: "Fooles, who doth it deny?" Song xi establishes the same claim with a tone of desperate pathos, but it is no less reproachful than the more belligerent sonnet. Stella's fickle aversion to Astrophil links her with the shallow, fashionable "fooles" of the court; neither she nor they can comprehend the deeper significance of Astrophil's love, for both are prompted by the most conventional motives and concerns.

For some, this moment in the sequence is a triumphant climax. Although Astrophil's despair verges toward recalcitrance in its allegiance to "night over day, dark over light, passion over reason," Rudenstine argues that "in the context of the sequence, Astrophil's ritual style lends him an important dignity and preserves him from mere frenzy or whining."[39] In the eleventh song, Stella's abrupt repudiation places Astrophil at an advantage because "his love is presented in terms of its fidelity, its capability of withstanding time and absence, whereas hers has clearly consisted of little more than those 'fancies' that have already changed."[40] His inability to control his feelings, for which he has been continually upbraided, by various authority figures and Stella herself, is now the source of virtue. Her rectitude seems by contrast merely priggish and hypocritical in its concern with reputation. The ceremonial tone of these closing sonnets and their assertion of unflagging constancy are seen as effective ways of achieving closure.

Others, however, have found little solace in these poems of complaint. David Kalstone feels that the "special ferocity" of Astrophil's sorrow prevents solution.[41] In his view, the narrative action dissolves in bitter disappointment and then "merely ends."[42] A fitting conclusion" must be sought elsewhere, and Kalstone, like many other readers of *Astrophil and Stella*, finds it in two sonnets "long printed as part of the sequence," but now detached from it.[43] The first renounces desire as:

> Thou blind man's marke, thou foole's selfe chosen snare,
>   Fond fancie's scum, and dregs of scattred thought,
>   Band of all evils, cradle of causelesse care,
>   Thou web of will, whose end is never wrought.
>
> (CS 31)

39. Rudenstine, *Poetic Development,* p. 267.
40. Ibid., p. 268.
41. Kalstone, *Poetry,* p. 177.
42. Ibid., p. 178.
43. Ibid.

The second evokes the solemn biblical tones of religious transcendence:

> Leave me ô Love, which reachest but to dust,
>   And thou my mind aspire to higher things:
>   Grow rich in that which never taketh rust:
>   What ever fades, but fading pleasure brings.
> Draw in thy beames, and humble all thy might,
>   To that sweet yoke, where lasting freedomes be:
>   Which breakes the clowdes and opens forth the light,
>   That doth both shine and give us sight to see.
> O take fast hold, let that light be thy guide,
>   In this small course which birth drawes out to death,
>   And thinke how evill becommeth him to slide,
> Who seeketh heav'n, and comes of heav'nly breath.
>   Then farewell world, thy uttermost I see,
>   Eternall Love maintaine thy life in me.
>
> *(CS 32)*

A grave Latin tag is appended to the latter sonnet: *Splendidis longum valedico nugis*. As Kalstone concedes, there is no sixteenth-century textual basis for the inclusion of these two sonnets in *Astrophil and Stella*, and Ringler, who places them at the end of *Certain Sonnets*, maintains they were written long before Sidney composed *Astrophil and Stella*.[44] Still, their air of resolute conviction draws many readers to this conclusion. J. W. Lever sees in them "Sidney's final attitude to romance," and he regards "Leave me o Love" as the paragon of poetic maturity in Sidney's development: "Released from its perplexities, his genius leapt forward and made this sonnet perhaps his greatest poetic triumph," one in which "the facility of his early work was transformed into power under perfect control."[45]

There is another final maneuver that has received less attentive acclaim. *AS* 107 seeks a more practical solution to Astrophil's

44. *Poems*, Ringler, pp. 423–424.
45. Lever, *Love Sonnet*, pp. 82, 91.

troubles, a solution less dramatic than despairing constancy or fierce renunciation. Astrophil's constancy begins to seem unhealthy in *AS* 106, for his fixation becomes an incurable affliction:

> But heere I do store of faire Ladies meete,
>> Who may with charme of conversation sweete,
>> Make in my heavy mould new thoughts to grow:
> Sure they prevaile as much with me, as he
>> That bad his friend, but then new maim'd, to be
>> Mery with him, and not thinke of his woe.
>
> (AS 106)

In *AS* 107, Astrophil seems to be striving to move beyond this wretchedness:

> Stella since thou so right a Princesse art
>> Of all the powers which life bestowes on me,
>> That ere by them ought undertaken be,
>> They first resort unto that soueraigne part;
> Sweete, for a while give respite to my hart,
>> Which pants as though it still should leape to thee:
>> And on my thoughts give thy Lieftenancy
>> To this great cause, which needs both use and art,
> And as a Queene, who from her presence sends
>> Whom she imployes, dismisse from thee my wit,
>> Till it have wrought what thy owne will attends.
> On servants' shame oft Maister's blame doth sit;
>> O let not fooles in me thy workes reprove,
>> And scorning say, 'See what it is to love.'
>
> (AS 107)

Astrophil renews his address to Stella directly, asking this time for release from bondage. This is a highly formalized, almost legalistic appeal, carefully outlining the terms and conditions of their relationship. Astrophil seeks to alter the absolute nature of his subordination, establishing some claims of his own against her "powers" as "Princesse." He pleads for the partial freedom and practical authority of "thy Lieftenancy," so that, once his wit is dismissed from her, he can turn his attention to another "great cause." The phrase is intriguingly cryptic; whereas some assign specific biographical significance, Ringler argues that this " 'great cause' more probably refers to public service in general."[46] In this laconic, glancing fashion, Sidney begins to return to the world of public and political concerns after deliberately banishing them from his protracted meditation on love. At the same time, he attempts one of the more explicit formulations of sexual politics, defining precisely the issues of power and autonomy. Within the constraints of Petrarchan tradition, Astrophil asks for the provisional power of a "Lieftenancy," a compromise between dominance and defeat. Yet this limited solution is apparently impossible. In the last poem, *AS* 108, "most rude dispaire my daily unbidden guest . . . makes me then bow downe my head." Astrophil is firmly held by the inescapable bonds of oxymoronic anguish: "That in my woes for thee thou art my joy. / And in my joyes for thee my only annoy." The final note is one of complete submission to romantic convention.

Once again a balance of power between sovereignty and submission proves impossible. The curve of his fictive courtship is drawn to more extreme postures of transcendence or noble pathos. Yet here, in *Astrophil and Stella,* Sidney handles these alternatives with an assurance and awareness unmatched in his other works. The sequence is a triumph of courtly wit and *sprezzatura* that can accommodate the tensions of sexual politics. Conflict is internalized and reduced to purely romantic concerns, and less is finally at stake. When the conflicts expand in the more open and inclusive narratives of the *Arcadia,* they become harder to comprehend or negotiate, revealing the limitations of wit. In *Astrophil and Stella,* contradiction and frustration are more readily accepted, and wit maintains its extraordinary composure and control.

46. *Poems,* Ringler, p. 490.

Chapter Four

Narrative Development
in the *Old Arcadia:*
Foul Ways and Fair Ends

F OR ALL ITS CONTRADICTIONS, *Astrophil and Stella* presents one of the most coherent sonnet sequences in English. Yet narrative development becomes far more problematic in the *Old* and *New Arcadia.* The simpler tale of the original proceeds smoothly, but the deus ex machina conclusion raises more questions than it answers. In the revision, the plot becomes more confusingly labyrinthine, making closure of any sort nearly impossible. When Musidorus first heard of Pyrocles' confusing difficulties in love, he "recommended to his best discourse, all which Pyrocles had told him," earnestly striving to arrive at a solution; "But therein he found such intricatenes, that he could see no way to lead him out of the maze" (*NA*, 94). Later, when Musidorus himself falls in love he finds its "intricatenes" even more perplexing: "O heaven and earth (said Musidorus) to what a passe are our mindes brought, that from the right line of vertue, are wryed to these crooked shifts? But ô Love, it is thou that doost it: thou changest name upon name; thou disguisest our bodies, and disfigurest our mindes. But in deed thou hast reason, for though the wayes be foule, the journeys end is most faire and honourable" (*NA*, 117).

This dichotomy increases as their love affairs develop, leaving the heroes still more helpless and confused. They find themselves bogged down along their various foul ways, while love's fair and honorable ends seem hopelessly remote. The plot's intricacies thwart the reader's comprehension as well. The fair ends of pastoral romance come as an abrupt non sequitur in the *Old Arcadia,* prompting questions and controversy about how they are obtained. In the revision, Sidney avoids coming to any conclusion. In both versions, Sidney's narrative sequence presents a pattern of ambivalence and irresolution, the same pattern encountered in his debates. The details of this complex narrative sequence are the subject of this and the next chapter.

In the *Old Arcadia,* the initial predicament is seemingly straightforward: Pyrocles and Musidorus must court the two princesses while circumventing the opposition of the girls' father. While the tactic of disguise solves this problem, it also creates further difficulties. For one thing, courtship becomes tortuously difficult, and the heroes must initially apply all their ingenuity to presenting their suits. Musidorus finds that his attentions are not taken seriously because he seems a mere shepherd; Pamela's disdain for a social inferior makes her immune to his charms. "He omitted no occasion whereby he might make Pamela see how much extraordinary devotion he bare to her service, and daily withal strave to make himself seem more worthy in her sight; that desert being joined to affection might prevail something in the wise princess. But too well he found that a shepherd's either service or affection was but considered of as from a shepherd, and the liking limited to that proportion" (*OA,* 98). Disconcerted at "finding his service by this means lightly regarded, his affection despised, and himself unknown," Musidorus devises a clever stratagem for "the manifesting of his mind" (*OA,* 98). He decides to court Pamela's chaperone, Mopsa, the foolish daughter of Dametas. Pamela is then piqued by curiosity and jealousy—"for indeed so falls it often in the excellent women that even that which they disdain to themselves yet like they not that others should win it from them"—and she listens more carefully to the declarations of this handsome shepherd; thus she begins to discern "a second meaning"

(*OA*, 99). By continuing to exploit "this fit occasion of Pamela's wit and Mopsa's ignorance" (*OA*, 102), Musidorus reveals his true status and identity through a series of guarded disclosures. His beloved is appropriately impressed, and his suit is thus advanced.

For Pyrocles these expository logistics are complicated even further by the intrusions of the king and queen. In the *New Arcadia* one is treated to an amusingly stylized account of his dilemma entitled "The Labyrinth of Zelmanes love":

> Zelmane returned to the Lodge, where (inflamed by Philoclea, watched by Gynecia, and tired by Basilius) she was like a horse, desirous to runne, and miserablie spurred, but so short rainde, as he cannot stirre forward: Zelmane sought occasion to speake with Philoclea; Basilius with Zelmane; and Gynecia hindered them all. If Philoclea hapned to sigh (and sigh she did often) as if that sigh were to be wayted on, Zelmane sighed also; whereto Basilius and Gynecia soone made up foure parts of sorow.
>
> (NA, 95–96)

In this witty scheme, the subject is reduced to an object, tugged and pulled symmetrically, a victim of both passion and aggression. In the *Old Arcadia*, Pyrocles seeks a way out of the "Labyrinth" by an ingeniously oblique maneuver. Exploiting the deluded infatuation of the king, Pyrocles suggests that Philoclea might intervene on her father's behalf: "Your words, mighty prince, were unfit either for you to speak or me to hear: but yet the large testimony I see of your affection makes me willing to suppress a great number of errors. Only thus much I think good to say: that these same words in my lady Philoclea's mouth, as from one woman to another, might have had a better grace, and perchance have found a gentler receipt" (*OA*, 115).

Basilius impulsively grasps at this lure, and rushes off to enlist his daughter as a go-between. He urges his need upon her in swooning clichés: "she would preserve his life in whom her life was begun;

she would save his grey hairs from rebuke, and his aged mind from despair; that if she were not cloyed with his company, and that she thought not the earth overburdened with him, she would cool his fiery plague, which was to be done with her breath" (*OA*, 115–116)'. His importunate desires become more unseemly when Basilius exploits his paternal authority as a means of obtaining them: "He concluded she should in one payment requite all his deserts; and that she needed not disdain any service, though never so base, which was warranted by the sacred name of a father" (*OA*, 116). What is meant to reinforce his pleas results in crude deflation, and the debasement of paternal sovereignty is conveyed through comic bathos.

The comedy is continued through Philoclea's confusion. She is elated by the chance to be alone with Cleophila, with whom she is thoroughly—if uncertainly—in love. Yet, however perplexing her own affections may be, she does not want them tainted by association with her father's coarse desires.

> Philoclea more glad than ever she had known herself that she might by this occasion enjoy the private conference of Cleophila, yet had so sweet a feeling of virtue within her mind that she would not suffer a vile colour to be cast over her high thoughts, but with an humble look and obedient heart answered her father that there needed neither promise nor persuasion unto her to make her do her uttermost for her father's service; that, for Cleophila's favour in all virtuous sort, she would seek it towards him; and that, as she would not pierce further into his meaning than himself should declare, so would she interpret all his doings to be accomplished in goodness. And therefore desired, if otherwise it should be, he would not impart it to her, who then should be forced to begin by true obedience a show of disobedience, rather performing his general commandment (which had ever been to embrace virtue) than any new particular sprung out of passion and contrary to the former.
>
> (*OA*, 116)

She knows too clearly what her father's feelings are and prefers to hear nothing more about them. Innocence is priggishly willed, becoming decorous, self-serving evasion. Basilius, who cares only for "a speedy return of comfort," ignores her reproaches, having "allowed her reasons and accepted her service" (*OA*, 116). The comedy of this exchange prompts a detached and somewhat cynical amusement at the same time it scores its ethical points with precision and subtlety. The contrast between the king's crude exploitation of his daughter, and Pyrocles' clever manipulation of the king, affords further entertainment.

The brief romantic interlude that results from all these maneuvers is chastely consummated by "the promise of marriage" (*OA*, 122). This is one of the work's few moments of unhindered joy, in which the hero actually gets what he wants and has worked for; it is not long sustained. When Gynecia is awakened by her nightmare and finds out that Pyrocles and her daughter are alone together, she comes dashing in "to separate them" (*OA*, 122). The pleasant harmonies of mutual affection are swiftly dispelled by jealous rage and lust. This intrusion is immediately succeeded by another, for just as Gynecia "began . . . to display to Cleophila the storehouse of her deadly desires," the Phagonian rebels attack, giving "just occasion to Cleophila to break off any such conference" (*OA*, 123). The rebellion is then dispersed by Pyrocles who turns the "many-headed multitude" against their leaders through his shrewd oratorical craft (*OA*, 131).

The pattern of this action is complex and unsettling, and some have seen in it an ominous significance. Franco Marenco observes that these "irruptions succeed each other with uniform consistency: they open a series of unhealthy parentheses in a state of normality which looks more and more precarious, until they lead to a final breakdown in the private life of the characters as well as in the life of the state."[1] The social order seems no less vulnerable than personal

1. Franco Marenco, "Double Plot in Sidney's Old *Arcadia*," p. 251.

composure as the turmoil of this scene increases. Yet Marenco's reading seems unduly alarmist, for disorder is averted and licentious impulse is always thwarted; even as it expands in its scope, the scene's chaotic energy seems oddly contained. There is nothing really final about any of these actions, inasmuch as none are carried through to completion, and the pattern is one of constant reversal rather than decline and breakdown. The romantic intrigue of the second "act" culminates in farcical frustration in which all attempts at control or assertion are reversed almost automatically.

The *Old Arcadia*'s third and fourth "acts" reach a similar climax. The machinations of the heroes achieve limited success, but they are swiftly overwhelmed by larger forces. Musidorus persuades Pamela to flee with him against her father's wishes. He plans further acts of aggression against the king, vowing to help Pyrocles "by bringing such an army hither as shall make Basilius (willing or unwilling) to know his own hap in granting you Philoclea" (*OA*, 173). Their romantic intrigue becomes increasingly belligerent. Musidorus manages his escape with Pamela by duping each of her guardians, designing his tricks to exploit their individual weaknesses. Dametas goes off in search of treasure, while his jealous wife, who is told he has a mistress, sets off to spy on him. Meanwhile the gullible Mopsa sits placidly in a "wishing tree" (*OA*, 195).

Pyrocles seeks to obtain his own desires by pretending to yield to those of Basilius and Gynecia. Having promised separately to meet each one in the same place, he tricks the unwitting pair into a "bed-switch," and he is left free to seduce Philoclea. Gynecia realizes she has been deceived immediately, for though the cave is dark, she can recognize her garrulous husband's voice. She cautiously remains silent and submits to his obtuse love making, while he exults in his presumed triumph, "more happy," Sidney slyly remarks, "in contemplation than action" (*OA*, 274). The comic irony is sustained in Basilius's apostrophe to night, "that hast with thy sweet wings shrouded me in the vale of bliss!" (*OA*, 274). His benighted raptures come to an end when the dawning light reveals that he has committed "adult'ry" with his wife; the oracle is thus ironically fulfilled.

While Basilius is reduced to abject prevarication, Gynecia seizes the initiative, posing as the ever-faithful wife. She is shrewdly restrained in her reproaches, compelling her spouse's grateful appreciation: "How much Basilius's own shame had found him culpable, and had already even in soul read his own condemnation, so much did this unexpected mildness of Gynecia captive his heart unto her, which otherwise perchance would have grown to a desperate carelessness" (*OA*, 278). Thus, they are "reconciled to Basilius's great contentation" (*OA*, 278), a reconciliation flawed, of course, by the craft and hypocrisy of Gynecia. This happy solution is dashed entirely when Basilius mistakenly drinks the love potion and drops suddenly to the earth. At the king's apparent death, Gynecia succumbs to the deepest remorse, for she sees this disaster as punishment for her sins, the "necessary downfall of inward wretchedness" (*OA*, 279).

For the other characters, the consequences of romantic intrigue are no less disastrous. Book IV, which depicts these disturbing results, begins ominously with an invocation of "everlasting justice" that makes "ourselves . . . the punishers of our faults, and . . . our own actions the beginning of our chastisement" (*OA*, 265). One is then treated to an amusing Oedipal imbroglio that is the result of Musidorus's trickery. Dametas, returning from his futile treasure hunt, sees his daughter up in a tree and tries to drag her down. When his wife sees them struggling together, she assumes this is his mistress and begins thrashing them both. Having escaped from this chaotic brawl, Dametas is further dismayed to find that Pamela is missing and Philoclea is sleeping with a greatly altered Cleophila. He still manages to steal away Pyrocles' sword, and locking them in their chamber, he runs out to spread the alarm. When the king's death is made known, panic and disorder increase.

Pyrocles, who is immediately suspected of all this treachery, awakens to find himself imprisoned and disarmed. He then realizes that they have been found out and recalls with horror "the cruelty of the Arcadian laws which, without exception, did condemn all to death who were found in act of marriage without solemnity of marriage" (*OA*, 290). Deprived of nearly every means of effective action, he decides that his own death is the only way he can spare his beloved Philoclea from the same fate. "For then he thought it would fall out that when they found his body dead, having no accuser but Dametas, . . . it might justly appear that either Philoclea in defending her honour, or else he himself in despair of achieving, had left his carcass proof of his fact but witness of her clearness" (*OA*, 291). Despite his careful deliberation and resourcefulness, even this plan miscarries. The weapon Pyrocles improvises is too blunt, and the noise of his efforts wakens Philoclea.

After she recovers from her astonishment, Philoclea engages with her lover in a dispute about the legitimacy of suicide. Philoclea claims that suicide is an abdication of our duty to God, who has "appointed us captains of these our bodily forts, which without treason to that majesty were never to be delivered over till they were redemanded" (*OA*, 294). In reply, Pyrocles maintains that his actions represent a last-ditch attempt at self-control. For Pyrocles, heroism requires strenuous exertion and autonomy. He tells Philoclea that she must not assume that "the valiant man is willingly to suffer any thing, since the very suffering of some things is a certain proof of want of courage" (*OA*, 297). Suicide affords a bold alternative to "submitting ourselves to each unworthy misery which the foolish world may lay upon us" (*OA*, 297). He concludes accordingly that "if God have made us masters of anything, it is of our own lives, out of which without doing wrong to anybody we are to issue at our own pleasure" (*OA*, 297). But Philoclea counters his argument on just these grounds, insisting that "it is not for us to appoint that mighty majesty what time he will help us. . . . That we should be masters of ourselves we can show at all no title, nor claim; since neither we made ourselves, nor bought ourselves, we can stand upon no other right but his gift, which he must limit as it pleaseth him" (*OA*, 297–298).

Whereas Pyrocles' bungled efforts to kill himself become subtly comic, the debate to which they give rise acquires gravity and significance. Some of the work's essential issues, bearing on the nature of heroism, are raised in this encounter between the active and the patiently submissive responses. Walter Davis, who assigns thematic primacy to "Christian patience,"[2] gives this exchange great importance: "Philoclea's arguments here reiterate those used by Pamela in the captivity episode" against the evil Cecropia,[3] but now they are directed toward the work's central figure, an auditor more virtuously responsive. Pyrocles must be drawn away "from the life of action to the life of contemplation" in Davis's scheme, a transition that he calls "the perfection of the hero through love."[4] The lovers' dispute is crucial, for it is here that the "way was paved by Philoclea, . . . where Pyrocles finally accepted Providence and thereupon acquired patience, the key to the virtues that purify the soul."[5]

Nancy Lindheim, however, points out that no such thing occurs; Pyrocles, in fact, is unaffected by his lover's arguments, and "his determination to commit suicide" is altered only "by Philoclea's passionately tearful assurance that she will kill herself as well."[6] He is patronizingly indifferent to her moral principles, "not so much persuaded as delighted by her well conceived and sweetly pronounced speeches" (*OA*, 298). Moreover, Pyrocles remains arrogantly con-

2. Walter R. Davis, "A Map of Arcadia," p. 75.
3. Ibid., p. 81.
4. Ibid., p. 68.
5. Ibid., pp. 162–163.
6. Nancy Rothwax Lindheim, "Vision, Revision, and the 1593 Text of the *Arcadia*," p. 141.

vinced of his own rectitude, blandly assuring her that "never can God himself persuade me that Pyrocles' life is not well lost for to preserve the most admirable Philoclea" (*OA*, 298). His change of mind is caused by calculation rather than conversion, for he sees through "a true use of reason" that his "way would not prevail" (*OA*, 299). This is, of course, a happy resolution of the immediate crisis, a resolution in which the conflict is gracefully muted and the hero preserved; yet it also begs the crucial questions of autonomy and submission. Pyrocles' ineptitude is mitigated by courtliness and comedy, and belief in his competence is sustained. Yet Sidney's hero is still thwarted in even the most limited exertions, and the questions concerning his capacity for control are deftly evaded.

The heroes' activities thus culminate in a familiar pattern. In seeking a way out of his labyrinthine difficulties through his own exertions, Pyrocles achieves only momentary success; his devious maneuvers eventually result in even greater difficulties, and he ends up disarmed and entrapped, the victim of circumstances he tried to control. Musidorus fares even worse. After he and Pamela have fled, he finds it increasingly hard to delay gratification. Gazing at his sleeping mistress, Musidorus is soon "overmastered with the fury of delight" and he seeks "'to take the advantage of the weakness of the watch" (*OA*, 202). He is just about to ravish her when, "to the just punishment of his broken promises, and most infortunate bar of his long-pursued and almost-achieved desires," he is overmastered by assaults from another quarter (*OA*, 202). The runaway lovers are seized and dragged back to the palace by the remnants of the Phagonian rebels.

The heroes have shown themselves incapable of achieving a solution, and their blunders have exacerbated the problem. The king, whose control and authority have been steadily deteriorating, is now eliminated altogether. The situation requires the intervention of a superior figure who will set these "crooked shifts" straight, and the character who takes on this role is the ultimate patriarch. Euarchus is not only the exemplary King of Macedon, "the line of his actions straight and always like itself, no worldly thing being able to shake the constancy of it" (*OA*, 357–358); he is also the father of Pyrocles and uncle to Musidorus. He enters the *Old Arcadia* in its final "act," a paternal deus ex machina, the only man capable of imposing a solution.

Euarchus has come here to urge Basilius to resume his royal responsibilities and renew an old alliance, an alliance that resembles the Protestant league. Greece is caught between "the Asiatics of the one side, the Latins of the other" (*OA*, 358). Sidney felt that the Protestant states were in the same predicament, and their disunity was a source of concern for him and his friends. In a letter written in 1574, Hubert Languet writes that he fears this disunity will open "a way for the Turks" into Europe.[7] Sidney expands the case for an alliance in the 1593 text, using the same arguments he had tried with Elizabeth and other Protestant rulers: "by uniting their strength, to make timely provision against this peril; by many reasons making them see that, though in respect of place some of them might seem further removed from the first violence of the storm, yet being embarked in the same ship the final wrack must needs be common to them all."[8]

When Euarchus arrives, he finds that his old friend is apparently dead and Arcadia is in turmoil. On behalf of the wretched citizens, Philanax asks Euarchus to assume rule of the country and administer the judicial inquiry. The force of the latter's authority is immediately apparent, for his arrival puts an end to the division some had thought to exploit. One of these men, Timautus, "still blinded with his own ambitious haste," tries to oppose the intervention of Euarchus, but he suffers the same fate as the Phagonian troublemakers:

7. *The Correspondence of Sir Philip Sidney and Hubert Languet*, trans. Stuart A. Pears, p. 44.

8. Cited in *The Countess of Pembroke's Arcadia (The Old Arcadia)*, ed. Jean Robertson, pp. 355–356.

for the people, already tired with their own divisions (of which his clampering had been a principal nurse), and beginning now to espy a haven of rest, hated anything that should hinder them from it. . . . And thus inflaming one another against him, they threw him out of the assembly, and after pursued him with stones and staves; so that, with loss of one of his eyes, sore wounded and beaten, he was fain to fly to Philanax's feet for the succour of his life—giving a true lesson that vice itself is forced to seek the sanctuary of virtue.

(*OA*, 354–355)

When Euarchus actually assumes the rule of the country, he takes firm steps to consolidate his authority, for he is concerned about further fluctuations in popular opinion. He tells Philanax that the Arcadians' "hasty drawing to me makes me think they may be as hastily withdrawn from me" (*OA*, 363). In addressing his new subjects, Euarchus urges them to "remember I am a man; that is to say, a creature whose reason is often darkened with error" (*OA*, 365). Yet even as he acknowledges his fallibility, he imposes absolute obedience. The Arcadians must abjure "foretaken opinions," further debates, and criticism of their new sovereign: "do not easily judge of your judge; but since you will have me to command, think it is your part to obey" (*OA*, 365). Only after he has imposed these strict conditions does Euarchus undertake "to be the judge of the late evils happened" (*OA*, 364–365).

Meanwhile, the two princes await their trial in jail, and within these straitened circumstances, they seem to regain their composure and authority. This confinement "they like men indeed (fortifying courage with the true rampire of patience) did so endure as they did rather appear governors of necessity than servants to fortune" (*OA*, 370). The heroes can regard their own death with tranquillity because they are convinced of their own justification: "We have lived, and have lived to be good to ourselves and others," Musidorus assures his friend; "Our souls . . . have achieved the causes of their hither coming. . . . And to many men (for in this time, place, and fortune, it is lawful for us to speak gloriously) it hath been behoveful that we should live" (*OA*, 371).

When they are drawn by these reflections into speculations on the afterlife, both youths anticipate some continuity between their heroic exertions in this world and their life in the next. Some philosophers contend, according to Musidorus, that "passions, thoughts, and imaginations" and the memory "(which riseth only out of them)" all die along with the body; "and then is there left nothing but the intellectual part or intelligence which, void of all moral virtues (which stand in the mean of perturbations) doth only live in the contemplative virtue and power of the omnipotent God (the soul of souls and universal life of this great work)" (*OA*, 372). The mundane "moral virtues," which consist in the Aristotelian "mean of perturbations," become obsolete when life's "perturbations" cease; mutability is supplanted by a stable, limpid transcendence. Pyrocles concedes that "sensible or passionate knowledge" is impossible in this state, but he insists on the endurance of individual perception: "it shall be a vital power of that very intelligence which, as while it was here it held the chief seat of our life" (*OA*, 372). He claims that a continuous perception "of things both present and past" will be maintained by this "right intelligence" (*OA*, 373).

Nancy Lindheim offers us the best analysis of this scene, an analysis that is cognizant of both the scene's specific contextual significance and its broader philosophical concerns. She shows that Sidney is making a case here for personal immortality; the integrity and endurance of the individual soul are his primary concern.[9] Again, Lindheim disagrees with Walter Davis, according to whom a contemplative "shift from the realm of the civic virtues to that of the virtues of the purified mind" occurs at this point in the story.[10]

9. Lindheim, "Vision," pp. 144–146.
10. Walter R. Davis, "Map," p. 65.

By the end of the heroes' exchange, song is supposed to replace "persuasive discourse with vision . . . and the struggles of the moral life fade before the slow opening up of the glorious light of heaven."[11] His Neoplatonic scheme prevents Davis from seeing the essential point of the pretrial scene. Pyrocles and Musidorus want to retain some memory of "the struggles of the moral life." As Lindheim shows, this is essential to their sense of justification, and the heroes remain consistently committed to the active life.[12] Musidorus establishes this commitment in his remarks about their past lives, and their ideas about the future sustain it.

The heroes' remarks also have an intriguing psychological significance, entirely consonant with their defense of the soul's integrity. The Averroistic doctrine of impersonal immortality, cited by Musidorus, poses the ultimate threat to individual autonomy. In this view, the soul is both absorbed and passively sustained by its progenitor, its own vitality extinguished by the "power of the omnipotent God" (*OA*, 372). The crucial psychological term is repeated in Pyrocles' reply: his inherent "vital power" (*OA*, 372) will not be relinquished even at death—the final encounter with the absolute authority.

Yet this scene, however ennobling, is still oddly incongruous. The heroes' lofty exchange may encourage one to forget the causes of their imprisonment, causes they completely ignore. They have been reduced to these mortifying straits by their blunders and misconduct, and it is certainly not unreasonable to expect some change of heart. Yet they do not repent or even reconsider any of their actions, consoling themselves instead with the memory of their many accomplishments and their unshakable self-esteem. Richard Lanham justifiably objects to such complacency: "They leave—so far as they know— a dead duke, a ruined queen, two princesses dishonored, and a

11. Ibid., p. 67.
12. Lindheim, "Vision," p. 146.

tumultuous kingdom ruled by a foreign king, as mementoes of their sojourn there. As we have seen, neither prince is wont to hide his light, but a reader may perhaps be forgiven for thinking them more pleased with themselves than the occasion warrants.[13]

The pretrial scene displays, I think, some of the fundamental contradictions in Sidney's treatment of his heroes. Their heroism requires self-assertion, but this gets them in trouble with paternal authority. Sidney cannot let them pursue their defiant activities, and so they are frustrated and immobilized, and submission to the father is enforced on them. At the same time, this expedient protects them from the guilt and dangers of continued defiance. There are still other advantages: accused of numerous crimes, the princes remain obdurately self-satisfied. In the face of annihilation, they are convinced of their immortal "vital power." Their arrogant immobility, another characteristic pose for Sidney's heroes, is both a kind of compromise and an impasse. Through this tense balance of power, certain checks are placed on paternal authority, and filial independence and integrity are maintained. Yet filial assertion is still extremely difficult, and the princes' status remains precarious. Sidney's treatment of them is inevitably evasive and ambivalent.

The trial itself becomes an occasion for a retrospective organization of the preceding events, and the reader is engaged in the process of judgment. Walter Davis has accurately noted the link between the trial's evaluative and narrative purposes: "From its very nature as a final act of order proceeds its main function in the book, which is to redefine and see the elements of pattern in the scattered events which have occurred since the princes penetrated the retreat. It asks, in effect, 'What has all this been about?' "[14] Davis finds that the answer emerges progressively from "three different versions of the plot of *Arcadia*."[15]

13. Richard A. Lanham, "The Old *Arcadia*," p. 288.
14. Walter R. Davis, "Map," p. 164.
15. Ibid.

The first of these is advanced by the counselor Philanax, who eagerly assumes the role of prosecutor. He begins his diatribe against Pyrocles by warning his auditors that they may "rather imagine you hear some tragedy invented of the extremity of wickedness" (*OA*, 386). He is clear about the generic principle of his narrative; yet he still faces difficulties in recounting these atrocities. The culprit's metamorphoses nearly confound Philanax, who must explain "such changes and traverses as a quiet poet could scarce fill a poem withal" (*OA*, 389). He explains things finally by attributing this inconstancy to one source: "But whosoever well weighs it shall find it sprung out of the same fountain of mischievous naughtiness: the killing of the father, dishonouring the mother, and ravishing the child" (*OA*, 390). For Philanax, these intricate shifts can only be understood in terms of a lurid perversity "that hath no restraint of shame" (*OA*, 387).

Pyrocles' rebuttal sustains the parallel between narrative and legal interpretation, for it offers the judge another "thread to guide you in the labyrinth this man of his tongue had made so monstrous" (*OA*, 393). He denies Philanax's sinister interpretation, "which he useth as the knot of all his wise assertions" (*OA*, 393), and advances love as his sole motivation and excuse: "I offered force to her; love offered more force to me" (*OA*, 394). Typically, Pyrocles' appeal is based on pathos, for he presents himself as passion's victim. He is overwhelmed by love, "whose violence wrought violent effects in me" (*OA*, 395). In this instance, passivity and displacement seem lame as a defense. Davis finds that his "story approaches the complexities and confusions of life as we know it, but the price we have to pay is that moral judgment is completely baffled."[16] Richard Lanham says more bluntly that this is "truth without consequences."[17]

Musidorus is more belligerently righteous in his own justification.

16. Ibid., p. 165.
17. Lanham, Old *Arcadia*," p. 305.

Philanax has infuriated him with charges of "treason," of "stealing away of the princess of this province" and violating his bond of "allegiance (having made himself a servant and subject)" (*OA*, 400). In reply, Musidorus boasts of their many heroic services to the royal family, and with brazen sophistry, he rationalizes his defiance of the king as service to the princess: "I pray you, then, whom should I wait of else but her that was my mistress by my professed vow, and princess over me while I lived in this soil? . . . taking me as her servant, then take withal that I must obey her" (*OA*, 402). When he turns his attention to his own motives—the "just excuses of love's force" (OA, 402)—Musidorus emphasizes the irreproachably heroic quality of these impulses: "those manlike courages that by experience know how subject the virtuous minds are to love a most virtuous creature . . . will deem it a venial trespass to seek the satisfaction of honourable desires—honourable even in the curiousest points of honour" (*OA*, 402).

Musidorus concludes his remarks with these instructions for Euarchus:

> Therefore, O judge, who I hope dost know what it is to be a judge, that your end is to preserve and not to destroy mankind . . . since that our doing in the extremest interpretation is but a human error, and that of it you may make a profitable event (we being of such estate as their parents would not have misliked the affinity), you will not, I trust, at the persuasion of this brabbler burn your house to make it clean, but like a wise father turn even the fault of your children to any good that may come of it, since that is the fruit of wisdom and end of all judgements.
>
> (*OA*, 402–403)

His defense vacillates between a blustering assertion of his virtue, honor, and services and a grudging admission of "a venial trespass" and "human error." Having acknowledged his misconduct, he asks that it be turned "to any good that may come of it," including, presumably his own good. For Walter Davis, this is the definitive version. Musidorus "presents us with a view of events that avoids both a theoretical singleness of scheme and the welter of unexamined experience, and in doing so offers us a brief experience of life seen *sub specie fictionis* as incomplete pattern. . . . This is a view we can rest content with, for it reflects what we have seen of the modified Platonic operation of love in the action of *Arcadia*."[18] Davis is satisfied because, as he says, Musidorus's defense somehow affirms his critical scheme. Euarchus, however, cannot "rest content" with this explanation, and his objections cannot be discounted even by the most sympathetic reader. Musidorus's version is too vague and self-serving to comprehend all the complexities of the preceding narrative; it glosses over the charges against them and ignores the problem of guilt. Nevertheless, the speech is very effective in other respects. Musidorus manages to redefine the implications of the trial by shifting attention from the filial offender's motives and responsibilities to those of paternal authority. He is raising a legitimate issue when he argues that justice should be remedial rather than punitive, and his demand that Euarchus should act "like a wise father" is especially compelling for the reader, who knows the true nature of his relation to the judge. This redefinition of the issues pertains for the remainder of the work, and most readers agree that the "real dilemma of the trial scene arises not from the conduct of the accused, but from that of the judge."[19]

In *An Apology for Poetry*, Sidney himself appeals to a higher standard of justice, one beyond mere legalism: "And for the lawyer, though *jus* be the daughter of justice, and justice the chief of virtues, yet because he seeketh to make men good rather *formidine poenae* than *virtutis amore* . . . so is he not in the deepest truth to stand in rank with these who all endeavour to take naughtiness away and plant

18. Walter R. Davis, "Map," p. 166.
19. D. M. Anderson, "The Trial of the Princes in the *Arcadia*, Book V," p. 411.

goodness even in the secretest cabinet of our souls."[20] He subordinates the superficial, punitive concerns of the law to poetry's more
humane commitment; moral edification takes precedence over retribution in this scheme.

Yet in another context, the implications of this ethical assumption
change. In a court of law one does not expect concern for moral
regeneration. Euarchus certainly adheres to a stringent legalism in
advancing his own ideas of "how to judge well" (*OA*, 404). Judgment cannot be reached "by a free discourse of reason and skill of
philosophy, but must be tied to the laws of Greece and municipal
statutes of this dukedom. For although out of them these came, and
to them must indeed refer their offspring, yet because philosophical
discourses stand in the general consideration of things, they leave to
every man a scope of his own interpretation" (*OA*, 404). This libertine variety prompts a conservative reaction. King James I was
drawn by similar apprehensions to the same conclusions: "Reason
is too large," he declared: "Find me a precedent and I will accept
it."[21]

In terms that explicitly invert the values of the *Apology*, Euarchus
confirms his commitment to the law and repudiates the free play of
wit: "the laws, applying themselves to the necessary use, fold us
within assured bounds, which once broken, man's nature infinitely
rangeth" (*OA*, 404). Whereas the poet, "disdaining to be tied to
any such subjection," goes "freely ranging within the zodiac of his
own wit," Euarchus, the man of law, strives to constrain this freedom, for he regards it as a threat to order and stability. In the *Old
Arcadia's* final scenes, Sidney seems to be defining the problem of
judgment and understanding in terms of two opposing systems.
Poetic vision and legal arbitration each have special value, appro-

20. Sir Philip Sidney, *An Apology for Poetry, or the Defence of Poetry,*
p. 106.
21. Quoted in Christopher Hill, *The Century of Revolution,* 1603–1714,
p. 179.

priate to their own context. But because Sidney's Arcadia is both a fictive utopia and a political state, the question of context stays open and the standards are uncertain.

Sidney gives even more explicit attention to another issue Musidorus raises: however affecting his appeal for paternal benevolence, it seems bound to fail, for the law is ruthlessly impersonal. Philanax has warned Philoclea shortly after her detainment to expect no sympathy from a court bereft of her father: "But since among yourselves you have taken him away in whom was the only power to have mercy, you must now be clothed in your own working, and look for no other than that which dead pitiless laws may allot unto you" (*OA*, 304). Her father's "strange humours" may have been irksome to Philoclea and her sister, but the girls' escape has unpleasant consequences. The law is harshly systematic, and its rigors make the quirks of personal authority seem more congenial.

For Euarchus, this contrast between the law and paternalism is especially significant. He is the father of one defendant and the guardian of another, and his ignorance of their identity heightens the dramatic irony of his dilemma. At the same time, his legal code is firmly patriarchal, possessing both a primitive, absolute force and a proprietary refinement. Musidorus is condemned to death for having "ravished her from him that owed her, which was her father" (*OA*, 406). Pyrocles' lust has threatened with force "that which, being holily used, is the root of humanity, the beginning and maintaining of living creatures, whereof the confusion must needs be a general ruin" (*OA*, 406). Sex must be contained within matrimonial bonds, for marriage is the basis of every other social tie: "the Grecian Helen, hath taught . . . what destroying fires have grown of such sparkles" (*OA*, 406).

The paternalism of Euarchus does not require him to "turn even the fault of your children to any good that may come of it" (*OA*, 403). For him, the intimate customs of the family must be upheld because our laws derive from them; society depends on these personal ties. Yet once this initial influence is established, public order attains preeminence over personal concerns and emotions. If these are not subordinated, "young men, strong men, and rich men shall ever find private conveniences how to palliate such committed disorders as to the public shall not only be inconvenient but pestilent" (*OA*, 407). Patriarchal authoritarianism acquires the ruthlessly impersonal significance of law; any attempt to escape it only makes its strictures more harsh and inflexible.

At the moment of anagnorisis, the crisis of paternal authority comes to a kind of climax. The disclosure of the princes' true identity poses with excruciating clarity the conflict between "fatherly love" and the requirements of "office" (*OA*, 411). Yet despite his anguish, Euarchus determines that "all private respects" must "give place to that holy name" of justice, and this dilemma is only fully resolved by renunciation: "I cannot in this case acknowledge you for mine; . . . Your vices have degraded you from being princes, and have disannulled your birthright" (*OA*, 411–412). At its harshest and most rigorous, paternalistic morality finally breaks off the connection of kinship on which it is based. The threat implied in Sir Henry Sidney's closing admonition to his son is here fulfilled: "Your loving father, so long as you live in the fear of God."[22] If the conditions are broken, love turns into a curse. Several readers have noted the parallels between Euarchus and Sir Henry. A. C. Hamilton has recently pointed out that both fathers were the same age when Sidney was writing the *Old Arcadia*, and he suggests that Sidney was trying to deal, in this tale of paternal judgment, with his own guilt about his unfulfilled expectations and prolonged idleness.[23] The responses to the father's wrath are varied and equivocal, and Sidney's treatment of filial guilt is, finally, obscure. Musidorus retaliates with a curse of his own, shouting, "Enjoy thy bloody conquest, tyrannical

22. Malcolm William Wallace, *The Life of Sir Philip Sidney,* p. 69.
23. A. C. Hamilton, *Sir Philip Sidney,* p. 41.

Euarchus" (*OA*, 412). Pyrocles, characteristically, is more plaintive and deferential, but Euarchus is unflinching. The tension of this scene spreads among the crowd of onlookers, and "most of them, examining the matter by their own passions, thought Euarchus (as often extraordinary excellencies, not being rightly conceived, do rather offend than please) an obstinate-hearted man, and such a one, who being pitiless, his dominion must needs be insupportable" (*OA*, 414). Sidney keeps his distance from the vulgar response, thwarting easy pity, for he cannot rely on feelings so shamelessly obvious.

There ensues the miraculous peripeteia with the "resurrection" of Basilius and the reversal of Euarchus's judgment. The restoration of Arcadia's "lawful prince" means that Euarchus must relinquish all control, but the latter is "more glad than of the whole world's monarchy to be rid of his miserable magistracy" (*OA*, 416). For Basilius this is a moment of contrition and increased awareness. Euarchus "with much ado made him understand how these intricate matters had fallen out," and Basilius, "remembering the oracle," thinks he sees the explanation for all these strange vicissitudes: "all had fallen out by the highest providence" (*OA*, 416). Humbled by this sense of superior forces at work and believing that "in all these matters his own fault had been the greatest," he attests to Gynecia's "excellent virtue" and begs his wife's forgiveness (*OA*, 416). At this point, one realizes that the final glimpse of providential order and purpose is sadly partial. As credulous as ever, Basilius still fails to understand Gynecia's conduct in the cave; he allows "her to receive the most honourable fame of any princess throughout the world, all men thinking (saving only Pyrocles and Philoclea who never betrayed her) that she was the perfect mirror of all wifely love . . . so uncertain are mortal judgements, the same person most infamous and most famous, and neither justly" (*OA*, 416). The *Old Arcadia* began by proclaiming that "there is nothing so certain as our continual uncertainty" (*OA*, 5), and now it ends on this same cautionary note. Even at the work's conclusion, there is no clear solution. On the contrary, the harmonies of the final scene are based on falsehood and evasion: the narrative's "crooked shifts" continue indefinitely.

"Then with princely entertainments to Euarchus, and many kind words to Pyrocles (whom still he dearly loved, though in a more virtuous kind), the marriage was concluded, to the inestimable joy of Euarchus (towards whom now Musidorus acknowledged his fault), betwixt these peerless princes and princesses" (*OA*, 416–417). In this way, with startling abruptness, the conflicts of the *Old Arcadia* are terminated. The narrative trails off with a summary of lives lived happily ever after and a promise of further Arcadian adventures. It is a notoriously problematic ending in which the contradictions between moral values and fictive rewards are glaring, and the conflict is barely diminished by the cryptic assertion of human uncertainty.

The critical response to the conclusion suggests the depth of its contradictions, for the ending has provoked considerable controversy. Some have played down the reversal and reward, apparently regarding these as a trivial anticlimax. In this view, the judgment of Euarchus stands as the definitive assessment. The princes are strenuously condemned by Franco Marenco as the "most evident examples of moral disintegration . . . beastly greed . . . riotous violence . . . [and] treachery."[24] For him, their adventures provide only a "negative *exemplum*," and "their experience remains unredeemed to the end; except in their muddled minds there is not the faintest trace of ideal or Platonic love."[25] If Marenco's response seems too stridently abusive, one should keep in mind Fulke Greville's opinion. Noting that the heroes stand "all accused and condemned of rape, paricide, adulteries, or treasons, by their own

24. Marenco, "Double Plot," p. 253.
25. Ibid. pp. 262–263.

Lawes," Greville exclaims, "who sees not, that these dark webs of effeminate Princes be dangerous forerunners of innovation, even in a quiet, and equally tempered people?"[26] In fact, Greville's discussion of the *Arcadia* poses an interesting critical problem. The presentation of Euarchus—"an image of more constant, pure, and higher strain, than nature makes those ordinary mouldes, wherein she fashioneth earthly Princes"—he sees as one of the work's conclusive accomplishments.[27] The original's subsequent developments, such as the resumption of responsibility by Basilius and "the marriage of the two sisters with the two excellent princes," he says are mere "ideas" that could have been realized "if this excellent Image-maker had liv'd to finish, and bring to perfection this extraordinary frame of his own Common-wealth."[28] By Greville's account, these events stand as loose ends.

Other readers have given more prominence to the *Old Arcadia*'s last scene, the implications of which cannot be ignored. Although their misconduct is established by Euarchus and assigned the gravest significance, Pyrocles and Musidorus easily escape punishment. In fact, they are rewarded with the girls, and their errors are ignored in a rush of paternal benevolence. Musidorus apologizes to Euarchus for losing his temper, but even this small act of repentance is engulfed parenthetically in the old man's "inestimable joy" (*OA*, 417). In an intriguing political analysis of Sidney's work, Piers Lewis attributes a boldly partisan bias to the author. He treats the conclusion as a clear instance of authorial favoritism; in the final confrontation with authority, the conventional moral standards are obscured or suspended. The heroes have enjoyed the privileges of Sidney's class throughout the *Old Arcadia,* and these privileges are extended to them even when they are wrong: "When aristocratic

26. Sir Fulke Greville, *The Life of The Renowned Sir Philip Sidney,* p. 13.
27. Ibid., pp. 13–14.
28. Ibid., pp. 14–15.

privilege collides with social order, social order must give way."[29] Lewis points out that, in these final scenes, "Sidney effectively decides against Euarchus without answering him, palliating the disorders of strong, rich, young aristocrats in defiance of the strongest case he can imagine against them."[30] The personal convenience of the overmighty subject, strenuously opposed by Euarchus, is indulged and vindicated through authorial intervention.

Finally, there are critics who find it unnecessary to take sides, for they place Sidney judiciously above these contradictions. They acknowledge that the conflict is never fully settled; yet they maintain that it is contained and clarified by ironic ambiguity. Elizabeth Dipple attributes the persistent "ambivalences and ironies" of the work to the complexities of its theme and tone.[31] Sidney's attitude toward his material is necessarily indeterminate, and Dipple sees this ambivalence as the source of the work's richness and realism. Similarly, Stephen Greenblatt finds great profundity in the *Old Arcadia*'s final scene: "The elusive tone of this passage—bordering at once on wry skepticism and sententiousness—is as complex and uncertain as the form of *Arcadia* itself. For in the mixed mode, to resolve is to lie."[32] Richard Lanham regards the bewildering abruptness of the final paragraphs as a stimulus to critical reflection. Convention requires Sidney to marry his characters off, "but he could at least show that it was a contrived solution, applied to a problem that in life has no end and no painless solution."[33] More recently, A. C. Hamilton has argued that the "work as a whole demands a divided response: the

---

29. Piers I. Lewis, "Literary and Political Attitudes in Sidney's *Arcadia*," p. 99.

30. Ibid., p. 76.

31. Elizabeth Dipple, " 'Unjust Justice' in the *Old Arcadia*," p. 86.

32. Stephen J. Greenblatt, "Sidney's *Arcadia* and the Mixed Mode," p. 278.

33. Lanham, "Old *Arcadia*," p. 375.

delight it affords constantly wars with its instruction in order to invite the reader's participation."[34]

In all these readings, ambiguity is the supreme artistic value, and "the onus of reconciliations . . . [is] laid very heavily on the receiving end."[35] Only through this kind of reader participation can the belief in artistic omniscience be sustained while the contradictions are acknowledged. These readings also share a distinctive critical bias, described with caustic accuracy by Rosemond Tuve: it is "the peculiar modern humility (arrogant enough) which thirsts for presentation of the whole baffling, ironic, conflict-filled complex of life"; so great is this thirst, that "we tend even to prefer reading around the resolutions of the ironies" and fixate on the "presentation of conflict."[36] The problem with the ending of the *Old Arcadia* is that it presents neither the coherent resolutions that Tuve expects nor the existential ironies imputed to it by others. Confronted with this hastily "contrived solution," Lanham, Hamilton, and others must assume some deeper meaning, which can only be inferred from the narrative's ellipses and inconsistencies. These provide scanty evidence for such grandiose conclusions.

There is, of course, the final aphorism about human fallibility: "so uncertain are mortal judgements, the same person most infamous and most famous, and neither justly" (*OA*, 416). This statement, however, follows directly after the reference to Gynecia's restored reputation: "all men thinking (saving only Pyrocles and Philoclea who never bewrayed her) that she was the perfect mirror of all wifely love. Which though in that point undeserved, she did in the remnant of her life duly purchase with observing all duty and faith, to the example and glory of Greece—so uncertain are mortal judgements . . . " (*OA*, 416). One is thus urged to apply the putative

34. Hamilton, *Sidney*, p. 56.
35. William Empson, *Seven Types of Ambiguity*, p. 193, n. 1.
36. Rosemond Tuve, *Elizabethan and Metaphysical Imagery*, pp. 48–49.

moral of the story to Gynecia alone. The lapses of the "peerless princes and princesses" (*OA*, 417) are entirely ignored here, and one is told instead of the magnanimous discretion of Pyrocles and Philoclea. One's attention is thus deflected from the questionable actions and motives of the heroes to problems of parental severity, ignorance, and hypocrisy. Sidney's irony about human uncertainty only reinforces the blatant favoritism of the conclusion and obscures its fundamental inconsistency.

The heroes should not be so easily forgiven for ravishing the girls and threatening the social order, but they still must be rescued from death at the hands of Euarchus. Basilius is restored, and Pyrocles and Musidorus receive the conventional rewards of pastoral romance as their paternal opponents are reduced to benign confusion. Yet these rewards cannot be administered within a clear or coherent ethical scheme. This would require a more explicit account of the desires and activities leading up to this conclusion and a clearer acknowledgement of their rebellious implications. The happy ending could not come as the result of the heroes' own exertions; instead, it must derive from the indulgent and confused good will of others. This is the nature of the "reader's participation" that Sidney invites.

The conclusion's incongruities finally do not sustain the cosmic ironies so frequently attributed to it. The ending of the *Old Arcadia* certainly does frustrate choice and resolution, but its purposes are more specific and immediate. The confusion is necessary because Sidney did not want to pursue these conflicts to a fully developed conclusion; this is as far as he takes it, and even this ending provokes all sorts of misgivings. Still, he gets away with several things: filial claims are satisfied without being fully vindicated, and paternal authority is thwarted without being denied. It is a kind of compromise solution, however precarious. Yet, the conflicts achieve an alarming intensity by the end of the *Old Arcadia,* and its contradictions come very close to the work's surface. Moreover, Sidney's attempt at closure, however equivocal, forces him to choose sides. The heroes' victory may seem harmlessly conventional and irrelevant, even anticlimatic, but they still win. No reference to human uncertainty can obscure that fact. The conflict could not be concluded like this, with all the rewards going to the disobedient sons, and when Sidney returned to it in the revision, he would never bring it so dangerously close to completion.

Chapter Five

THE *New Arcadia*'s EPISODES:
"THE JORNEY OF HIGH HONOR"

T HE EPISODES THAT DOMINATE the *New Arcadia*'s second book greatly expanded the short, simple narrative of the *Old Arcadia.* Sidney seems to have adopted this device for several reasons. Each of the episodes shows the heroes exhibiting courage, virtue, and acumen in various military and political exploits, thus allowing a display of expansive heroic qualities within a pastoral context. Musidorus initiates the episodic sequence in order to make his "estate knowen" to Pamela. In his accounts of his own adventures, as well as his displays of horsemanship and "Matachine daunce in armour" (*NA,* 178–180), he is intent on the same demonstrative purpose. He seeks to display to her his noble qualities and heroic endeavors, having been deprived of the opportunity for heroic exertion by his peculiar situation.

Consistent with the demonstrative purpose of the episodes is their amplification of the narrative scope and structure. This effect, which implies both expansion and intensification, was greatly favored by the Renaissance, and its connection to episodic construction was presumed by many to be integral. "Since it is the poet's aim to amplify the action and to strengthen it with every ornament," argued a sixteenth-century Italian critic, "he will adorn the subject most wonderfully with digressions, and he will separate and rejoin one thing with another in such a way that the action, through the episodes, will appear more beautiful and clear."[1] Amplification acquires a special significance for Sidney, given both his conception of heroism and his intellectual and evaluative ambitions in both versions. The episodes provide a greater variety of issues and situations, and the tests of heroic skill and intelligence are correspondingly increased. Sidney's expansion of the simple, linear pastoral of the *Old Arcadia* broadens and exalts the significance of his heroes' adventures.

The special significance of this episodic elaboration is made clearer by certain distinctive characteristics. Sidney's episodes feature the distressed maidens, monstrous foes, feats of superhuman prowess, and exotic settings of earlier chivalric adventures. Similarly, the warrior ethos of arms, glory, and personal honor prevails. Yet the first episode indicates that his interests are more explicitly intellectual, as is his notion of heroism. He gives much attention to Pyrocles' and Musidorus's princely education (*NA*, 189–190), and he credits the excitement of their first adventure to the opportunity offered to "fall to the practice of those vertues, which they before learned" (*NA*, 191). Political expertise is the primary educational attainment, and it is amply demonstrated by Musidorus's remarks. His eulogy of King Euarchus contains a highly theoretical discourse on the evils of oligarchy, and the astute maneuvers of Euarchus on his ascension to the throne are described in detail (*NA*, 185). The reader is also involved in this enterprise, as A. C. Hamilton points out: "The larger purpose of the stories of the princes is to serve the reader even as stories of princes served them during their early education: 'the delight of tales being converted to the knowledge of all the stories of worthy princes, both to move them to do nobly, and teach them how to do nobly; the beauty of virtue still being set before their eyes' ([*NA*,] 190)."[2] Indeed, the acts of heroism and reading share the same goal of intellectual mastery. "Sidney's em-

1. Roberto Maggi, quoted in Bernard Weinberg, *A History of Literary Criticism in the Italian Renaissance*, pp. 410–411.

2. A. C. Hamilton, *Sir Philip Sidney*, p. 152.

phasis," David Kalstone explains, "is never on simple participation in the stream of events, or even simple delight in or fear of the images before one, but rather on control and mastery. His heroes become *readers* of their experience."[3]

The most striking display of political sophistication occurs in Musidorus's account of the rebellion of the Phrygian citizens against their tyrannical king. Dissension breaks out among the soldiers during their battle with Pyrocles and Musidorus, and rumors of the king's death ensue. Elated, "certaine yong men of the bravest minds, cried with lowde voice, Libertie; and encouraging the other Citizens to follow them, set upon the garde, and souldiers as chiefe instruments of Tyrannie" (*NA*, 200). When this action begins to get out of hand, "some of the wisest (seeing that a popular licence is indeede the many-headed tyranny) prevailed with the rest to make Musidorus their chiefe" (*NA*, 201). Things become more complicated when the citizens' army learns that the king is still alive, and he is "gathering forces in all speed possible to suppresse this mutinie. But now they had run themselves too farre out of breath, to go backe againe the same career . . . therefore learning vertue of necessitie, they continued resolute to obey Musidorus (*NA*, 201). Under his guidance, the rebels win, the tyrant is slain, and Musidorus gives legitimacy to the rebellion by appointing a good man, "of the bloud Roiall, & next to the succession," to be monarch (*NA*, 201).

What is distinctive in this military adventure is the peculiar nature of the hero's authority. He relies as much on a shrewd understanding and exploitation of human motivation as he does on valor or charisma. Heroic action involves an application of sophisticated political insights and principles. This is the crucial difference between the *New Arcadia* and such chivalric sources as *Amadis de Gaule*. Erich Auerbach's description of earlier Arthurian

3. David Kalstone, "Sir Philip Sidney," p. 49.

adventures clarifies the contrast: "these perilous encounters called *avantures* now have no experiential basis whatever, . . . it is impossible to fit them into any actual or practically conceivable political system . . . [and] they commonly crop up without any rational connection."[4] The earlier chivalric romance is unified by its magical setting and an ethos of idealized egotism; the extended series of adventures provides an occasion for almost random self-assertion. The adventures of Pyrocles and Musidorus, on the other hand, constitute a more systematic test of political wit.

In their next adventure they rid the country of Pontus of a cruel tyrant and his wicked giants. Once again they are careful in their choice of a successor, demonstrating their capacity for "publike actions, of princely, and (as it were) governing vertue" (*NA*, 204). Subsequently, they concur in a striking resolution. Realizing that honor cannot be securely sustained without constant risk, "they determined in unknowne order to see more of the world, & to imploy those gifts esteemed rare in them, to the good of mankinde; and therefore would themselves . . . goe privately to seeke exercises of their vertue; thinking it not so worthy, to be brought to heroycall effects by fortune, or necessitie (like Ulysses and Aeneas) as by ones owne choice, and working" (*NA*, 206). The contrast between deliberate choice and exertion and deference to fortune and necessity introduces a central ambiguity in Book II. Without being fully deprived of choice, the heroes immediately begin to lose control over events. Later developments seem intended to humble an overweening heroic ambition. That Pyrocles and Musidorus might be guilty of hubris is certainly implied by their self-conscious desire to surpass Ulysses and Aeneas. There is, however, a further tendency of subsequent events to frustrate understanding as well as practical mastery, resulting in a nearly complete incapacitation. Such a result is confusing inasmuch as understanding is the work's essential virtue

4. Erich Auerbach, *Mimesis*, p. 135.

and an ambition one shares with the characters. The causes of this far more unsettling defeat are suggested by the patterns of the later episodes.

As the third episode begins, the reader is alerted immediately to the diminished influence of the heroes. Having just informed Pamela of their heroic decision to employ their talents for "the good of man-kinde," Musidorus remarks that their next adventure was "not so notable for any great effect they perfourmed" as for "the un-used examples therein" (*NA*, 206). The Prince of Paphlagonia is blinded and deposed by his bastard son Plexirtus. Alone and despairing, he is prevented from committing suicide by his legitimate son, Leonatus. The epitome of filial piety, Leonatus has come to his father's assis-tance, despite the old man's earlier banishment of him, a result of his stepbrother's treachery. Pyrocles and Musidorus come upon them during a storm, in time to hear their wretched tale and assist them against the troops of the evil Plexirtus. The battle is so diffi-cult a test of their military skill, that "Pyrocles & Musidorus had never till then found any, that could make them so well repeate their hardest lesson in the feates of armes" (*NA*, 212). Despite their frustration in single combat, they help rally the populace and eventually defeat Plexirtus. The blind king bequeaths his newly restored crown to Leonatus and dies, "his hart broken with un-kindnes & affliction, stretched so farre beyond his limits with this excesse of comfort, as it was able no longer to keep safe his roial spirits" (*NA*, 212).

A moving figure even in Sidney's brief tale, the blind king is the model for both Lear and Gloucester. Shakespeare amplifies the character of the old patriarch until his follies and sufferings become terrifying enormities; yet Lear's death still brings the same simple symmetry of feeling:

> But his flawed heart—
> Alack, too weak the conflict to support—

'Twixt two extremes of passion, joy and grief,
Burst smilingly.

(*King Lear*, V. iii. 198–201)

For both characters, death constitutes a tragic resolution of life's painful contrarieties. Both Sidney and Shakespeare effect an extraordinary resolution of contrasts by an intensification of them. Their concise, symmetrical formulation of an old king's mortal conflict is an extremely bold and profound example of wit's capacities. This play of wit is an essential element of *King Lear*'s "gaiety transfiguring all that dread," whose awesome serenity Yeats celebrates in "Lapis Lazuli."

The settlement between the two brothers after their father's death has precisely the opposite effect. It represents an intensification of conflict by a merely superficial resolution. Leonatus and Plexirtus are reconciled, but their reconciliation is false and destructive, based as it is on the former's gullible lenience and the latter's deceitful craft. Their story is allowed neither a moral nor a formal conclusion, and their conflict is renewed with broader, more devastating repercussions in later episodes.

The fourth episode is a tale of romantic perversity in which Queen Erona falls in love with a base, unworthy subject as a punishment for her opposition to Cupid's worship. She, in turn, is loved by King Tiridates, who wages an especially cruel and destructive war for her favor. The two princes, "longing to have some triall of their vertue" (*NA*, 214), arrive in Lycia hoping to assist the besieged queen. Their arrival threatens to lengthen the savage war, so settlement by personal combat is decorously agreed upon. Unfortunately, the terms are not adhered to by their opponent, and Antiphilus is taken and used to force Erona's surrender. The heroes then resort to "witty dissimulation" (*NA*, 236), slay Tiridates, defeat his forces, and restore Antiphilus to Erona. Their marriage, however, represents another false settlement, in political and romantic terms.

Antiphilus's villainy is apparent to everyone, and his elevation to power over the queen and her subjects allows him greater opportunity for evil. In the previous episode the princes had been unable to avert such a conclusion because of the inadequacies of their virtuous ally. Now, in a far more sinister development, they are forced into assisting an evident villain, and they participate directly in the advancement of a corrupt cause. The episodic sequence begins to trace, in Peter Lindenbaum's apt phrase, a "pattern of decline and increasing complication."[5] The efficacy of heroic activism is clearly declining, yet the significance of this trend is still not clear. The problems encountered in the next adventure should help to clarify its meaning.

Plangus is the hero of the next episode, one who becomes the central figure of the entire episodic sequence. Sidney gives his predicament, which is a variant on that of Hippolytus, considerable attention, for Plangus is a sort of counterpart to Pyrocles and Musidorus. There is a versified account of his disputation with Basilius (*NA*, 226ff), and Pamela later relates Plangus's history in the fifth episode. Zelmane describes the heroes' involvement in Plangus's difficulties in a subsequent episode, and Plangus is finally shown wandering bereft and helpless in search of Euarchus in Basilius's narrative at the end of Book II.

The son of the King of Iberia, Plangus becomes entangled with Andromana, the wife of a subject, "while yet the errors in his nature were excused by the greenenes of his youth, which tooke all the fault upon it selfe" (*NA*, 243). This narrative emphasis on extenuating circumstances makes several points at once. While insisting on indulgence of his youthful venialities, Sidney also immediately establishes Plangus's pathos and vulnerability. With his responsibility for the initial event diminished, he is so much less to blame for its ultimate consequences. His father eventually finds them out, but

5. Peter Alan Lindenbaum, "The Anti-pastoral Pastoral," p. 103.

the son manfully takes all blame on himself and strives to exonerate his partner. Soon, the older man "founde himselfe warme in those desires, which were in his sonne farre more excusable" (*NA*, 244). The indulgence of the son is given further point by this contrast. It is another example of Sidney denying the father what is permitted the son. Once again, he adopts an aggressively moralizing tone toward the father.

His father sends Plangus off to battle, "because he would avoide the odious comparison of a yong rivall" (*NA*, 244), and pursues his foolish infatuation. Andromana, now conveniently a widow, responds cleverly, using every wile to dupe the old man and advance her ambition. After their marriage and her ascent to the throne, Plangus returns. She attempts to renew their old affair, but he, "for the reverence of his fathers bed," spurns her (*NA*, 245). Furious at this rejection, Andromana plots an ingenious and highly significant revenge, seeking to "overthrow him in the foundation of his strength, which was, in the favour of his father" (*NA*, 245). She does so, paradoxically, by praising him to her husband, implicitly accusing him of a subversive ambition and antagonism. Beginning with remarks on "the liberty of his mind, the high flying of his thoughts, [and] the fitnesse in him to beare rule," she contends that "he was not borne to live a subject-life" (*NA*, 246). She manages "by putting-of objections, [to] bring in objections to her husbands head, already infected with suspition" (*NA*, 246). Finally she becomes even bolder in her insidious maneuvers, forcing the king to contemplate the most terrifying prospects.

Nay (woulde she say) I dare take it upon my death, that he is no such sonne, as many of like might have bene, who loved greatnes so well, as to build their greatnes upon their fathers ruine. Indeed Ambition, like Love, can abide no lingring, & ever urgeth on his own successes; hating nothing, but what may stop them. But the Gods forbid, we should ever once dreame of any such thing in him, who perhaps might be content, that you & the world should know, what he can do: but the more power he hath to hurte, the more admirable is his praise, that he will not hurt.

(NA, 246)

This is a passage of extraordinary brilliance and force. Of course, in its immediate context, the rhetoric works with evil genius to push the old king into paranoid hatred of his son. Yet, in its sharp and deliberate ambiguity, it has a far more profound impact on the reader. One's detachment from the conflict and sympathy for Plangus enable one to see other, more essential implications. Sidney shows with ironic clarity the tragic predicament of the son and subject, "not borne to live a subject-life." His youth and vigor involve him in an inevitable conflict with his father and sovereign. How is it possible for such majestic potency to surrender to subjection? The explicit parallel of Ambition and Love works with striking cogency to conflate erotic and political energy, suggesting the irrepressible vigor of both. The last sentence manages to convey all at once the threat, innocence, and awesome glory of Plangus's position.

Sidney depicts a situation almost identical to the one Shakespeare describes in his famous Sonnet 94. It seems that Shakespeare probably drew on this passage for his initial poetic premise, given the striking similarity of Sidney's last phrase to "They that have pow'r to hurt and will do none."[6] Each writer deals with the peculiar problem of aristocratic power, exposing its disturbing sexual and psychological implications from different points of view. Shakespeare observes his young lord from the outside, combining acute sympathy with subtle reproach. The young man's distinction consists in an uncorrupted, and undefined, potential; and his power is restricted in sinister ways to the power to hurt. Aristocratic potency is paradoxically limited and vulnerability increased by his singular

---

6. See J. W. Lever, *The Elizabethan Love Sonnet*, p. 217.

position. As Empson says in his essay on this sonnet, *"any* contact with infection is fatal to so peculiarly placed a creature"; such a flaw is part of "the hubris and fate of greatness."[7] Shakespeare's feelings for his subject are mysteriously complex, but he is painfully aware of the difficulties of becoming involved with such a person—particularly as a political and sexual subordinate. There is an undertone of resentful antagonism that is given ominous expression in the poem's concluding lines: there Shakespeare warns the young man that his dazzling attractions are precarious and susceptible to "base infection." From his point of view, the youth's dominant characteristics are egotism and dangerous potency, and they inspire feelings of distance and distrust.

Sidney, naturally enough, writes from a different perspective, for the young aristocrat's situation resembles his own. He acknowledges the problems that the young lord causes for others, but he is intent on showing how hard it is to be such a person. His heroes are almost always drawn into sexual and political intrigue against their will, and they are frequently victims of others' aggression. For all his strength and glamour, the hero's essential characteristic in Sidney's account is vulnerable subordination. Here pathos prevails instead of the mood of apprehension and resentment in Sonnet 94.

If Sidney's passage lacks the dark emotive mystery of Shakespeare's poem, it compensates with a resonant, forceful clarity, carefully illuminating the causes of his hero's predicament. On its surface the speech flatters to destroy, exposing the ironies of Shakespeare's poem, but the final intention is clearly sympathetic. Conflict begins with the basic urges of desire, as it does throughout the *Arcadia.* The innocence of youthful impulse is also emphasized by its contrast with the depraved lust and envy of the older characters, just as it is in the main plot. Finally, generational rivalry leads to intense political hostility, as the conflict escalates. The young man's

7. William Empson, *Some Versions of Pastoral,* p. 99.

147

princely power threatens his father in new ways, increasing the latter's antagonism. Plangus forgoes any act of resistance out of filial piety, but like all the heroes, he finds conflict inescapable. He is drawn into a harrowing contest with his father, "the foundation of his strength" (*NA*, 245), in which he must either hurt or be hurt.

Sidney's continuing account probes still further into the complexities of this double bind. Plangus's stepmother exploits both aspects of his dilemma, contriving to make his deference look ominous while having him "imployed in all such dangerous matters, as ether he should perish in them, or if he prevailed, they should increase his glory: which she made a weapon to wound him" (*NA*, 246). Plangus eventually realizes that "even contraries [were] being driven to draw one yoke of argument" in his father's mind, an argument consistently directed against him, "which though Plangus found, yet could he not avoid" (*NA*, 247). The treacherous stepmother finally accuses Plangus directly of plotting to murder the king and marry her, prompting his father to apprehend him and sentence him to death. When Plangus escapes, he momentarily considers revenge, but his long-suffering "naturall love of his father" causes him "to choose a voluntarie exile, then to make his fathers death the purchase of his life" (*NA*, 249). His options are thus reduced to the bleakest terms possible. Plangus flees, persisting in his course of passive withdrawal, but his afflictions continue, for his father suspects his flight is prompted by "a fearefull guiltines" (*NA*, 250). Plangus avoids direct conflict by ceasing to exert himself altogether, yet persecution and suffering cannot be escaped.

For all its painful consequences, Plangus's response to conflict has certain peculiar advantages. While he loses control, he also abdicates responsibility for a terrible situation. All aggressive impulses are assigned to his parents. Even the suspicion that his actions or intentions are aggressive is imputed to others, and "fearefull guiltines" is thus projected outward as the malicious and paranoid construction of his enemies. Alien to the innocent hero's mind, these ideas reflect only on those who entertain them: *honi soit qui mal y pense.* The compensations for all this suffering are varied. Plangus's pathos allows a kind of latent moral aggression and relief from guilt, for he is the image of wronged innocence. One is encouraged to feel as much contempt for his persecutors as one feels sympathy for him. Moreover, his retreat into passivity enables him to abstain from any further dangerous acts of engagement or assertion. He can preserve something of the static, insular innocence and undiminished potential of an earlier, presexual period. Finally, Plangus achieves a secure, if oppressive, control over his Oedipal hostility and rebellious impulses. Restraint and pathos firmly establish the young lord's innocence, preserving him from all means of "base infection."

Filial submission allows Plangus to escape the guilt and risks and onerous responsibilities of conflict with paternal sovereignty, but there are, of course, grave problems with his purity. The young lord's integrity requires a restraint so absolute that it approaches immobility and impotence. For Plangus, helpless anguish becomes the predominant characteristic, and he is debilitated in all his further undertakings.

Even after Plangus leaves Iberia, his romantic and political endeavors still come to grief, and he becomes entangled in the chaotic passions of another episode. His love for Queen Erona is unrequited, but he must, for her sake, rescue his despicable rival, Antiphilus. His assistance to Erona incurs the hatred of his only ally, Artaxia, sister to the slain Tiridates. Artaxia had befriended Plangus after his exile, but now she turns against him for seeking to aid the woman who caused her brother's death. She has Antiphilus executed and captures Erona, intending to do the same to her. Plangus, unable to fulfill the conditions for his beloved's release or to free her by force, is entirely helpless. Confounded by these subsequent developments and still cursed with the enmity of his own father, Plangus's only resort is an appeal to "the mighty and Good King Euarchus" (*NA*, 338).

Plangus's resolution clarifies a marked heroic tendency in the *New*

Arcadia, evident in Pyrocles and Musidorus as well. The two princes could assist inasmuch as one of the conditions for Erona's deliverance is their conquest of two of Artaxia's knights, but Plangus assumes they are dead after hearing of their shipwreck, and he turns, in his despair, to their father. Pyrocles subsequently hears from Basilius about Plangus's quest for Euarchus, but he is too preoccupied with his own problems to be of any immediate help. He is grieved by the plight of Plangus and Erona, yet he leaves it to Euarchus "to take in hande the just delivering of her, joyned with the just revenge of his childrens losse" (*NA,* 338). Like so many others, this episode is marked by the heroes' inability to conclude it; either they simply cannot resolve the conflicts that confront them or they contrive a solution that collapses immediately after their departure. This sequence of frustrations and defeats is almost embarrassing. Like the farm boy whom Don Quixote "rescues" from a beating, most of those Pyrocles and Musidorus succor have their calamities subsequently redoubled. Although one does not regard the heroes as foolish or blameworthy, one is impressed with an increasing sense of filial inadequacy.

Consonant with this decline in heroic prowess is the heroes' increasing dependence on a benign, judicious patriarch, a dependence that both Plangus and Pyrocles acknowledge. The father eventually emerges as the only one capable of sorting out all these tortuous contradictions. This figure, however, engenders a high degree of ambivalence. In his absence, he becomes the heroes' only resource, and even the narrator awaits his arrival. Both works seem to require this personified deus ex machina in order to impose order and clarity on the narrative's hopeless confusion. In the unfinished *New Arcadia,* Euarchus never materializes, and these episodic contingencies are left unconcluded. This is, in a way, an improvement on the *Old Arcadia*'s frantic vacillations. When Euarchus does assume control, the heroes are threatened with extinction; he must then be arbitrarily refuted and the heroes must be rescued by Sidney's sudden reversal. Narrative confusion is abruptly renewed in the original's final paragraphs. In the *New Arcadia*, Sidney's strategy is more diffuse and less obvious. The episodic sequence still affirms filial dependence; at the same time, paternal control is held in abeyance, and antagonism is muted. Incompletion allows Sidney to have it both ways in less explicit fashion. Two essential narrative tendencies are still clear in these episodic developments: for better or for worse, the heroes are eventually overwhelmed by the difficulty of their adventures and reduced to dependence on paternal authority; and at the same time, the father to whom they submit evokes great ambivalence. His authority is clear, whereas its nature is not.

Plangus's disputation with Basilius reveals another essential feature of the heroic character and suggests something further of the nature and degree of Sidney's ambivalance. Their exchange presents an abstract perspective on the narrative's vicissitudes, as each character attempts to formulate the existential implications of his experience. The issue is, appropriately, the opposition between the human will and the forces of fortune and necessity. This conflict was evoked earlier by Pyrocles' and Musidorus's prideful voluntarism in their choice of a heroic course. Their subsequent experience, however, has tended to decide the issue in favor of fortune. In the debate, man's lack of control is immediately conceded, and the question is one of appropriate attitude and response. Plangus's feelings are immediately clear from his lament that men are mere "thralles to Fortune's raigne" (*Poems* 30.17).[8] Basilius is moved by Plangus's misfortunes but urges on the younger man resignation and equanimity:

8. In the *New Arcadia*, the debate occurs in chapter 12 of Book II, pp. 227–231. In the *Old Arcadia*, it appears in the second eclogues as a debate between Plangus and Boulon, recited by Histor. William Ringler lists it as #30 in *The Poems of Sir Philip Sidney*, pp. 57–62. I am using Ringler's text and line numbers for clearer reference, e.g., *Poems* 30.17, to indicate line 17 of #30.

Yet Reason saith, Reason should have abilitie,
> To hold these worldly things in such proportion,
> As let them come or go with even facilitie.
But our Desire's tyrannicall extortion
> Doth force us there to set our chiefe delightfulnes,
> Where but a baiting place is all our portion.
But still, although we faile of perfect rightfulnes,
> Seeke we to tame these childish superfluities:
> Let us not winke though void of purest sightfulnes.

> > > > (*Poems* 30.131–139)

It is surprising to hear such wisdom emanating from Basilius. The pompous banalities of Geron might seem more appropriate to his character. Nevertheless, he does not sententiously exhort his auditor to emulate his own "constant temper," as Geron does with Philisides (*OA*, 72). Rather than persisting in the polarized opposition of Reason and Desire encouraged by the terms and structure of debate, Basilius seeks to get beyond categorical antitheses. He acknowledges the imperatives of each and their inevitable, paralyzing clash. Formulating his resolution in moderate, deliberately non-categorical terms, the older man argues for accommodation and compromise. His acceptance of life's vicissitudes implies a humane self-acceptance. He can thus renounce the inhuman "perfect rightfulness" that stringent rationalism encourages, while still opposing the "superfluities" of desire, because both are impulses originating in presumptuous delusions of control. Having dismissed these yearnings for absolute autonomy, distinct but essentially parallel, Basilius encourages a tempered yet responsible self-control.

Basilius's practical advice is grounded in a benign, providential view of cosmic order, which he earnestly urges on his young auditor. Plangus, in his frustration and distress, has succumbed to extravagant "Despaire" (*Poems* 30.53), as sinful for the pagans of this pre-Christian idyll as it was for Sidney's contemporaries. Sidney makes the implications of these excesses alarmingly clear. Plangus proceeds from a pessimistic view of man's life as a doomed "pilgrimage" (*Poems* 30.5), through parenthetical doubt of heaven's existence (*Poems* 30.59), to a scandalous attack on divinity: "Let doltes in haste some altars faire erect / To those high powers, which idly sit above, / And vertue do in greatest need neglect" (*Poems* 30.62–64). Shocked at these "blasphemous words" (*Poems* 30.67), Basilius insists on the "high Justice" of Providence (*Poems* 30.71), which surpasses human understanding. This transcendent order assures the ultimate usefulness of adversity and significance of contingency: "But still our dazeled eyes their way do misse, / While that we do at his sweete scourge repine, / The kindly way to beate us on to blisse" (*Poems* 30.74–76).

Plangus's despair originates in two essential aspects of heroic experience in the *Arcadia*. One is romantic, the Petrarchan exaltation of the beloved. He enshrines her as a goddess and a "saint," whose misfortune is a greater "sacriledge" (*Poems* 30.97) than his own blasphemy: "The world the garden is, she is the flower / That sweetens all the place; she is the guest / Of rarest price, both heav'n and earth her bower" (*Poems* 30.98–100). Basilius, in turn, insists that "passions do deceave" (*Poems* 30.69), distorting one's perception of higher ends by concentrating entirely on personal attachments. The other essential factor is the hero's experience of his own helpless inadequacy. Unable to assist his beloved, Plangus laments human impotence in general terms. His difficulties are largely attributed to the forces of change, which subvert the stability of human relations and the effectiveness of the individual. These disruptive forces range from the internal, organic shifts of the body's "elements" (*Poems* 30.29) to the vast, cosmic flux of "Fortune's raigne" (*Poems* 30.17).

Plangus grapples with one of the *Arcadia's* central issues and, indeed, a basic concern of the entire period with its fascination with mutability. In the clash of human will with fortune, the essential problem is change. Sidney deals with this problem in several ways.

He attempts to show how one can sustain some sort of stability in the midst of life's relentless vicissitudes, or, as Fulke Greville says, "how to set . . . a stay upon the exorbitant smilings of chance."[9] The *New Arcadia* begins with an artful state of innocence in which circumstantial arrangements attain harmonious stability. Basilius's first response to Plangus invokes this condition, whose perfection is natural, political, and existential: "How long wilt thou with mone-full musicke staine / The cheerefull notes these pleasant places yeeld, / Where all good haps a perfect state maintaine?" (*Poems* 30.38–40). This "perfect state" has been drastically altered with the progression of the narrative. An accommodation to changed circumstances, one that regains some part of this lost stability and balance, is now required.

A different accommodation is proposed by each of the disputants. Basilius emerges as the spokesman for wit, a sane balance of flexibility and principle. His tolerance of human inadequacy—our failure to attain "perfect rightfulness"—is achieved through his belief in providential "high Justice." This belief in God's omnipotence diminishes the fear of mutability, assuring mankind of an ultimate, if inscrutable, stability. Pamela's forceful defense of "constancie in the everlasting governour" (*NA*, 407) establishes this as the essential attribute of divine authority. Moreover, this providential "constancie" sustains man's finite powers.

Plangus's response is disturbingly ambiguous. He obdurately rejects the wisdom of Basilius, spurning the latter's efforts to contain "raging woes" within "morall rules" (*Poems* 30.151). His blasphemy and despair stir no remorse, and he proudly refuses all "consolacyons" (*Poems* 30.143). Neil Rudenstine accurately establishes the seriousness of this obstinacy: "If Plangus achieves a form of poetic vindication by virtue of his constancy and noble sorrow, Boulon [i.e., Basilius] compels us to view him more soberly *sub*

---

9. Sir Fulke Greville, *The Life of The Renowned Sir Philip Sidney,* p. 16.

specie aeternitatis."[10] Plangus's excesses are, to some extent, merely Petrarchan histrionics, but they are also based on his own genuinely grim experiences, and in this respect, these excesses are justified: "Curst be good haps, and curst be they that build / Their hopes on haps, and do not make despaire / For all these certaine blowes the surest shield" (*Poems* 30.41–43). Plangus's life has involved little except an oppressive sequence of "certaine blowes," and despair is certainly an appropriate, if not inevitable, response; indeed, it is his "dayly lesson" (*Poems* 30.53), imposing on him a sense of his own wretched impotence. At the same time, "love . . . forcethe" him to persist in a futile commitment to activism (*Poems* 30.57). His is an odd, affecting stance, fusing agonized pathos with a tense, defiant energy, and it is characteristic of each of Sidney's heroes (including Astrophil).

Plangus's peculiar posture constitutes an ambiguous solution to heroic difficulties, an alternative to the accommodations of wit. It sustains a fiercely symmetrical balance of passive and aggressive impulse. The effects of each are neutralized by their opposition. Tension supplants the equanimity of wit, and conflict is resolved by the more obscure operations of the ambivalent will. His solution is effective in several ways. Excessive passivity runs the same risks as heedless self-assertion. Plangus's belligerent tone allows a limited sense of potency and guards against the potential consequences of total vulnerability to fortune's "certaine blowes." Even as he writhes in anguished abasement to superior forces, he defiantly resists them. Pyrocles' and Musidorus's adventures terminate in an equally frustrating impasse, which allows a similar compromise between passivity and activism. This resolution also obviates, to a large degree, the need for further choice and action, as both become increasingly difficult. Their failure to conclude their adventures also arrests the process of change and development by blocking its results; thus, the

10. Neil L. Rudenstine, *Sidney's Poetic Development*, p. 40.

compromising effects of this process are forestalled, and the heroes retain the disengaged innocence and stability of untried potential.

Whatever their odd advantages may be, the heroes' vacillations ultimately derive from ambivalence and distrust of authority. Their subordination to a higher power, either the personal control of an actual father or the transcendent power of providence, is firmly established. Sigmund Freud suggests the inevitability of this linkage: "The last figure in the series beginning with the parents is that dark supremacy of Fate, which only the fewest among us are able to conceive of impersonally."[11] Affectionate trust and dutiful submission are the required filial responses in Sidney's world; yet his protagonists are increasingly victimized by paternal and providential abuse. Despite assurances that this "sweet scourge" will beat them "on to blisse," their difficulties go unrelieved and unconcluded. Despair is a powerful reproach to divine authority, exalting filial hostility to a cosmic level. Plangus carries this to more strident lengths, going as far as direct blasphemy. Pyrocles and Musidorus are more restrained, but their flirtation with despair becomes serious enough to prompt thoughts of suicide in the *Old Arcadia*. Similarly, another heroic counterpart carries their filial aggression at the practical level to its logical conclusion. Amphialus's rebellion represents a more direct assault on the father's sexual and political authority. Such filial defiance can never meet with success in Sidney's *Arcadia*, and, for Plangus and Amphialus, defeat is especially severe. Nevertheless, their belligerent resistance allows a striking, if ultimately innocuous, expression of filial hostility.

The remaining episodes consist of the adventures of Pyrocles, and they culminate in the same balanced ambivalence of feeling. Pyrocles undertakes the sixth and seventh adventures on his own, but as they continually interrupt one another, he becomes thoroughly confounded by their complexities. He begins by accepting the

11. Sigmund Freud, "The Economic Problem in Masochism," p. 198.

challenge of Anaxius, nephew to Tiridates, welcoming this opportunity "to do something without the company of the incomparable
Prince Musidorus" (*NA*, 263). He admits to "a kind of depending
upon him, as without him I found a weakenesse, and a mistrustful-
nes of my selfe, as one strayed from his best strength, when at any
time I mist him" (*NA*, 264), and his resolve is strengthened by a
desire to break free of this dependence. On his way to Anaxius, he
witnesses the assault by Dido and eight other women upon Pamphilus, whom they have bound with garters and are pricking with
bodkins. Pyrocles intervenes, slaying their bodyguard and driving
away the other women, but Dido, single-minded in her hatred of
this man, stays behind and persists in her torture. The paragon of
libertine egotism, Pamphilus is "a man in nothing, but in deceaving
women" (*NA*, 265), she exclaims. He delights in sadistic sexual
conquests, seducing and jilting one woman after another. Most of
his victims are fully aware of his character but enter into relations
with him as a sort of courtly "sport" (*NA*, 267), intent on their
own competitive sexual triumphs—"like them I have seene play at
the ball, growe extremely earnest, who shoulde have the ball, and
yet every one knew it was but a ball" (*NA*, 267). What began as
an amatory game becomes furiously cruel in its consequences, with
the embittered women, their honor lost, plotting to castrate Pamphilus: "beginning at first but that trifling revenge, in which you
found us busie; but meaning afterwardes to have mangled him so,
as should have lost his credit for ever abusing more" (*NA*, 269).

Yet, however grave its consequences, the conflict retains the essentially trivial and degraded quality of its central cause. Dido's
anger is provoked by vanity, and that "scorne of al scornes" driving
her to such fury is Pamphilus's flippant remark that there are
"many fairer" (*NA*, 269). This excellent satire of the court's sexual
rites provides a curious case of "vanishing distinctions," in which
conflict is balanced by equally corrupt motivations. Pyrocles' intervention is determined almost exclusively by the simple criterion of

who is being victimized. The situation is entirely reversible, as developments indicate, for on the arrival of his friends, Pamphilus leads an attack on Pyrocles and Dido. Although "a faithfull peace [is] promised of all sides" after Pyrocles' chivalric exertions on Dido's behalf (*NA*, 269), it cannot long endure, given the nature of the conflict and the opponents.

Pyrocles arrives at the appointed place and awaits Anaxius's arrival, but as soon as they begin single combat, Pamphilus is seen tormenting Dido. Anaxius will not agree to postponing their duel, and Pyrocles must run away from him to assist the distressed woman, as a crowd of spectators jeer at him "as at the arrantest coward" (*NA*, 271). Choice is possible, as "the Ladies misery overbalanced my reputation" (*NA*, 272), but the terms become extremely difficult. Her difficulties are said to derive from "too soone trusting to the falshood of reconcilement" (*NA*, 272), a remark generally applicable to the developments of every episode; the settlements of every adventure since the third are fraudulent and ephemeral. Not only are opponents incapable of any authentic amity, but values become disturbingly irreconcilable as well. Conflict, which has been a constant and central concern in the *Arcadia,* threatens to overwhelm and defeat the work's evaluative framework, dominating and diminishing wit's resources. This unsettling tendency is further accelerated by the final developments of the episodic sequence.

Plexirtus's malicious ambitions eventually destroy his deceptive truce with Leonatus. Despite Plexirtus's incorrigible villainy, Pyrocles finds himself bound to rescue him from a well-deserved death. He has given his word to the dying Zelmane, Plexirtus's daughter. She is innocent of her father's evil nature and so enamored of Pyrocles that she disguises herself as a page to accompany him. He reciprocates by assuming her name and by promising to save her father. The episodic intricacies need not be further explored. Of primary importance is the absolute dilemma of priorities. Immediately after Pyrocles and Musidorus decide to split up, a messenger arrives to summon them to Pontus, where they have been pledged to join with the king against three of his enemies:

> Now the day was so accorded, as it was impossible for me both to succour Plexirtus, & be there, where my honour was not onely gaged so far, but (by the straunge working of unjust fortune) I was to leave the standing by Musidorus, whom better then my selfe I loved, to go save him whom for just causes I hated. But my promise given, & given to Zelmane, & to Zelmane dying, prevailed more with me, then my friendship to Musidorus: though certainely I may affirme, nothing had so great rule in my thoughts as that. But my promise caried me the easier, because Musidorus himselfe would not suffer me to breake it.
>
> (*NA*, 299)

This passage elaborates a painfully problematic situation, with its syntactic ramification of every antithesis. The heroes' decision to split up to redress the calamitous developments of earlier adventures initiates their difficulties. Previously, Pyrocles had welcomed such an opportunity for autonomy, but now it generates anxiety and conflict; indeed their decision to "divide our selves" immediately acquires still more conflictual overtones as soon as the messenger arrives (*NA*, 299). Nevertheless, Pyrocles' predicament is methodically ordered and eventually resolved. This is effected by a progressive intensification of the conflict, culminating in the penultimate sentence: his oath is stronger than his friendship though nothing is stronger than his friendship. Just as this excruciating contradiction threatens to thoroughly stupefy the subject, it coalesces into a single imperative: his friend orders him to keep his promise. Thus, the passage effects a deft synthesis of seemingly irreconcilable directives. Freedom of choice and action emerge from a context that threatened to strangle it in contradictions. Yet it does not seem merely incidental that Pyrocles can act only by regressing to that dependence on Musidorus he had sought to escape. His freedom is to that extent diminished. More significantly, one derives from this passage a familiar sense of the subject as object, caught by the tug and pull of symmetrically opposed forces. Control and choice are relinquished to others, and the hero's dilemma is resolved by a lapse into passivity and dependence. This in turn makes the deft accommodation of wit seem thin and contrived, a rationalization rather than a probing resolution.

Pyrocles' hopeful assertion that "the jorney of high honor lies not in plaine wayes" provokes similar misgivings (*NA*, 301). He is trying to assure himself of the legitimacy of his final mission, the rescue of Plexirtus. Honor binds him to fulfill his oath to Zelmane, yet his success in this enterprise insures the survival and freedom of a malicious villain. The outcome is disastrous, for Plexirtus treacherously plots the heroes' destruction. There ensues the "most confused fight" at sea and the shipwreck that brought Pyrocles and Musidorus to Arcadia. This chaotic fight, the episodic catastrophe that concludes their adventures and returns the story to the main action, reduces the heroes' effectiveness to its lowest point: "truly I thinke we never perfourmed lesse in any place" (*NA*, 305). They are capable of certain minimal ethical decisions—"we thought it lesse evill to spare a foe, then spoyle a friend" (*NA*, 305)—but wit's effects are, finally, negligible. They escape with their lives, but everyone else is destroyed in a horrifying, Hobbesian struggle. "For the narrownesse of the place, the darkenesse of the time, and the uncertainty in such a tumult how to know friends from foes, made the rage of swordes rather guide, then be guided by their maisters" (*NA*, 305). In this final episode, the intensity of the conflict renders mastery impossible, choice specious, and survival the sole heroic accomplishment.

So how is one to comprehend the meaning of this "jorney of high honor," culminating as it does in ignominious confusion? Despite its assuring tone, Pyrocles' aphorism about the labyrinthine complexities of adventurous pursuits is not very illuminating. His statement is finally no more persuasive than Musidorus's justification of foul ways through fair ends. Both represent attempts to clarify and resolve the narrative's "crooked shifts," romantic and political. Although reminded that honor is the ultimate goal, the reader is still left with the sense of its unattainable transcendence. The actual conclusion of the episodic sequence suggests quite another goal. Chaotic conflict, heroic inadequacy, and vulnerable subordination to fortune prevail in each of these final adventures. From the shipwreck to the resumption of the tale of Plangus and Erona, related by Basilius at the end of Book II, the mood is one of failure and defeat.

These impressions of the final episodes are the basis of my objection to a more positive interpretation of their development. Nancy Lindheim advances such an argument, consonant with her generally high estimate of Sidney's sophistication. For her, the increasing complexity indicates a tough-minded appreciation of the problematic, which does not diminish the efficacy of the *New Arcadia*'s ethical imperatives: "the principles of their education cannot be applied stringently or automatically, but they can still serve as a guide through the maze of semi-truths and partial goods. The principles remain as standards and goals even in a complex, ambiguous world."[12] I agree that the work's standards are unaltered by the narrative's vicissitudes, and their urgency is undiminished; yet these standards seem to me increasingly inadequate as actual resources. They allow only negligible choice and action, and their slight effects are neither edifying nor instructive. Lindheim, like Pyrocles, wishfully insists on the supremacy of standards the viability of which has been severely reduced.

What is the significance, then, of this pattern of increasing complication and irresolution? The emphasis on heroic vulnerability and impotence, the dissipation of previous settlements and failure to

12. Nancy Rothwax Lindheim, "Sidney's *Arcadia*, Book II, p. 170.

achieve a final settlement, and the increasing intensity and eventual predominance of conflict, all of these narrative tendencies suggest difficulties with the material that frustrate comprehension and closure.

Some of Sidney's difficulties are simply technical, as Richard Lanham suggests: "with its five acts swamped by precisely that episodic construction Aristotle excoriates," the plot becomes too unwieldy to control or unify.[13] The complex requirements of Sidney's narrative scheme reflect some general literary developments of the late sixteenth century. On the one hand, enthusiasm for magnificence and copiousness persisted; on the other hand, there was an increasing concern for systematic literary standards, a demand reflected in the growth of critical controversy and reinforced by a commitment to ethical precision. Artists like Sidney, Tasso, and Guarini were strongly influenced in the process of composition by these formal and thematic responsibilities; specifically, they tried to impose a more coherent organization on the materials of chivalric and pastoral romance. The variety of Ariosto and Montemayor retained its basic appeal, but amplification had to be unified and contained.

The stringencies of this narrative approach diminished its feasibility and reduced its influence on subsequent forms such as the novel. As Auerbach explains in his essay on *Don Quixote,* the novel reaches back to the older romance sources infusing "the element of genuine everyday reality into that brilliant and purposeless play of combinations" of "the older tradition of the romance of adventure."[14] The exacting requirements of late sixteenth-century narrative preclude the more relaxed and truly open-ended approach of Cervantes. Tasso's anxieties about his work show that these requirements involved more than technical difficulties, whereas Guarini's

13. Richard A. Lanham, "The Old *Arcadia,*" p. 236, n.5.
14. Auerbach, *Mimesis,* p. 355.

success approaches a kind of academic virtuosity. Sidney seems to have tried this kind of work twice, achieving modest success with the first attempt and, perhaps, taking on too much in the second. Finding that "his original plan was no longer workable,"[15] and tiring of its increasingly difficult complexities, he quit writing.

The final impression of agonized conflict and confusion derives in part from this failure to complete the *New Arcadia*; one is left at midpoint in the process of increasing complication. One's perception, however, is not entirely determined by the absence of a conclusion or some other structural deficiency. The contradictions of the *Old Arcadia* indicate that a simple ending is an insufficient resolution, affording little relief from the pervasive sense of conflict and confusion. Perhaps Sidney hoped to obtain more satisfying results in a second attempt. Whatever his reasons, he undertook an extensive revision in which he planned an altered, and thematically improved, ending; and he failed to finish this project. In some senses his approach to the material resembles the heroes' conduct in the adventures: the initial settlement proves to be false and inadequate; contradictions emerge and intensify; and Sidney is finally unable to resolve these renewed conflicts.

The parallel between heroic and authorial frustrations suggests a common source: Sidney's ambivalence is another cause of the work's persistent conflicts. This pattern of narrative irresolution reveals deep, unsettling doubts about autonomy and social order and their ultimate compatibility. The heroes' adventures call into question their capacity for self-control and assertion. On the other hand, their difficulties provoke anxiety about control by higher forces. Distrust of authority at all levels—parental, political, even providential—pervades this work. By simply ending the tale at midpoint, Sidney avoids coming to any harrowing conclusions, and the

15. Nancy Rothwax Lindheim, "Vision, Revision, and the 1593 Text of the *Arcadia*," p. 147.

conflicts remain moot. Heroic ambitions are left unfulfilled, for the protagonists remain defiant but helpless victims. Control from above is forestalled, nonetheless, for there is no restoration to the status quo ante. Sidney ultimately prefers the security of this narrative impasse to the dangers of a clearer resolution.

Chapter Six

REBELLION IN ARCADIA

T HE THIRD BOOK OF THE *New Arcadia* is Sidney's most interesting and complicated piece of work. The book's scope is again expanded from pastoral romance to epic combat, and the war between Amphialus and Basilius, like the episodes in Book II, allows narrative and thematic amplification. Its conflicts are intensified and charged with a broader, more public significance, for rebellion by an overmighty subject sharply defines the work's political issues. Alternately, another conflict is sustained within Amphialus's fortress between his mother, Cecropia, and their three captives, Pyrocles-Zelmane and the two princesses. This conflict is more inwardly focused though no less intense, and the terms of the antagonism are moral and theological. To further complicate matters, the book abruptly ends before concluding either conflict. Sidney's failure to complete Book III makes it difficult to fully understand the connections between its different perspectives.

In an effort to establish narrative continuity, many critics regard the work's theological sections as the culmination of its conflicts. E. M. W. Tillyard was the first to assign thematic primacy to the captivity. This closing segment presents, in his view, the "theme of a supreme test of character and of martyrdom."[1] Thus, the *New*

1. E. M. W. Tillyard, *The English Epic and Its Backgrounds*, p. 298.

Arcadia's final perspective shifts from political to religious, from the order of nature to that of grace.[2] Heroic activism is ultimately subordinated to patient endurance, and the two princesses emerge as the work's paragons. Tillyard contends that if the *New Arcadia* had been completed, the two male heroes would have undergone similar religious development:

> When the revised version breaks off, Pyrocles and Musidorus have not yet reached the degree of perfection to which their betrothed princesses have arrived. . . . It is probable that if Sidney had carried through his revision he would have made the patience of Musidorus and Pyrocles under the mistaken sentence of Euarchus match the patience of Pamela and Philoclea when in captivity to Cecropia.[3]

J. F. Danby also sees the *New Arcadia* as an increasingly transcendent work whose "plan requires that the classical, romance and chivalric schemes should be brought within the orbit of an instructed renaissance Christianity."[4] The most fervent exponent of this point of view is Walter Davis. He insists on the full realization of this religious scheme in the 1593 composite, "as complete a version of Sidney's masterpiece as exists in our imperfect world."[5] In their prison colloquies, the two heroes attain the same "harmony of soul" that their mistresses achieved in the captivity.[6] This "final reintegration" is profoundly religious, even mystical; and Davis, echoing Tillyard, defines the process as a "shift from the realm of the civic virtues to that of the virtues of the purified mind."[7]

This approach has several advantages, not the least of which is

2. Ibid., p. 309.
3. Ibid., p. 308.
4. John F. Danby, *Poets on Fortune's Hill*, p. 71.
5. Walter R. Davis, "A Map of Arcadia," p. 4.
6. Ibid., p. 52.
7. Ibid., pp. 51, 65.

the lofty coherence it imparts to the expansive complexity of Book
III; Davis's study imparts to the entire work an impressive consistency and order. Moreover, it advances an explanation of the
heroines' importance, placing their peculiar triumph in a broader
thematic context. Nevertheless, this interpretation leaves certain intractable narrative concerns unassimilated; it imposes order on this
book through an evasion or distortion of some of its essential aspects. An approach that sees only a pattern of contemplative ascent
cannot explain the persistence of heroic assertion or the concern
with the legitimacy of resistance. Although thwarted and embar-
rassed for much of the captivity, Pyrocles' activism is vindicated in
the final chapters; indeed, it compares favorably with the sisters'
quietism.

Nancy Lindheim has pointed out some of the problems of such
an approach. In an excellent article discussing the implications of
Sidney's revisions, she rejects the interpretations of Danby and
Davis and suggests that neither text will "bear the particular freight
of religion and neo-Platonism that is being thrust upon it by analogy
with the expanded scope of the Captivity"; she is referring specifically to the text of Books III through V, but she finds the notion of
a final religious conversion irrelevant to either text: "debatable
even for the *New Arcadia;* it is totally unjustified for the *Old.*"[8]
Lindheim refutes such claims by showing that no character undergoes a religious conversion. In fact, all remain obdurately in character throughout, "constant" in all their impulses and convictions.

Lindheim explains that "Sidney's idea of development seems to
call for realization of attributes that have a latent or embryonic
existence in the character rather than envisioning some basic change
in outlook or understanding."[9] While all characters remain con-

8. Nancy Rothwax Lindheim, "Vision, Revision, and the 1593 Text of the
Arcadia," p. 140.
9. Ibid., p. 141.

sistent, their exemplary status varies according to their changing circumstances; "some situations call for courage, strategy, resistance; others for undespairing acceptance."[10] Again, coherence depends on wit, on a flexible discernment of what is called for; and Lindheim's term for this unifying principle is "ethical decorum."[11] In her view, the work does not evolve toward a transcendent, unitary vision like that described by its religious critics. Instead, its development is diffuse, and ethical flexibility is sustained throughout.

Lindheim has restated the *New Arcadia*'s informing principle in terms particularly appropriate to Book III. The work's conflicts acquire special intensity in the political and religious crises of this section, and she strives along with Sidney to sustain a broadened "understanding of the complexity of heroic and moral experience."[12] Decorum is one of the essential Renaissance resources in this endeavor, for this rule of rhetoric had acquired the highest ethical significance for Sidney and his contemporaries. Hanna Gray expands on the ultimately existential importance of eloquence:

> The terms "*decorum*" and "*imitatio*," for example, are central in both rhetoric and moral philosophy, and the humanists often appear to fuse their meanings whatever the context. Thus, the imitation of stylistic and ethical models are spoken of in identical terms; or the idea of always speaking appropriately, of suiting style and manner to subject, aim, and audience is treated as the exact analogue of behaving with *decorum*, of choosing the actions and responses which are best in harmony with and most appropriate to individual character and principles on the one hand, the nature of circumstances on the other.[13]

The principle of decorum allows for a more sophisticated and practical notion of virtue than hieratic schemes of transcendence.

10. Ibid., p. 142.
11. Ibid.
12. Ibid., p. 147.
13. Hanna H. Gray, "Renaissance Humanism," p. 208.

Sidney adheres to the former standard explicitly in his advice to his father concerning the latter's difficulties as Lord Deputy of Ireland:

> So strangely and dyversely goes the cource of the worlde by the enterchanginge humors of those that governe it, that thoughe it be most noble to have allweyes one mynde and one constancy, yet can it not be allwaies directed to one pointe; but must needes sometymes alter his cource, accordinge to the force of others changes dryves it. . . . Particularly to yowr lott, it makes me change my style, and wryte to your Lordship, that keepinge still yowr minde in one state of vertuouse quietnes, yow will yet frame yowr cource according to them. And as they delay yowr honorable rewardinge, so yow by good meanes to delay yowr returne, till either that ensue, or fitter tyme be for this.[14]

For an active man of the world, integrity depends on flexibility and sensitivity to circumstance. Yet such enlightened adaptability should not become mere pragmatic expediency; or rather, as Cicero and his humanist disciples insist, "expediency can never conflict with moral rectitude."[15] Thomas More's praise of "civil philosophy" in the *Utopia* is intriguing in this respect. His narrator repudiates "this scholastic philosophy which thinks that everything is appropriate everywhere. But there is another philosophy of a more civil kind, which knows the stage it should act on, adapts itself accordingly in the play it has in hand and plays its part appropriately and with decorum."[16] More's habitual irony makes it hard to gauge the degree of ambiguity in these remarks. Nevertheless, there is still some protection against the slide into simple opportunism in the religious underpinnings of this "civil philosophy." A man's course is not determined solely by his own fallible judgment and will; God also determines the range and variety of choices. Life's "scattered" and

14. "Correspondence," XXXV, "To Sir Henry Sidney" (Apr. 25, 1578), in *The Prose Works of Sir Philip Sidney,* ed. Albert Feuillerat, III, 122.

15. Cicero, *De Officiis,* III, iii, cited in Hiram Haydn, *The Counter-Renaissance,* p. 450.

16. Thomas More, *Utopia,* p. 34.

perplexing "second causes" are finally coherent, as Francis Bacon explains, "the chain of them, confederate and linked together" by providence.[17] Sidney's belief in "constancy in the everlasting governour" (*OA*, 407) restricted the demands of his adaptive capacity, assuring him that life's vicissitudes were both short term and manageable.

The problems with this ethic are obvious, particularly for those committed to its political applications. The gap between circumstance and providence seems to widen with engagement, and despite the exercise of considerable flexibility, reconciliation can be nearly impossible. Sidney's balancing act finally failed at Elizabeth's court, landing him outside the sphere of practical influence and effectiveness. Nevertheless, he retained his belief in the ultimate compatibility of human endeavor and God's will; his letter to Francis Walsingham is a compelling testament to his conviction.[18]

The strength of Sidney's faith still did not enable him to realize fully its promise in his life or his art. With characteristic ambition, he applied himself to this task in the *Arcadia*, seeking, as Greville reminds us, "to limn out such exact pictures, of every posture in the minde, that any man being forced, in the straines of this life, to pass through any straights, or latitudes of good, or ill fortune, might (as in a glasse) see how to set a good countenance upon all the discountenances of adversitie, and a stay upon the exorbitant smilings of chance."[19] Yet Greville concedes the "imperfection" of the work and the inevitable defeat of these ambitions, repeatedly emphasizing Sidney's intention rather than his accomplishment.[20] In Book III one confronts the most dramatic instance of this "imperfection": Sidney's failure to complete the work.

17. Francis Bacon, "Of Atheism," in *Francis Bacon: A Selection of His Works*, p. 86.
18. "Correspondence," LXXXIX, "To Sir Francis Walsingham" (Mar. 24, 1586), *Prose*, Feuillerat, III, 166–167.
19. Sir Fulke Greville, *The Life of The Renowned Sir Philip Sidney*, p. 16.
20. Ibid.

This failure derives, in part, from the inherent difficulties of his approach. Thematically, Sidney seeks to project an image of constancy and balance in a context of expanding contingency. This process corresponds to the narrative's formal development in which a unified organization is supposed to keep pace with expansive amplification. Sidney certainly assumed the existence of an order capable of embracing all this complexity, but in the end, he could not trace its operations. Lindheim explains his defeat in organizational terms, suggesting that his narrative expansion may have posed problems no longer soluble in the framework of his earlier composition. Because he did not approach his increasingly complex material "as though he already knew all the answers,"[21] he would not impose those that no longer applied. Lindheim is, of course, sympathetic to this failure of omniscience, and she finally exults in this assertion of Sidney's fallibility. She shares with Greville an appreciative understanding of certain limitations; yet these limitations do not hold her interest, and she does not probe beneath their surface.

In Book III, where Sidney's syncretistic ambitions sustain their most dramatic extension and defeat, insight into wit's limitations is crucial to an understanding of the text and of his failure to conclude the third book. The nature of wit's limitations is, in turn, clearest in Book III. Its climactic character and narrative and speculative breadth reveal varied sources of confusion and difficulty. This section's political speculation reveals theoretical uncertainty typical of sixteenth-century thought. During the transition from feudalism to nationalism and a centralized monarchy, the issue of sovereignty became increasingly important; yet its terms were never established with any real clarity, particularly in England. There was a strong inclination toward royal absolutism, reinforced by circumstances and moral sentiment, but as J. W. Allen asserts, this "was no more than a tendency and it was not very strong"; in much of sixteenth-century

21. Lindheim, "Vision," p. 147.

political thought "the tendency to illogical compromise" was pre-dominant.[22] In Allen's stern judgment, most political theory, except for Richard Hooker's, was "timid and inconclusive and more or less incoherent."[23] Subjects in the ambiguous position of proximity to the throne found that the nature of their relation was quite problematic; the uncertainty of the courtier's status and circumstances contributed to the confusion of the courtly code. The *New Arcadia's* inquiry into the nature of sovereignty and subjection must be analyzed within this broader context, for despite his temporary withdrawal from Elizabeth's court, Sidney could not completely escape its perplexing effects.

The recurrent psychological obstacles to wit's comprehensive resolutions are also manifest in Book III. Underlying Sidney's ideological and intellectual confusion is a basic ambivalence toward authority. This attitude is most apparent in the third book because the nature of authority becomes increasingly clear as the conflicts are escalated. Chaotic complexity and confusion persist despite Sidney's conscious intentions because of an unconscious preference for these conditions. The terms of an orderly solution have become far too oppressive and absolute by the book's end, so its imposition is finally resisted. Sidney's abrupt termination of the revision is an oddly appropriate resolution of his difficulties with the material, combining qualified assertion with a defensive obscurity. It is the last in a sequence of telling narrative evasions. The influence of ambivalence, as well as more conscious sources of confusion, become clearer from an analysis of the text.

The book begins with the seizure of the princesses and Zelmane initiated by the evil Cecropia. Amphialus, for a time, remains passively "amazed" by her treachery (*NA*, 363). Sidney again takes

22. J. W. Allen, *A History of Political Thought in the Sixteenth Century,* p. 268.

23. Ibid., p. 250.

pains to mitigate his male protagonist's guilt by assigning much of the blame to a bad parent. Thus, he asserts that Amphialus "was utterly ignorant of all his mothers wicked devises; to which he would never have consented, being (like a rose out of a brier) an excellent sonne of an evill mother" (*NA*, 363). He is, of course, driven to collaborate in her schemes by his unrequited love for Philoclea, but his innocence is sustained by several devices, such as his extraordinary ignorance of his mother's abuses of their captives. The most important basis is a sharp distinction between Cecropia's and Amphialus's motives for rebellion.

Both mother and son ultimately defy authority and violate the bond of subjection, but their reasons are completely opposed. Cecropia is driven by pride, envy, and ambition; and her brutal hatred of submission and lust for power free her from every inhibition. The daughter of the King of Argos, Cecropia had enjoyed sovereignty for a time as the wife of Basilius's younger brother and "apparant Princesse" of Arcadia (*NA*, 364). Then Basilius's marriage and the birth of two heirs to the throne blasted her aspirations. Her fury at finding her "Royall bloud . . . stained with the base name of subjection" drives her to conspire against Basilius and his daughters (*NA*, 364). She released the savage beasts in Book I and instigated the revolt through Clinias in the second book, but her efforts to destroy the royal family have all failed.

Cecropia is dismayed by the discovery of her son's "childish passion of love," fearing that it will thwart her schemes, and she urges him to dispense with these feelings: "For Hate often begetteth victory; Love commonly is the instrument of subjection" (*NA*, 365). Love is indeed his only motivation, and its effects are ambiguous. It certainly induces a profound subordination and mitigates his aggression. Cecropia, however, shrewdly adjusts her plans for attaining power, exploiting her son's desire for an Arcadian princess as a means to the throne. Thus, mother and son are united in a rebellious alliance against Basilius for entirely different motives. Amphialus

quickly recovers from his initial shock and organizes an army to resist the efforts of Basilius to retrieve his daughters. Despite his innocence of ambition, he becomes involved in a massive defiance of
authority.

The vast, protracted war that ensues dominates much of the third
book. For some time the rebels sustain the initiative, with the son's
military preeminence and the mother's seditious "wit-craft" the
decisive factors (*NA*, 464). In describing their resistance, Sidney
devotes attention to the war's political and strategic aspects, and his
narrative is informed by a lucid, critical intelligence. As the war advances, however, these strategic concerns recede, their urgency fad-
ing in the dreamy, episodic encounters of chivalric romance. This
results in a peculiar blurring of focus and dissipation of aggressive
energy. The conflict is muted and its implications are avoided by this
subtle narrative shift.

Initially, Amphialus displays the skill and patience of a sound
strategist. His preparations for Basilius's assault are both scrupulous
and sensible:

> Then omitted he nothing of defence, as wel simple defence, as
> that which did defend by offending, fitting instruments of mis-
> chiefe to places, whence the mischiefe might be most liberally
> bestowed. Nether was his smallest care for victuals, as wel for the
> providing that which should suffice both in store & goodnesse, as
> in well preserving it, and wary distributing it, both in quantitie,
> and qualitie; spending that first which would keepe lest.
>
> (*NA*, 373)

Engagement in battle provokes a simpler, less sophisticated response, however. In his prudent strategic calculations, "before the
enimies came," Amphialus "was carefull, providently diligent, and
not somtimes without doubting of the issue; now the nearer danger
approched . . . the lesse still it seemed: and now his courage began

to boile in choler, and with such impatience to desire to powre out both upon the enimie" (NA, 386).

The contrast of martial virtues suggests potential difficulties, and the conclusion of the first day's battle seems to confirm their opposition. Amphialus confronts the mysterious Black Knight, but their protracted struggle is disrupted by "an olde Governour of Amphialus" (NA, 393). The older man wounds the other knight, actually Musidorus, and slays his horse. "Amphialus cried to him, that he dishonoured him: You say well (answered the olde Knight) to stande now like a private souldier, setting your credite upon particular fighting, while you may see Basilius with all his hoste, is getting betweene you and your towne" (NA, 393). The contrast between courage and calculation is thus given admonitory significance by the directives of this old general. Sidney received the same warning from Languet, who wrote him, "It is the misfortune, or rather the folly of our age, that most men of high birth, think it more honorable to do the work of a soldier than of a leader, and would rather earn a name for boldness than for judgment."[24]

The old governor seems to speak for Sidney because the description of the first day's battle suggests that the author shares with his character a thoroughly practical and impersonal notion of warfare. Indeed, in his opening account, Sidney deprives knightly valor of its glamor as well as its effectiveness. Amphialus's belligerence becomes bestial: he is "like a Tigre, from whome a companie of Woolves did seeke to ravish a newe gotten pray; so he (remembring they came to take away Philoclea) did labour to make valure, strength, hatred, and choller to answere the proportion of his love, which was infinit" (NA, 388). Achilles is the obvious prototype for Amphialus; by the conversion of their love into brutal ferocity both heroes attain an awesome, terrifying force. Yet their wrath also makes their triumphs

---

24. *The Correspondence of Sir Philip Sidney and Hubert Languet,* trans. Stuart A. Pears, p. 137.

repellent. A clear example is Amphialus's first victim, the beautiful young Agenor, "lately growne a Lover" (*NA*, 386). In his romantic innocence the youth approaches battle as if it were a tournament. He charges the enemy, "neither staying the comaundment of the captaine, nor recking whether his face were armed" (*NA*, 387). Amphialus's lance splinters at their clash, and Agenor's heedless bravery earns him "not onely a suddaine, but a fowle death, leaving scarsely any tokens of his former beautie" (*NA*, 387).

Agenor's gruesome death and disfigurement afford an appropriate beginning for this battle. The carnage that ensues is equally grotesque: "In one place lay disinherited heades, dispossessed of their naturall seignories: in an other, whole bodies to see to, but that their harts wont to be bound all over so close, were nowe with deadly violence opened: in others, fowler deaths had ouglily displayed their trayling guttes" (*NA*, 388). Sidney's hideous imagery forcibly alters the appearance of war. His description becomes emblematic at the battle's conclusion, exposing the sordid brutality beneath the glamorous façade: "For at the first, though it were terrible, yet Terror was deckt so bravelie with rich furniture, guilte swords, shining armours, pleasant pensils, that the eye with delight had scarce leasure to be afraide: But now all universally defiled with dust, bloud, broken armours, mangled bodies, tooke away the maske, and sette foorth Horror in his owne horrible manner" (*NA*, 392). These harsh pictorial contrasts amplify one's perception of combat in precisely the way Sidney describes in the *Apology*: his artful "speaking picture" has a powerful impact on both "the imaginative and judging power."[25]

Agenor's death has further effects on the reader's conception of warfare. His reckless bravery is obviously foolish, and his demise is the cruelest reproach for such romantic hubris. Yet, despite his

---

25. Sir Philip Sidney, *An Apology for Poetry, or the Defence of Poetry*, p. 107.

superior strength, Amphialus has similar difficulties imposing his will upon their struggle. Agenor's appearance stirs Amphialus's "Compassion"; yet the latter's feelings are ineffectual against the forces unleashed by his rebellious "Choller"; even his lance is infused with a "pittilesse" and "unsparing" spirit (*NA*, 387). The chivalric standards simply fail in this context, as all personal intentions are engulfed in the unmitigated, impersonal violence of troops and arms. "But by this time there had bene a furious meeting of either side: where after the terrible salutation of warlike noyse, the shaking of handes was with sharpe weapons" (*NA*, 387). Sidney's figure emphasizes the inhumanity of this encounter with pointed irony. Individual passions—honorable or wrathful, compassionate or simply vain—are submerged in the clash of objects; "the justling of bodies" (*NA*, 388) is only one of many such insensate collisions. Along with the "clashing of armour, and crushing of staves" (*NA*, 388), the soldiers' exertions are governed by larger forces and objectives than chivalric intent.

The next major engagement encourages similar conclusions. Amphialus and his followers have remained within their fortifications under seige. Phalantus, an idle gallant of the Basilian camp, grows bored with inaction and challenges Amphialus to private combat. In doing so, he insists he is a "hateless enemie" motivated solely by a "liking of martiall matters without anie mislike of your person" (*NA*, 413). Sidney subtly satirizes their mannered chivalric gestures, the "noble gentleness" and "honourable speeches" exchanged.

Phalantus's motto, *"The glorie, not the pray"* (*NA*, 416), succinctly defines the basic issue. The categorical separation of military objectives is complete, making the cult of personal glory a vacuous ritual. Devoid of any serious intention, their fight becomes frivolous, even decadent. Moreover, it constitutes a serious breach of the public responsibilities of command. Thus, when Amphialus accepts the challenge, he is chastened once more by "his olde governour" for seeking "rather . . . the glorie of a private fighter, then of a wise Generall" (*NA*, 414).

It is surprising, then, to find that subsequent narrative developments are unaffected by these seemingly definitive attitudes. Amphialus continues to succeed in war, and his disregard for the old governor's sound advice has no consequence whatsoever. Indeed, the latter is never heard from again, and his point of view is only sporadically presented. Moreover, the scale of the war is drastically diminished, and every subsequent conflict is decided by single combat. Sidney makes these six contests the center of attention for the remainder of Book III. This means that the military forces so obtrusively operative in the beginning of the book are suspended, as the principals return to chivalric ritual. Amphialus is no longer obliged to consider fortifications, provisions, or military discipline. He is now free to concentrate on the decoration of his armor and horse in order to impress his beloved. Personal, romantic concerns regain their primacy as public and political issues recede.

The next encounter involves Amphialus in an extraordinary conflict with Argalus and his wife, Parthenia, and its resolution reveals fully the ambiguities of Sidney's military attitudes. The perfect harmony of Argalus's and Parthenia's marriage is threatened by war, when Basilius summons this brave knight to do battle with the indomitable Amphialus. Parthenia strives against the rigors of duty and honor, and he mildly chastens her for her opposition. Their crisis engenders a characteristic antithesis of values—"Affection" against "Honour" (*NA*, 420)—yet Parthenia's final assertion of affectionate attachment anticipates an eventual reciprocity: "Parthenia shalbe in the battle of your fight: Parthenia shall smart in your paine, & your blood must be bled by Parthenia" (*NA*, 421).

Amphialus and Argalus begin their struggle courteously, but once they are engaged in combat, their belligerence escalates. Indeed, their fight proceeds toward a typically excruciating knot of antagonism, providing a "notable example of the woonderfull effectes of

Vertue, where the conquerour, sought for friendship of the conquered, and the conquered woulde not pardon the conquerour: both indeede being of that minde to love eche other for accepting, but not for giving mercie, and neyther affected to over-live a dishonour" (*NA*, 426). Argalus dies, still struggling, and Parthenia is overwhelmed with grief.

The grim pathos of this situation, relieved for a time by the mock chivalries of the "combate of cowardes" (*NA*, 428–434), is finally resolved by the ensuing combat between Amphialus and the mysterious "Knight of the Tombe." This latter fight is exceedingly one-sided, and Amphialus magnanimously abstains from pressing his advantage. His pity is scorned by his opponent, and Amphialus, "in whome abused kindenesse became spitefull rage," overwhelms the other knight, mortally wounding him for his "discourtesie" (*NA*, 446). Only then does he discover that he has slain Parthenia. She dies thanking him for this "service," which will reunite her with her beloved (*NA*, 447), "since whose death I have done nothing but die. . . . O sweete life, welcome (saide she) nowe feele I the bandes untied of the cruell death, which so long hath helde me" (*NA*, 448).

The denouement of this segment pushes the conflict to the limits of pathos and paradox. Honorable courtesy and cruel violence, harmony and discord, beauty and mortal horror, all the essential contrasts of Sidney's vision of war, are symmetrically at play here. The extraordinary synthesis effected by Parthenia's death depends on Sidney's unique point of view, which is defined in his description of her appearance:

> her necke, a necke indeed of Alablaster, displaying the wounde, which with most daintie blood laboured to drowne his owne beauties; so as here was a river of purest redde, there an Iland of perfittest white, each giving lustre to the other; with the sweete countenance (God-knowes) full of an unaffected languishing: though these thinges to a grosly conceaving sense might seeme disgraces; yet indeed were they but apparailing beautie in a new

fashion, which all looked-upon thorough the spectacles of pittie, did even encrease the lynes of her naturall fairenes, so as Amphialus was astonished with griefe, compassion, & shame, detesting his fortune, that made him unfortunate in victory.

(*NA*, 447)

This ghastly "speaking picture" is designed to elicit a more discerning response than horror or disgust. Although one may feel something like the "griefe, compassion, & shame" of Amphialus at first, one is finally meant to regard this scene with detached fascination. In one's distance from the turbulent passions of the principals, even the mild stirrings of pity are finally subdued by an appreciative wonder. In *AS* 34 of *Astrophil and Stella*, Sidney remarks, "Oft cruell fights well pictured forth do please," and his understanding of the ironies of this phenomenon is manifest in *AS* 45, where he mocks Stella's indifference to real suffering and her susceptibility to "imag'd things." Yet one finds one's response to suffering here is the same as it is with Argalus and Parthenia: one is moved more by the clever wit of the image than by the pain it depicts.

Robert Kimbrough insists rather incongruously on the "forthrightly realistic" nature of the clashes between Amphialus, Argalus, and Parthenia; and he maintains that they represent a break from "the customs and ceremonies of chivalry."[26] Yet these battles are presented much less realistically than the earlier image of war, which "sette foorth Horror in his owne horrible manner." In the earlier instance, Sidney's exposition is probing and analytic, emblematically unmasking some latent significance. The contrasts are jarring and exclusive, and their terms are irreconcilable. His description of Parthenia's wounds presents no such contrast; instead Sidney devises complex, inclusive formulations the terms of which are complementary and equally engaging. Although new aspects are revealed, one does not judge or choose among them. One's

26. Robert Kimbrough, *Sir Philip Sidney*, p. 140.

perception plays on the surface of these antitheses. Here war's splendid, beautiful "maske" is not repudiated as a distortion of its true aspect, for it is no less essential or authentic to this view of combat.

Ultimately, it is the latter point of view that governs Sidney's presentation of the war, despite the reservations revealed in the earlier passage. From this perspective every casualty resembles Parthenia: their wounds "to a grosly conceaving sense might seeme disgraces; yet indeed were they but apparailing beautie in a new fashion." Thus even the impact of the first battle's imagery is muted. Death and mayhem are stylistically assimilated to a pattern of "curious" and "witty" conceits. Horses lying dead on their masters afford a notable inversion, for "in death [they] had the honour to be borne by them, whom in life they had borne" (*NA*, 388). The earth is said to be buried with men, and "legges . . . contrarie to common nature, by being discharged of their burthen, were growne heavier" (*NA*, 388). In the end, Sidney intends one to regard all this with a steady, admiring gaze, to be no less intrigued with combat's "horrible manner" than with its delightful appearance. Such serene equanimity is a mark of exquisite taste and sophistication, beyond the comprehension of "a grosly conceaving sense." Sidney would contemplate his own impending death with the same aesthetic detachment. The gangrenous stench of his wound was almost overpowering, but he could still compose a song entitled "La cuisse rompue."[27] The contradictions of chivalry are nowhere more apparent. Sidney's cavalier wit allows him to face death with elegant composure and style, and he imposes a graceful order on the grotesque and pointless accidents of battle. Yet it was this same chivalrous style that caused the fatal wound. In his writing, Sidney's outlook poses obstacles to wit's more purposeful applications; this calm acceptance of war's "horrible manner" obscures real conflicts and prevents clear assessment.

27. Greville, *Life*, p. 138.

This shift in perspective affects narrative developments in similar ways. An expansive synthesis is finally sustained within the terms of chivalric romance. This loose narrative mode incorporates the grotesque and satiric material of the earlier battles, even the harsh contradictions of which are reconciled and assimilated by this diffuse genre. Moreover, as the war proceeds through a protracted sequence of encounters between single combatants, interest in its purpose and results diminishes. Despite their initial prominence, tactics and issues vanish as narrative concerns, whereas details of ornament and gesture absorb all one's attention. Freed of their ultimate consequences, the warriors' exertions become a self-contained spectacle rather than a functional tactic. This development contributes to the tone of appreciative neutrality. Conflict and defeat are isolated from a broader consequential context by this mode of narration, and their harsher aspects are mitigated.

This benign resolution of conflict barely skirts certain thematic difficulties. Sidney relinquishes the critical acuity of his early accounts of battle. By harsh and satiric contrast, he had clarified the war's basic issues and principles; these are subsequently obscured by his glorification of single combat. Still more problematic is the effect on the work's development. Neither the narrative nor the battle it seeks to describe advance according to any systematic, sequential plan. Instead, they proceed through a series of episodic, disconnected struggles, eventually culminating in irresolute stasis. The *New Arcadia* is not completed, nor is anything decided by this war, practically or theoretically. Sidney's chivalric equanimity involves him in profound irresolution. Once again he confronts the reader with a powerful and significant conflict that is never clearly developed or decided.

This ambiguity has several sources, among which the confused military notions of Sidney's class are certainly influential. For Sidney, as I have shown, war remained an "occasion for honorable self-display and the public performance of "fine deeds.' "[28] The cult of martial glory could, of course, encourage vainglorious idiocy, as Sidney demonstrated in his portrayal of Phalantus. Alternately, it might stir men to acts of exemplary selflessness. Nevertheless, the effectiveness of personal heroism was ultimately limited. *Sprezzatura* and the code of fair play might not only diminish the aristocracy's zeal and belligerence but also prove self-destructive. Another source of confusion was the concentration on the immediate encounter and the individual performance. Heroic adventurism prevailed over systematic campaign, preventing a more consistent, impersonal discipline. While it allowed Sidney an impressive bravura in his approach to warfare, the chivalric style also proved problematic. It seems to have confused both his attempts at military command and his attempts at epic composition. Sidney's confusion was in no way unique. Michael Walzer, in his explanation of the Calvinists' opposition to chivalric romance, cites the admission by a Huguenot officer "that the medieval romances of Amadis still caused 'un esprit de vertige' among the men of his generation."[29] Seen in this context, Don Quixote's madness becomes a comic exaggeration of a fairly common weakness. This weakness for chivalric fiction was one to which the aristocracy was especially susceptible.

A similar irresolution governs Sidney's political speculation in the revision, generating contradictions more intense and intricate. These are apparent from the beginning of his account of the rebellion. Responsibility for the rebellion's political aspects is immediately assigned to Cecropia. Although Amphialus displays considerable guile in his defiance of Basilius, all his maneuvers are made "according to the counsell of his mother" (*NA*, 371). Under her tutelage, he learns to exploit factional motivations, manipulating the "humors" of each group (*NA*, 371). His leadership offers something

28. Michael Walzer, *The Revolution of the Saints,* p. 272.
29. Ibid., p. 72, n. 14.

for everyone: "To his friends, friendlines; to the ambitious, great expectations; to the displeased, revenge; to the greedie, spoyle: wrapping their hopes with such cunning, as they rather seemed given over unto them as partakers: then promises sprong of necessitie" (*NA*, 371).

Far more significant than these tactics is the "justification" of rebellion published by Amphialus. This overmighty subject declares his motives for aggression to be purely official, concealing their origins in private ambition or desire. By rationalizing defiance in public, ethical terms, he employs a weapon far more seditious than feudal militarism or conspiratorial calculation. Amphialus attacks Basilius ideologically, undermining his legitimacy as a ruler while usurping it for himself. This document sets forth clearly the problem of the monarch's moral authority, one of the *Arcadia's* central concerns; it concludes, characteristically, with a deft circumvention of this same problem.

In his "justification," Amphialus bases all his arguments on a teleological notion of value. He assigns primacy to the abstract "ende whereto any thing is directed" rather than to the concrete "thing thereto directed" (*NA*, 371). In political terms, this requires that "the weale-publicke was more to be regarded, then any person or magistrate that thereunto was ordeined" (*NA*, 372). This functional definition of political priorities allows an impersonal conception of authority and its claims. The "duetie which is owed to the countrie, goes beyond all other dueties" (*NA*, 371), and it is opposed to the older, feudal loyalties to the ruler's sacred person. Such rational abstraction is a powerful solvent of traditional loyalties to "all tender respects of kinred" and "long-helde opinions" (*NA*, 371). Indeed, the latter are said to be pernicious tools of oppression, "rather builded upon a secreate of governement, then any ground of truthe" (*NA*, 371).

Having established these principles, Amphialus persuasively applies them to the Arcadian political crisis. Because Basilius has "given over al care of government" and neglects "the good estate of so many thousands," the country founders in a "dangerous case" (NA, 372). The commoners' insurrection in Book II is simply one symptom of misrule, but Sidney dismisses their response as inadequate and illegitimate, a sort of muddled reflex reaction; rather than redressing the country's chaotic conditions, it simply exacerbated them. Amphialus proposes a more authoritative solution, more conservative in its reapportionment of power. He advances a theory first adopted by the Huguenot aristocracy in their efforts to secure independence from a centralized, Catholic monarchy. Responsibility for the commonwealth was to be shared by the ruling classes; "The care whereof, did kindly appertaine to those, who being subalterne magistrates and officers of the crowne, were to be employed as from the Prince, so for the people" (NA, 372). Sidney's knowledge of this doctrine is attributed to his acquaintance with François Hotman's *Franco-Gallia* and with the *Vindiciae Contra Tyrranos,* presumably written by his friend, Philip de Mornay. Both works oppose the nobility's constitutional claims to the potentially tyrannical impulses of the crown, cautiously explaining their own right to resistance.[30]

At this point in the "justification," the rigor of Amphialus's argument breaks down. He shifts from legal prerogatives to ancient claims of blood. His position is preeminent because he is "descended of the Royall race, and next heire male" (NA, 372). This polemical expedient has several advantages. It allows him to challenge the status of Philanax, Basilius's duly appointed regent. Philanax is noble and, according to the terms of the "justification," entitled to assume governmental responsibility. Consequently, Amphialus reverts to more arbitrary standards, impugning the other's birthright as well

30. See William D. Briggs, "Political Ideas in Sidney's *Arcadia,*" pp. 141–142, 150. For a more comprehensive account of Huguenot theory, see J. W. Allen, *Political Thought,* pp. 302–331, and Walzer, *Saints,* pp. 74–87. The major primary documents can be studied in Julian H. Franklin, trans. and ed., *Constitutionalism and Resistance in the Sixteenth Century.*

as his administration: Philanax is "a man neither in birth comparable to many, nor for his corrupt, prowde, and partiall dealing, liked of any" (*NA*, 372). By deflecting his aggression to a social inferior, Amphialus avoids a direct assault on the king; he even pretends concern for Basilius, "since all that was done, was done for his service" (*NA*, 372). This was the habitual defense of aristocratic rebels, used in both the Pilgrimage of Grace and the Huguenot rebellion. In England the rebels claimed to be acting against Cromwell rather than Henry VIII, and in France the Huguenots professed their loyalty to King Charles and directed their attacks on the hated Guises. The justification ends with this equivocal challenge to royal control, thus seeking to have it both ways. The argument it advances alternately depreciates and depends on feudal standards of sovereignty.

The inconsistencies are to some extent calculated, duplicitously concealing the true intentions of a rebellious subject; but they also reflect the essential contradictions of this political theory. The Protestant aristocrat remained, as Walzer notes, "a man of established (if often decaying) position, possessed of practical military skills and a mind to accompany them—a combination of status, function, and mentality not conducive to extended or radical speculation."[31] The nobility's stake in the status quo prevented them from carrying this redefinition of authority to its logical conclusions. Obviously their own authority was based on the same feudal and hierarchical standards as the monarch's, or as one shrewd Huguenot noted: "The nobility alone has not deviated from the correct path, . . . it has understood that if there were no longer a king, each village would free itself from its gentleman."[32] Too rigorous an assault on royal prerogative by the aristocracy would clearly subvert their own position. The inherent inconsistencies in the doctrine of subaltern

31. Walzer, *Saints,* p. 77.
32. Quoted by Walzer, in *Saints,* p. 92.

magistracy—its reliance on both ancestral and legalistic claims—allow the continuity and endurance of their essentially feudal power. At the same time, they clearly diminish the nobility's capacity for autonomy and resistance to increasing royal control. The aristocracy could never obtain the revolutionary fervor and freedom of the more alienated and religiously fanatical lower orders.

Aristocratic defiance was restrained by another historical factor, implied in Sidney's account of this rebellion. The "justification" sways some, "of more quicke then sounde conceipte," to the cause of Amphialus (*NA*, 373), but many remain indifferent to its arguments. These latter are more susceptible to the straightforward suasions of rude power. In this group, Amphialus's actions "breed a coolenesse, to deal violently against him, and a false-minded neutralitie to expect the issue" (*NA*, 373). This pliant neutrality poses another threat to the security of the monarch and the government. When strength is the sole determinant of loyalty, all other constraints are removed from the overmighty subject. The result is the chaotic free-for-all that dominated England in the fifteenth century, in which the crown became a kind of political "football."[33] Philip Sidney was undoubtedly affected to some extent by what Irving Ribner calls "the great fear of Tudor Englishmen," and he may have been drawn toward a belief in "the superiority of the king to human law and the necessity for absolute and unquestioned obedience to him."[34] Despite its constraints, Tudor supremacy had sustained order and stability and won the loyalty of its subjects, whose loyalty to the throne, combined with their enduring distaste for the results of noble presumption, posed a serious obstacle to lordly ambition.

Amphialus's subsequent characterization is significantly altered

33. S. T. Bindoff, *Tudor England*, p. 8. See also Lawrence Stone, *The Crisis of the Aristocracy*, pp. 96–97, and Allen, *Political Thought*, pp. xv, 121.
34. Irving Ribner, "Sir Philip Sidney on Civil Insurrection," pp. 262, 264.

after these early forays into politics and warfare, and he becomes a suppliant courtier. His Achillean wrath is mollified by the return to chivalric ritual, so that the character of the warrior, like that of the war, is altered by this shift. At the same time, the ruse of magistral ambitions, adopted only at his mother's instigation, is abandoned. In a maneuver typical of the other young heroes, the declared terms of his conflict with authority are subsequently ignored. His belligerence and his cunning diminish as the conflict advances, and Amphialus emerges in his true aspect as plaintive supplicant. The pathos of futile courtship becomes his definitive characteristic.

Unrequited love is the true motive for his actions; the political "justification" is an empty subterfuge, the terms of which he neither fully embraces nor pursues. His romantic impulses afford Amphialus an authentic justification, compelling even to Philanax. This stern counselor to Basilius, captured during the first battle, appeals to Amphialus to surrender. The king would surely forgive him, inasmuch as his "fault passed is excusable, in that Love perswaded, and youth was perswaded" (NA, 401). His transgressions are diminished by the increasing emphasis on romantic compulsions; he elicits sympathy from all, even the most punitively righteous. Amphialus, like Pyrocles, is regarded throughout "with more affection then judgement" (NA, 84).

Besides its sentimental appeal, Amphialus's dilemma has another, more ambiguous feature that makes forgiveness natural. His affection cripples and finally defeats him, enforcing a pathetic—and reassuring—impotence upon this fierce warrior; he can be easily indulged because he is ultimately harmless. Later in the story, a typical exchange occurs between Amphialus and Cecropia, occasioned by the unyielding resistance of his beloved. His mother urges him to exert that "imperious maisterfulnesse, which nature gives to men above women. For indeede (sonne, I confesse unto you) in our very creation we are servants" (NA, 453). She chastens him for "seeking to have that by praier, which he should have taken by authoritie" (*NA*, 451). Cecropia's anxieties are vindicated, for love indeed proves an "instrument of subjection" (*NA*, 365); her son willingly embraces the abject condition she so frantically seeks to escape.

This abasement culminates in the familiar self-destructive reflex in which aggression is turned back upon itself. Disclosure of Cecropia's abuse of their prisoners causes Amphialus to attempt suicide. His last act affords a "pittiful spectacle, where the conquest was the conquerors overthrow, and self-ruine the onely triumph of a battaile, fought betweene him, and himselfe" (*NA*, 494). The book's vast conflict is completely internalized, and Amphialus becomes its only victim in one of the boldest distortions Sidney makes on behalf of his heroes. Amphialus commands awe as well as pity, for, like Othello, he grandly usurps all punitive authority: "he needed no judge to goe upon him: for no man could ever thinke any otherworthy of greater punishment, then he thought himselfe" (*NA*, 492). By his masochism, Sidney's hero secures an even greater advantage than indulgent admiration, namely, his survival. Amphialus's wound is not fatal, and he is entrusted to the care of Helen of Corinth (*NA*, 496). Like many self-inflicted punishments, his is not as damaging as those administered by others. By these drastic measures, Amphialus preempts punitive control from higher authorities and mitigates its severity. At the same time, the painful costs of this defensive posture are obvious: abject restraint and deference simply intensify Amphialus's anguish and frustration.

I discern one more, probably inevitable, evasion of conflict in Sidney's handling of Amphialus. The shifts in heroic posture parallel some of the vicissitudes of Sidney's career, and cumulatively, they effect a peculiar resolution. Amphialus strikes out with activist assurance, his ambitions bolstered by the intellectual influence of others. In Sidney's life, these inchoate theories were assimilated to an older, more nebulous ethos of courtship and submission; in his characters, the dominance of the traditional attitude is even more pronounced. The impact of these ideological shifts is diminished in the *New Arcadia* by depriving them of political content. Claims to magistral authority are shown to be a pretext for romantic motives. The latter impulses reassuringly contradict the former presumptions; Amphialus seeks only to make "all his authoritie to be but a footestoole to Humblenes" (*NA*, 370). The courtly posture of submission and servitude is, in turn, presented exclusively in its original erotic terms. Its disconcerting political implications, so obvious in the lives of Sidney and other courtiers, are obscured in the revision. In his treatment of Amphialus, Sidney makes a romantic virtue of political necessity, resorting to the conventional mystification. The courtly tradition never fully subdued conflict at court; even in fiction, it still only partially reduces the pain of subjection.

Whereas Amphialus is both crippled and redeemed by his ambivalence, Cecropia, "whose thoughts were unperplexed" (*NA*, 375), relentlessly pursues her villainous destiny. In the *Arcadia,* the gravest risks are sustained by women and commoners, whose defiance of authority incurs severe punishment. The rebellious activities of Amphialus and the two protagonists are hedged by equivocation, and they are spared the fate of these sexual and political scapegoats. Sidney's treatment of these figures reveals intriguing shifts in characterization and narrative development.

In the *Old Arcadia,* Gynecia takes on the perilous role of untrammeled aggression. Vowing that she will "stir up terrible tragedies rather than fail of her intent" (*OA*, 96), Gynecia nearly overwhelms all with the force of her desire for Pyrocles. She is freed from all inhibitions, intent on the elimination of all obstacles to her lusts, including her daughter: "it is Philoclea his heart is set upon; . . . it is my daughter which I have borne to supplant me. But if it be so, the life I have given thee, ungrateful Philoclea, I will sooner with these hands bereave thee of than my birth shall glory she hath bereaved me of my desires" (*OA*, 92). She concludes her soliloquy with this triumphant declamation: "In shame there is no comfort but to be beyond all bounds of shame" (*OA*, 92). The same vehemence of yearning and resolve mark her speech in the cave scene: "I would I might be freely wicked, since wickedness doth prevail" (*OA*, 183). Dedicating herself to the "infernal furies," she dispenses with enfeebled virtue: "Let my rage be satisfied . . . I desire but to assuage the sweltering of my hellish longing. Dejected Gynecia!" (*OA*, 183).

Natalie Zemon Davis has studied the prominent historical role of women in various assaults on the established order, examining both actual insurgencies and festive simulations. She has found that, during the Renaissance, conventional assumptions of female "unruliness" and irresponsibility often allowed them a unique revolutionary license. Freed from social constraints by discriminatory assumptions, women could be more disruptive than men.[35] Recognizing this advantage, men sometimes sought to exploit it through transvestite disguise on both festal and revolutionary occasions. Such disguises abound in literature, and Davis mentions Pyrocles as one of the many "literary examples of male transvestitism."[36] His attack on the king's authority is, however, covert and equivocal; with the *Arcadia's* older women, this "unruliness" is genuinely dangerous. As her name implies, Gynecia is the epitome of full-blown feminine sexuality. Her erotic energy and lusts are generalized into a radical willfulness, making her the most forceful figure in the *Old Arcadia*, a distinction C. S. Lewis notes in comparing her to Phèdre.[37] In the *New Arcadia*, her villainy is surpassed by that of Cecropia, another evil mother.

Yet, for Sidney, the salient feature of such power is its reversibility. Disruptive force turns back on itself in circular fashion and its ob-

---

35. Natalie Zemon Davis, "Women on Top," in *Society and Culture in Early Modern France*, p. 131.

36. Ibid., p. 132.

37. C. S. Lewis, *English Literature in the Sixteenth Century*, pp. 335, 338.

jectives are completely thwarted. Heroic ambivalence is also circular in its oscillations between pathos and assertion, but these are more securely contained by inhibition, insuring a basic safety and stability. For Gynecia, the shifts resulting from the absence of restraint lead only to precipitous defeat. In Sidney's treatment of his villains, the reversal of impulse is more abrupt and its containment more brutal. This reversibility is graphically illustrated in Sidney's description of an earlier rebellion, the scenes of which clarify Sidney's attitude toward his inferiors.

The sequence of events is described in both versions of the *Arcadia*, beginning with Pyrocles' desperate need to express his feelings: "Cleophila thus at one instant both beseiged and banished, found in herself a daily increase of her violent desires which, as a river, his current being stopped, doth the more swell, so did her heart, the more impediments she met, the more vehemently strive to overpass them" (*OA*, 113). For the moment, romantic expression is restricted to conversation with Philoclea, and these feelings are channeled and subdued in courtly discourse. Gynecia's rude intrusion releases a more powerful flood, threatening to engulf them all. She dismisses her daughter and turns on Pyrocles, "when suddenly the confused rumor of a mutinous multitude gave just occasion to Cleophila to break off any such conference (for well they found they were no friendly voices they heard)" (*OA*, 123). Torrential emotion climaxes in anarchy, as Gynecia and Pyrocles are engulfed by the rebellious mob:

> they were overtaken by an unruly sort of clowns which, like a violent flood, were carried they themselves knew not whither. But as soon as they came within the compass of blows, like enraged beasts, without respect of their estates or pity of their sex, they ran upon these fair ladies, to show the right nature of a villain, never thinking his estate happy but when he is able to do hurt. Yet so many as they were, so many almost were the minds all knit together only in madness. Some cried 'take!', some 'kill!',

some 'save!'; but even they that cried 'save!' ran for company with
them that meant to kill. Everyone commanded, none obeyed. He
only seemed to have most pre-eminence that was most rageful.
(*OA*, 123–124).

The "infected will" moves through these scenes with a disembodied,
irrepressible force. It spills over from courtly dalliance, the temperate
balance of which cannot be sustained, into brazen lust. This leads
immediately to the chaotic assault of the Phagonians upon the
king's sovereign authority. Political and sexual rebellion are fused
strikingly by this sudden transition. In Sidney's account, "more and
more wickedness opened itself" to the rebellious will, "once past the
bounds of obedience" (*OA*, 128). Inner harmony and social order
are demolished by its thrust.

Yet even more astonishing than the will's cataclysmic force is its
absurd impotence: "mischief," Sidney explains, must "multiply in
itself till it come to the highest, and then fall with his own weight"
(*OA*, 128). A momentary lull affords Pyrocles a chance for some
manipulative oratory, and the mob is cajoled back into submission.
Those who stirred up this revolt learn the volatile "inconstancy" of
"the many-headed multitude" in painful fashion (*OA*, 131):
"their fellows, that were most glad to have such a mean to show
their loyalty, dispatched most of them with a good rule: that to be
leaders in disobedience teacheth ever disobedience to the same
leaders. So was this ungracious motion converted into their own
bowels, and they by a true judgement grown their own punishers"
(*OA*, 131–132). Rebellious assaults on hierarchy do not reduce all
to chaos and confusion as they initially threatened; instead, these
attacks are automatically turned back against the subject by a
rigid reflex reaction. The will's erotic and political aspirations are
thwarted by this reflexive aggression. The description of the mob's
assault in which "this ungracious motion [is] converted into their

own bowels" portrays this process in its grisliest, most severe aspects.

The crushing defeat of the Phagonians involves yet another shift in narrative distance in which guilt is displaced onto mere commoners. Pyrocles and Musidorus are engaged in a more subversive, if less direct, assault on the sovereignty of Basilius, yet they escape retribution. Indeed, in the *New Arcadia*, they can even mete out punishment. The battle with the Phagonians is prolonged, providing an occasion for much ponderous and sadistic drollery. Both Sidney and his heroes plunge gleefully into slapstick mayhem. A tailor loses his nose, bends down to pick it up, and ends up losing his head (*NA*, 312). Another rebel's "butcherly eloquence" is stilled though his "tongue still wagged" after his decapitation (*NA*, 312). A painter who wanted to see battle scenes firsthand "returned, well skilled in wounds, but with never a hand to performe his skill" (*NA*, 313). Presumably such humor would be less offensive to his aristocratic audience at Wilton than it is today; yet, even allowing for a change in tastes, the wit seems excessively brutal. Sidney's heroes abandon themselves to an obviously gratifying, if somewhat displaced, aggression against the king's enemies, thus allaying somewhat their own guilt. The effectiveness of such a tactic is, finally, rather crude.

When the system is challenged by subordinates, rebellion is crushed with all the force of moral absolutism and displaced aggression. When such impulses originate in Sidney's heroes, the issue becomes more problematic. The Huguenot theory of subaltern magistracy was an attempt to deal with this problem by sanctioning only "official" disobedience led by noble authorities. As I have shown, this justification was only partially successful. Amphialus finally abandons the theory, and Sidney's hero is protected by more evasive narrative expedients. More severe consequences befall those whose gender or status permits Sidney to feel greater detachment. Cecropia is ultimately responsible for her son's actions, having organized and directed his amorphous energies, and she bears the brunt of the wrath his actions provoke. The circumstances of her death are wonderfully appropriate. She dies fleeing from her own son as the latter, the paragon of passive aggression, pursues her with sword drawn, intending only "to kill himselfe in her presence" (*NA*, 492). Frightened and guilt-stricken, Cecropia falls to her death. She is destroyed by the punitive forces she and her son have released, while Amphialus maintains a kind of covert control. Her own ruthless potency makes the evil mother a scapegoat for the more timorous filial offenders.

Cecropia's villainy reaches its apex during the captivity. She plans to break the resistance of their captives easily and takes "the charge upon her, not doubting the easie conquest of an unexpert virgin, who had alreadie with subtiltie and impudencie begun to undermine a monarchy" (*NA*, 376). Indeed, her approach to both undertakings is the same: Cecropia reasserts the seditious tenets of the "justification" and pursues them to their logical conclusion. Seduction, no less than sedition, leads to a direct assault on authority. The transgressive implications of their activities, obscured by Amphialus, are amplified by Cecropia, and the lines of conflict are clearly drawn.

Cecropia begins by expounding a naturalism alternately libertine or deterministic, a position that allows polemical flexibility. She can oppose Philoclea's chastity as a willful "private choise" made in defiance of anatomical destiny (*NA*, 378): "Nature, when you were first borne, vowed you a woman, & as she made you child of a mother, so to do your best to be mother of a child" (*NA*, 379). As in Milton's *Comus*, chastity consists of a spiritual freedom from the order of nature, and Philoclea opposes all "constraints" with an insistence on "her libertie" (*NA*, 380). Cecropia alters her approach with Pamela, emphasizing the freedom and "preheminence" allowed by nature's generosity to women (*NA*, 404). Nevertheless, the tone of the *carpe diem* passage that follows becomes subtly mandatory.

The basic issue is broached when Pamela invokes her father's strictures against her marriage. When reminded of Basilius's eccentricity, she asserts his absolute patriarchal authority: "If he be pevish (said Pamela) yet is he my father, & how beautiful soever I be, I am his daughter: so as God claimes at my hands obedience, and makes me no judge of his imperfections" (*NA*, 405). Cecropia professes unctuous admiration for "such zeale of Devotion," but her tone becomes increasingly patronizing and critical (*NA*, 406). The girl's filial devotion has a naïve charm in Cecropia's view, but it is also "the best bonde, which the most politicke wittes have found, to holde mans witte in well doing" (*NA*, 406). She urges Pamela to put such childish fears behind her and embrace a higher virtue, one that is skeptical and self-reliant, and she concludes with a profession of exuberant atheism:

> For, as children must first by feare be induced to know that, which after (when they doo know) they are most glad of: So are these bug-beares of opinions brought by great Clearkes into the world, to serve as shewelles to keepe them from those faults, whereto els the vanitie of the worlde, and weakenes of senses might pull them. But in you (Neece) whose excellencie is such, as it neede not to be helde up by the staffe of vulgar opinions, I would not you should love Vertue servillie, for feare of I know not what, which you see not: but even for the good effects of vertue which you see. Feare, and indeede, foolish feare, and fearefull ignorance, was the first inventer of those conceates. . . . so as it is manifest inough, that all things follow but the course of their own nature, saving only Man, who while by the pregnancie of his imagination he strives to things supernaturall, meane-while he looseth his owne naturall felicitie. Be wise, and that wisedome shalbe a God unto thee; be contented, and that is thy heaven.
>
> (*NA*, 406)

This is an extraordinary declaration, its philosophical force and scope couched in the breezy, cajoling tones of seduction. Indeed its radical implications are expanded rather than obscured by this immediate purpose, and their impact is increased by Cecropia's conviction: she is "speaking the more earnestly, because she spake as she thought" (*NA*, 406).

She continues the demystification and rationalization of authority initiated in the "justification." Though less formal, Cecropia's argument is more inclusive and explicit. The "justification" alluded only briefly to the oppressive effects of "long-helde opinions" and "all tender respects of kinred" (*NA*, 371); in her session with Pamela, Cecropia delves more deeply into the origins of this "secreate of government" (*NA*, 371). She traces these origins back to primitive superstitions and fears that keep men in a childish state of dependence. Although all forms of government exploit this condition, she puts special emphasis on the genius of religion for enforcing servility. Cecropia's psychological insights into politics are even more subversive than the functional abstractions advanced in the "justification."

Cecropia's atheism has both ancient and contemporary sources. Epicurus and his Roman disciple, Lucretius, were both considered notoriously irreligious thinkers. Condemning religion as a source of morbid fears, Epicurus expounded his materialist philosophy largely in order to oppose superstitious beliefs in the immaterial. Lucretius felt an even more impassioned antipathy to religious mystery, and he celebrated Epicurus as Promethean savior of mankind: " 'Not the fam'd stories of the Deity / Not all the Thunder of the threatning Sky / Could stop his rising Soul.' "[38] Cecropia also attacks the "foolish feare, and fearful ignorance" that posit miraculous for natural causes. Her pagan hubris and her insistence that self-contentment is heaven enough identify her as an unabashed Epicurean.[39]

It is Machiavelli, however, whose formidable presence dominates

38. Quoted by George T. Buckley, *Atheism in the English Renaissance*, p. 10.

39. See Edwin Greenlaw, "The Captivity Episode in Sidney's *Arcadia*," pp. 59–63.

in this passage. His influence was far more sinister for the Renaissance, for his thought went beyond the libertine hedonism of Epicurus. Its political and psychological implications were profoundly unsettling. Sidney may have been more discriminating and less easily scandalized than most in his attitude toward Machiavelli. Irving Ribner has argued that Sidney shows a similar understanding of the difference between public and personal virtue, and his interest in political history is also secular and systematic.[40] Yet Sidney remains firmly moralistic in his approach to politics, and Ribner acknowledges that Sidney shared the conventional Tudor hatred for Machiavellian thought and drew on this hatred in his portrayal of villainy.[41] Machiavelli's indifference to religious mystery was considered particularly blasphemous, for despite his cautionary disclaimers, he probed its sources and effects with extraordinary speculative freedom. He restricted his remarks to pagan religious practices, but the scandalous point was lost on few; it involved what Hooker termed the "politic use of religion" and its unique disciplinary hold on believers: "for a politic use of religion they see there is, and by it they would gather that religion itself is a mere politic device, forged purposely to serve for that use. Men fearing God are thereby a great deal more effectually than by positive laws restrained from doing evil; inasmuch as those laws have no farther power than over our outward actions only, whereas unto men's inward cogitations, unto the privy intents and motions of their hearts, religion serveth for a bridle."[42] In his *Discourses*, Machiavelli praises Numa for fabricating miraculous tales about himself in order to impose his rule on the early Romans. This shrewd and ambitious charlatan "had recourse to religion as the most necessary and assured support of any civil society," and his task was made consider-

---

40. Irving Ribner, "Machiavelli and Sidney," p. 153.
41. Ibid.
42. Richard Hooker, *Of the Laws of Ecclesiastical Polity, Book V,* p. 19.

ably easier by the "untutored and superstitious" nature of his subjects.[43]

Such irreverence was, of course, the cause of the Elizabethans' excessive vilification of Machiavelli; their outrage, an indication of their obvious fascination. He and his disciples were accused of claiming " 'that the Scriptures were devised by men, only for policy sake, to maintain peace in states and kingdoms, to keep subjects in obedience to laws and loyalty to magistrates, by thus terrifying them from enormities when their consciences are possessed with an opinion of hell fire, and alluring them to subjection by hope of eternal life.' "[44]

This is, of course, precisely the claim Cecropia makes, and her entire argument follows from this impious premise. The subversive demystification of all authority, even God's, is the inevitable result of a purely rational conception of authority. The "justification" initiated this analytic assault, but Cecropia presses it to its limits. Her "politic" atheism is the most radical and thorough attack on the claims of sovereignty. She is, in fact, one of the few who follow their ideas through to a logical conclusion, pressing her rebellious claims with uncommon intellectual rigor. Pamela and Euarchus argue the case for obedience no less forcibly, but all the heroes waffle safely between these two poles. Cecropia's fate reveals the risks of logical consistency, and her ideas are discredited by their blasphemous implications.

Pamela then proceeds to annihilate her opponent, attacking Cecropia's atheism on all counts. Nature is governed by necessity rather than chance, Pamela insists, for the "goodly worke of which we are, and in which we live" is eternal, coherent, and invariable

43. Niccolo Macchiavelli, *Discourses on the First Ten Books of Titus Livius,* pp. 146–148.

44. John Dove, *Confutation of Atheism* (1605), quoted in Ernest A. Strathmann, *Sir Walter Ralegh,* p. 88.

(*NA*, 407–408). These qualities culminate in "perfect order, perfect beautie, perfect constancie" (*NA*, 408). Philosophically, Pamela is seeking to refute the Epicurean naturalism, the assumptions of which inform her opponent's argument. She goes right to the heart of the issue by focusing on necessity, for this was precisely the force Epicurus sought to deny. As Bertrand Russell explains, "Epicurus was a materialist, but not a determinist," for his atomic theory, unlike that of Democritus, proposes a random cosmology rather than one governed by natural law. "The conception of necessity in Greece was, as we have seen, religious in origin, and perhaps he [Epicurus] was right in considering that an attack on religion would be incomplete if it allowed necessity to survive."[45] Pamela's metaphysical abstractions acquire greater force with their translation into political terms. God is personalized as an "everlasting governour" whose "constancie" inspires Pamela's "true & lively devotion" (*NA*, 407). Greatest attention is given to the character of his providential government. Cecropia's nature, a random and relative "mingling of many" (*NA*, 409), evokes a horror of cosmic anarchy: Pamela contends that natural order could not possibly follow from

> many natures conspiring together, as in a popular government to establish this fayre estate; as if the Elementishe and ethereall partes should in their towne-house set downe the boundes of each ones office; then consider what followes: that there must needes have bene a wisedome which made them concurre: for their natures beyng absolute contrarie, in nature rather woulde have sought each others ruine, then have served as well consorted partes to such an unexpressable harmonie. For that contrary things should meete to make up a perfection without a force and Wisedome above their powers, is absolutely impossible; unless you will flie to that hissed-out opinion of Chaunce againe.
>
> (*NA*, 408)

45. Bertrand Russell, *A History of Western Philosophy*, p. 246.

Pamela's cosmology affords a telling contrast to the *New Arcadia*'s opening pastoral vision. At first glance, nature had appeared to be functioning in interdependent autonomy, with each organic impulse easily coordinated:

> There were hilles which garnished their proud heights with stately trees; humble valleis, whose base estate semed comforted with refreshing of silver rivers: medows, enameld with al sorts of ey-pleasing floures: thickets, which being lined with most pleasant shade, were witnessed so to by the chereful deposition of many wel-tuned birds: each pasture stored with sheep feeding with sober security, while the prety lambs with bleting oratory craved the dams comfort: here a shepheards boy piping, as though he should never be old: there a yong shepherdesse knitting, and withall singing, & it seemed that her voice comforted her hands to work, & her hands kept time to her voices musick. As for the houses of the country (for many houses came under their eye) they were all scattered, no two being one by th'other, & yet not so far off as that it barred mutual succour: a shew, as it were, of an accompanable solitarines, & of a civil wildnes.
>
> (*NA*, 13–14)

In this scene both physical and human nature contrive through mutual collaboration to produce the most pleasing ecological effects. Sidney presents a miniature of the chain of being in which the material, social, and aesthetic realms harmoniously combine. The lower orders, inanimate and vegetable, delight the eye by embellishing the scene with trees, rivers, flowers, and shady groves. Both man and the animals make music, but human music is enriched with a more complex and artful purpose. The shepherdess lightens her labor with song while the rhythm of her knitting gives measure to her music. The shepherd boy's piping, "as though he should never be old," makes one aware of the timeless and idealizing power of art. The houses (a circular return to inanimate objects, at this point shaped by conscious human purpose) are the final image of the intricately

organized synthesis. Their distance allows an "accompanable soli-
tarines, & . . . a civil wildnes," social advantages further sustained
by Arcadia's humane political order. This latter is said to derive
from "the well tempered minds of the people" and "the good lawes"
set down by "former princes" (*NA*, 19).

The actual basis of this order is revealed in Pamela's declamation,
which Lindheim calls the *New Arcadia*'s "doctrinal center."[46]
Pamela's theological authoritarianism provides a gloss of the narrative's political events, illuminating the source of all conflict and
difficulty. The harmonious collaboration of the work's opening
scenes is shown to require the constant exertion of providential control. The country's natural order is not the result of pastoral sym-
bioses, an active and organic reciprocity of natural elements, nor is
its utopian society the creation of its constituents. Only through
despotic organization can these "many contraries . . . proceede still
kept in an unitie" (*NA*, 409).

Pamela's theology reflects a general tendency of Calvinism toward
divine despotism; in Walzer's excellent phrase, "the chain of being
had been transformed into a chain of command."[47] "Only God's
command," he continues, "only the perpetual struggle of his saints,
imposed some minimal order on earth . . . the unity of the uni-
verse was imposed from above and was neither natural nor inherent;
it too depended directly and continuously upon the commands of
God, imagined as the chief magistrate of a cosmic city."[48] The theological tract translated by Sidney, de Mornay's *Trewnes of Christian
Religion*, is quite clear on this point, insisting on the need for a
divine "Governer" and Superiour":

> whence commeth this goodly proportion, and this orderly pro-
> ceeding of things by degrees? . . . Commeth it of the things

46. Nancy Rothwax Lindheim, "The Structure of Sidney's *Arcadia*," p. 43.
47. Walzer, *Saints*, p. 166.
48. Ibid., p. 161.

themselves? How can that bee? For seeing that nothing doth willingly become an underling unto others why bee not the heaviest masses allotted to the best shares? . . . Then is there a devider or distributer of these things, who having imparted them too others, had them first himselfe, and that most aboundantly; and who moreover is of necessitie, almightie, seeing that in so unequall partition, he holdeth them neverthelesse in concorde.[49]

The treatise repeatedly insists that "nothing moveth it selfe," for, if anything did, cosmic anarchy and "continual warre" would result.[50] De Mornay's treatment of Aristotle is interesting in this respect. Aristotle is included among the other sages of antiquity who give philosophic evidence of God's existence; his view of providence is based on the traditional chain of being. God is "the breeder and Mainteyner of all the things whereof this world is composed; and yet for all that, he entreth not into them, but his power and providence oversitting them from above . . . make all and every thing to doe according to their nature."[51] Aristotle is subsequently chastened, however, for giving "him self more to the seeking and searching of Naturall things, than to the mynding of the Author of them."[52]

Of course, "perfect order, perfect beautie, perfect constancie" do not prevail in a fallen world, and only fragmentary evidence of God's providence survives. In the New Arcadia, an idealized harmony is briefly sustained at its outset, but the country's pastoral order proves as evanescent as the beatific "Remembrance" of Urania that opens Book I. Protracted political upheaval and erotic tension

49. Philip de Mornay, A Woorke concerning the Trewness of the Christian Religion, "Begunne to be translated into English by Sir Philip Sidney Knight, and at his request finished by Arthur Golding," in Prose, Feuillerat, III, 205–206.
50. Ibid., pp. 207, 219.
51. Ibid., pp. 240–241.
52. Ibid., p. 285.

dominate the remainder of the narrative. According to Pamela, this increasing confusion is the inevitable consequence of leaving creatures to their natural devices: "their natures beyng absolute contrarie, in nature rather woulde have sought each others ruine, then have served as well consorted partes to such an unexpressable harmonie" (*NA*, 408). For orthodox Calvinists, the point of this doctrine is the natural depravity of each creature. Although Sidney gives this due emphasis, other irregular implications emerge from his narrative, causing problems of responsibility.

Pamela's "divinitie" establishes the enormity of Basilius's abdication, for one thing. In Sidney's fictive Eden, paternal negligence, rather than filial disobedience, is the original sin; the latter is simply one of several inevitable consequences of the former. No matter how "well-tempered" the minds of his subjects, or sound the constitutional order, or felicitous the natural advantages, pastoral concord can be sustained in Arcadia only by the constant predominance of patriarchal sovereignty. Its relaxation reduces all to chaotic confusion, and its restoration is essential to the renewal of the primal harmony briefly glimpsed in the opening scenes. Having effected this relaxation of paternal control, Sidney never allows its full restoration in his Arcadia. The revision breaks off in the midst of continuous conflict and chaotic dissolution. The *Old Arcadia's* conclusion represents another abdication of disciplinary control similar to Basilius's initial relinquishing—which, of course, started the entire process.

Thus the revision betrays a profound ambiguity in the Calvinist cosmology. The emphasis on God's absolute sovereignty has always been problematic. Seventeenth-century theologians, according to Perry Miller, realized the difficulty of establishing "any grounds for moral obligation," for without some modification, "Calvin's splendid vision of God's omnipotence would become, when taught to men of weaker resolution, an excuse for their licentiousness and a justification of their indolence."[53] Sidney's *Arcadia* represents, I think, an unconscious exploitation by an otherwise scrupulous and resolute moralist of this famous loophole in the Calvinist covenant. Though his heroes are hardly licentious or indolent, they tend toward an ethical inertia; their aberrations are indulged as the automatic consequence of the lapses of their sovereign. Son and subject are thus freed of considerable responsibility.

Yet, even with its compensatory ambiguities, this solution is too drastic for Sidney. While it relieves the heroes of all responsibility, it also reduces them to passive vulnerability. The risks of total submission to despotic sovereignty are at least as great as its advantages. Similarly, the starkly defined terms of the conflict between Cecropia and Pamela are also too absolute. Neither Sidney nor his heroes can emulate the women's rigor, Pamela's resignation being no less unfeasible than Cecropia's aggression. The remainder of the work backs off from these disturbing tendencies and evades the implications of Pamela's ultimate, despotic solution. The narrative plunges back down from this unitary transcendence to the realm of contingency and dissolution. One becomes absorbed again in the plot's sudden shifts and the heroes' oscillations. Despite its confusing ambiguities this ambience is what Sidney finds the most viable; the painful clarities of Pamela's "divinitie" are finally unacceptable to him.

The superiority of the heroines during their captivity has been noted by several critics.[54] Once again Sidney makes his women sustain greater risks, but this time it works to their advantage. Because more is risked, more is triumphantly gained in the *Arcadia's* most grueling struggle. The heroines fulfill the requirements of submis-

---

53. Perry Miller, *The New England Mind,* pp. 367–368.
54. See Tillyard, *English Epic,* p. 308, and Myron Turner, "The Heroic Ideal in Sidney's Revised *Arcadia,* p. 71.

sion and self-control, requirements that prove impossible for their male counterparts. Yet these feminine virtues, as Sidney depicts them, are in some ways rather ambiguous. In the *Old Arcadia,* the heroines' passive dependency receives much greater emphasis. Pamela may strive against her attraction to Musidorus "with a true-tempered virtue" (*OA,* 98), but when he discloses his true identity, she is brought near to a "dull yielding-over her forces" by a well-timed love song (*OA,* 107). Philoclea first appears as an infantile ingenue of "unspotted simplicity" (*OA,* 108), whose innocence is simply a point of departure for an abrupt, impassioned fall.

In the *New Arcadia,* love's conquest is not so complete. Musidorus's revelation of his identity elicits no sign of weakness from Pamela, as she questions her suitor "with a setled countenance, not accusing any kind of inwarde motion" (*NA,* 163), and she responds to his love song "without shew either of favour or disdaine" (*NA,* 164). The poise manifest in this scene is the basis for her awesome serenity later on when she is held captive. Philoclea is still more docile than her sister, and she concedes "victorie" to Pyrocles immediately after he makes known his identity and declares his love. Yet she orders him to "use it with virtue" (*NA,* 260), and by maintaining her composure she insures fulfillment of this condition. Pyrocles wants to consummate their "imbracements . . . with the chiefe armes of his desire" on the spot, "but Philoclea commaunded the contrary" (*NA,* 261). Despite her lover's nominal authority, Philoclea retains command in their relationship.

Sidney thus recreates his heroines in the second version, allowing them a significant edge on their lovers and far more self-control. Their composure in love allows them to withstand far more violent pressures during their captivity. Yet their exemplary virtue remains essentially passive, tending near the very end toward a dangerous quietism. Their triumph consists of saintly endurance, and although they resist the assaults on their integrity, they abstain from any action. As Pamela's speech makes clear, they are exalted by their trusting obedience to paternal and providential authority.

Their posture in captivity, although exemplary in many respects, cannot be emulated by the heroes. For Sidney, the virtues of hero and heroine are mutually exclusive. Nancy Lindheim has shown how this distinction is maintained in two crucial scenes of the *Old Arcadia*. In the first, Pyrocles and Philoclea are caught in the bedchamber by Dametas, and they argue about what to do next. Pyrocles insists that "the very suffering of some things is a certain proof of want of courage," and he rejects her course of "submitting ourselves to each unworthy misery which the foolish world may lay upon us" (*OA*, 297). His sense of mastery requires action, even if it means suicide, for "if God have made us masters of anything, it is of our own lives" (*OA*, 297), and he is unpersuaded by her argument. Her threatening to kill herself if he does is the only thing that prevents Pyrocles from braining himself. Subsequently, the heroes' commitment to the active life persists during their own "captivity" as they await trial. In their reflections on the afterlife, they argue for the endurance of the individual's "vital power" and "moral virtues" (*OA*, 372). Lindheim's analysis of these scenes clearly shows that Pyrocles and Musidorus undergo no conversion to the virtues of their female counterparts.[55] Just as they escape the consequences of untrammeled aggression, the heroes also avoid the risks of submissive obedience. Sexual distinctions are maintained with schematic precision, for the heroes' virility precludes subjection "to each unworthy misery" (*OA*, 297).

The conflict between the women becomes still more brutal before the reader escapes its rigors. When Cecropia resorts to physical torture, the heroines simply endure. Philoclea writhes in thrilling agonies of pathos, but this is Cecropia's only satisfaction: "as for the graunting your request, know for certaine you lose your labours, [I] being every day furtherof-minded from becoming his wife, who

55. Lindheim, "Vision," pp. 141–142, 146.

useth me like a slave" (*NA,* 471). Cecropia is denied even this pleasure by Pamela who endures all with regal dignity and yields nothing: "And then, Beastly woman (saide she) followe on, doo what thou wilt, and canst upon me: for I know thy power is not unlimited. Thou maist well wracke this sillie bodie, but me thou canst never overthrowe. For my part, I will not doo thee the pleasure to desire death of thee: but assure thy self, both my life and death, shall triumph with honour, laying shame upon thy detestable tyranny" (*NA,* 472–473). Their exemplary endurance secures them an impressive ascendancy.

In sharp contrast is the behavior of Pyrocles. He succumbs to a degraded confusion and anxiety, and his frantic exertions are both excessive and ineffectual:

> But Zelmane (who had from time to time understood the cruell dealing they had used to the sisters, & now had her own eies wounded with the sight of ones death) was so confused withall (her courage still rebelling against her wit, desiring still with force to doo impossible matters) that as her desire was stopped with power, so her conceit was darkned with a mist of desire. For blind Love, & invincible valure stil would cry out, that it could not be, Philoclea should be in so miserable estate, and she not relieve her: and so while she haled her wit to her courage, she drew it from his owne limits."
>
> (*NA,* 479–480)

For him, the captivity confounds his faculties, not only rendering them inadequate but throwing them into opposition. Pamela's "Reason taught her there was no resistance," after brief consideration, "(for to just resistance first her harte was enclined)" (*NA,* 472). Not so Pyrocles, from whom tyrannical power elicits willful opposition as it thwarts his will; indeed, will desperately opposes wit, obscuring all "with a mist of desire" (*NA,* 479). Pyrocles subsequently vacillates between defeatism and desperate intrigue. Deprived of all its resources, his will is initially overwhelmed: "her [i.e., Zelmane's] valure overmastred, her wit beguiled" by the "fetters of servitude," he succumbs to depression: "griefe gat seate in her softned minde" (*NA*, 436). He is nearly stupified by his "solitarie Sorrowe, with a continuall circle in her selfe, going out at her owne mouth, to come in againe at her owne eares" (*NA*, 436). While the women channel their troubles into a contemplative ascent, Pyrocles' feelings turn back on themselves, stagnating in their circular self-enclosure.

His melancholy ruminations are relieved only by the treachery of Artesia, for she provides him with an opportunity for action. This alone restores a fragile balance to Zelmane's character: she returned "the government of her courage to wit, & was content to familiarize herselfe" (*NA*, 437) with Artesia's conspiracy against their captors. The princesses, however, will not share in such base machinations, and they expose the entire scheme. Pyrocles' exertions meet with a similar reproach when he again proposes deceit as the only solution to their plight. He pleads with Philoclea to "pretend a yeelding unto Cecropias request" (*NA*, 480). She refuses even at the risk of losing her life: "for dissimulation, my Pyrocles, my simplicitie is such, that I have hardly bene able to keepe a straight way; what shall I doo in a crooked?" (*NA*, 481). Her persistence in the "straight way" embodies the *Arcadia*'s cardinal virtue; Philoclea rejects all her lover's proposals, "sweetly continuing constant" by this means alone (*NA*, 482).

Nevertheless, Pyrocles' deviations "from the right line of virtue" do not provoke one's contempt (*NA*, 117). Instead, one delights in the exciting "contrarietie in passions" (*NA*, 490) and admires his frantic impulses and stratagems. These have, in fact, engaged one's sympathy throughout the *Arcadia*, even when they are dangerously wayward. Even when his degradation is complete near the end of the captivity, this continues to be true. Cecropia has arranged two macabre spectacles to unnerve her captives thoroughly. She fails to shake Philoclea, but Pyrocles is completely defeated. Although Philoclea's composure "wavered" at the moment of her sister's simulated death, she finally withstands this cruel shock:

> There was no assault given to the sweet Philocleas mind, that entered so far, as this: for where to all paines and daungers of her selfe, foresight with (his Lieutenant Resolution) had made ready defence; now with the love she bare her sister, she was driven to a stay, before she determined: but long she staied not, before this reason did shine unto her, that since in her selfe she preferred death before such a base servitude, love did teach her to wish the same to her sister. Therefore crossing her armes, & looking sideward upon the ground, Do what you wil (said she) with us: for my part, heaven shall melt before I be removed.
>
> (*NA*, 475-476)

When Pyrocles is presented with the sight of Philoclea's head in a bloody basin, he succumbs to blasphemous, suicidal despair. His is the same "wilde furie of desperate agonie" all Sidney's heroes must ultimately suffer (*NA*, 483). This strenuous, forceful anguish, first evinced in the histrionics of Plangus, is consummated by the actions of Amphialus. With all of them, filial hostility acquires an apocalyptic intensity, but heaven's punitive wrath (as well as the reader's disapproval) is forestalled by several typical devices, beginning here with an unsuccessful suicide.

After several furious reproaches to "tyraunt heaven, traytor earth, blinde providence" for allowing Philoclea's death—"no justice, how is this done? how is this suffered? hath this world a government?" (*NA*, 483)—Pyrocles inevitably attempts an "unnaturall murdering of him selfe" (*NA*, 483). With equal inevitability, he bungles it, and he concludes this scene with an overwrought oath of revenge and restitution. Like Amphialus, he secures one's sympathy initially through his suffering. Yet Sidney's presentation of Pyrocles is far more complex in its procedures, and his defense of his principal hero is both more subtle and more adroit. Sidney shows Pyrocles, after his rather slapstick suicide attempt, deciding "first to destroy, man, woman, and childe, that were any way of kinne to them that were accessarie to this crueltie; then to raze the Castle, and to builde a sumptuous monument for her sister, and a most sumptuous for her selfe; and then, himself to die upon her tomb" (*NA*, 483–484). Pyrocles becomes laughably compulsive and hyperbolic in sorrow, his grief degenerating to ranting bathos: "wo be to me, if any exceede me in wofulnes" (*NA*, 484).

Pyrocles' blasphemous belligerence, already muted by pathos and reflexive aggression, is still further obscured by his comic excesses. Sidney appeals first to sentiment and then to humor in an attempt to spare his hero from the consequences of his conduct. However humiliating, Pyrocles' absurdity gets him off the hook on which Cecropia impales herself. As I have indicated previously, these devices are essential to Sidney's Arcadian fantasies. Sidney urges all his readers, along with his sister, to regard Pyrocles' antics as mere "follies," which we "blame not, but laugh at" (*OA*, 3). The comic bathos of this scene makes it even easier to regard the main character "with more affection than judgement" (*OA*, 26).

Sidney's final intervention on his hero's behalf is still more dramatically beneficent. Just before the abrupt termination of Book III, he allows Pyrocles a brief heroic recovery. The young hero commands not only indulgence but respect in these final scenes. Once Amphialus is dispatched from battle, his brutal ally, Anaxius, threatens to kill them all. The captives respond to this "new alarum" along characteristic lines (*NA*, 503), and one assumes the issue will be the same. Once again, the heroines' "minds, which were so unconstantly dealt with" remain unshaken, and their "constancy" is increased still further by adversity (*NA*, 503). Pyrocles, in turn, is "winded . . . againe into the former maze of perplexitie" (*NA*, 504). The heroines are serenely resigned to chaste martyrdom, while the hero desperately strives for their escape.

The upshot of this crisis, however, is completely different. In this context, Pyrocles' "perswasions to temporize" are shown to be neither ineffectual nor corrupt (*NA*, 508). In fact, it is now the women whose impulses lead them into error, for their saintly zeal tends toward a dangerous quietism. Pyrocles prevents these "excellent Ladies from seeking by the pasport of death, to escape those base dangers whereunto they found themselves subject" (*NA*, 512). By persuading them "to overpasse many insolent indignities" (*NA*, 512), he gains time and a chance for effective action.

This all comes to pass when events bring them "to the streight she [i.e., Zelmane] most feared for them, either of death or dishonor" (*NA*, 512). Pyrocles rises grandly "to attend the uttermost occasion," sustained by his "heroicall courage" and "wit" (*NA*, 512–513); having been frustrated for so long, both faculties are finally given an appropriate outlet. Similarly, his virile identity emerges from its oppressive disguise, and he is at last permitted to act "according to the Pyroclean nature" (*NA*, 518). When passive "abiding no longer abroad in the matter, she that had not put off, though she had disguised, Pyrocles" (*NA*, 513), emerges for a fully masculine fight, "where manhood blew the trumpet" (*NA*, 516). Just before the narrative abruptly ends, the hero's aggressive potency is dramatically expressed and morally vindicated.

But not quite. As in all of Sidney's expressions of aggression, ambivalence again prevails, and the action is denied consummation. Pyrocles and Anaxius, like Amphialus and Musidorus, fight to an enervated standstill, and their struggle ceases. This last struggle is intense but static, culminating in an emblematic impasse. The reasons for this sudden break in midsentence are, of course, obscure. William Leigh Godshalk argues that Sidney must have at least completed the last sentence and attributes this interruption to the loss of some pages "from the end of the MS."[56] A. C. Hamilton sug-

56. William Leigh Godshalk, "Sidney's Revision of the *Arcadia*, Books III–V," p. 177.

gests that the break could be blamed on the scribe, or the foul papers, or the difficulties of revision, or simply Sidney's death.[57] Or it may be deliberate: "It is unfinished because his life was unfinished, and he expected always to be summoned to virtuous action; but chiefly because it is to be finished by the reader";[58] in other words, its true completion is the practical application of its lessons and examples to our lives. Hamilton also claims that the "triumph of love and virtue in Book III, in both the princes and princesses, now resolves the moral argument of the original, so that even in its unfinished state, the *New Arcadia* is unified and essentially complete."[59] This assessment is, however, qualified, if not contradicted, by his discussion of the "limitations of masculine virtue," for he acknowledges that neither hero "is able to free the princesses despite his utmost endeavour" and says that the "explanation for their failure would seem to be that love and virtue remain divided in them, as they do in Amphialus."[60] Thus the conclusion's "triumph" is not so inclusive or definitive as Hamilton implies, and a central problem is left unresolved. Indeed, even if one allows for the possibility of some sort of immediate conclusion to this scene, now lost, it is doubtful that the missing pages would settle many of the issues left dangling. I suspect that the break is deliberate in another sense. This last scene represents, I think, the *New Arcadia's* final evasive compromise. The hero's potency is contained and neutralized without being crushed, and his circumscribed virility is, in turn, vividly sustained. Moreover, the issues raised in the captivity are ignored in the agitation and sword play of the final chapters. Sidney's vision of an embattled—and arrested—heroism may afford him the most tenable resting place. Despite all the commotion and ambiguity, this

57. A. C. Hamilton, *Sir Philip Sidney*, pp. 172–173.
58. Ibid., p. 173.
59. Ibid., p. 159.
60. Ibid., p. 163.

last scene is more acceptable than the work's "doctrinal center" and its stark certitudes.

The *New Arcadia* concludes with a suspension of action—probably the most appropriate resolution. The revision's third book is in many ways the most interesting, for its various narrative shifts clearly reflect the evasive, contradictory tendencies of Elizabethan culture. The strategic force and critical clarity of Sidney's early military accounts are diminished by a subsequent absorption in chivalric adventure and romantic pathos. The more speculative assault on authority is discredited by its villainous associations and logical consistency. Finally, the captivity evokes an increasingly apocalyptic view of politics, defining subjection in absolute, religious terms. For many in the sixteenth century, this constituted the ultimate solution of life's complexities, and many of Sidney's critics display evidence of its enduring aesthetic appeal. Sidney, however, does not sustain such a perspective despite its edifying prospects. Instead, the book moves away from this absolute, seemingly inevitable solution and returns to the arena of contingency and confusion. The work ends with a vision of dramatic but ineffectual heroism.

In this last respect, the book's end resembles Sidney's own. His death may also represent a kind of compromise between irreconcilable contradictions, the same contradictions encountered in his works. Sidney had proved an unhappy and inept courtier because his insistence on his "native, & legall freedom" had provoked the Queen's hostility and diminished his political influence.[61] His desire for autonomy was further hindered by guilt and uncertainty because ambition could readily decline into mere "selfnesse." Military adventure finally offered an escape from these frustrations, and Sidney plunged into the freedom and glories of battle. His fame was secured by his reckless bravery and deeds of exemplary selflessness. "I understand I am called very ambitious and prowd at home," he wrote not

61. Greville, *Life*, p. 69.

long before his death, "but certainly if thei knew my ha[rt] thei woold not altogether so judg me."[62] His demise at Zutphen would clear him of those charges.

Sidney's was indeed a splendid end, with its acts of bravery and self-sacrifice. His concern for others, his stoical endurance, his earnest repentance and theological concern were held up as a model for all. His prolonged decline was an extraordinary performance, for as Stephen Greenblatt explains in his study of Sir Walter Ralegh, "a 'good death' was no accident of blind courage; it was the result of discipline, intelligence, timing, and careful preparation. The truly memorable death scenes of the age, on the scaffold, at home, or even on the battlefield—Sir Thomas More, Mary Queen of Scots, Sir Philip Sidney, John Donne, Ralegh, Charles I—were precisely that: *scenes,* presided over by actor-playwrights who had brilliantly conceived and thoroughly mastered their roles."[63] Yet, for all its splendor, there is something wrong with Sidney's death: an absence of true purpose, a tinge of reckless waste and self-destructiveness. His dying in this way had little to do with his long-range goals; it really served no political or military purpose. Cleared thus of charges of ambitious calculation, Sidney was reduced to a kind of glamorous irrelevance. Languet had warned him that "young men who rush into danger incautiously almost always meet an inglorious end, and deprive themselves of the power of serving their country; for a man who falls at an early age cannot have done much for his country."[64] Languet was wrong about "an inglorious end," but in its practical respects, his warning was fulfilled. Elizabeth had the last word. In reprimanding Sir Charles Blount, Lord Mountjoy for dashing off to battle without her permission, she admonished him with Sidney's example: "Serve me so (quoth she) once more, and I will

62. "Correspondence," LXXXIX, "To Sir Francis Walsingham" (Mar. 24, 1586), *Prose,* Feuillerat, III, 167.
63. Stephen J. Greenblatt, *Sir Walter Ralegh,* p. 15.
64. *Languet,* Pears, p. 137.

lay you fast enough for running; you will never leave it untill you are knockt on the head, as that inconsiderate fellow Sidney was."[65]

In my interpretation, Sidney's death presents a pattern encountered throughout his literature. His end is dramatically impressive, stirring admiration and sympathy, and it releases him from the conflicts between autonomy and submission. But Sidney's final performance neither confronts nor resolves those conflicts, and at Zutphen, of course, it cost him his life. In his poetry and fiction, the conclusions are less grim, but they still leave matters dangling; one has doubts about their relevance to the persistent contradictions of the text. All of Sidney's stories trace a movement to and away from domination, never breaking free and never completely submitting. Astrophil's oscillations between abject devotion, importunate desire, and bitter despair sustain the tensions of the sequence through to the end. The abrupt and arbitrary triumph of the heroes in the *Old Arcadia* does nothing to alter their subordination and dependence, and the terms of this triumph are never made clear. The epic conflicts of the revision are suspended in midsentence. All Sidney's stories culminate in a pattern of ambivalence and evasion. No resolution is possible, the conflicts are partly side-stepped, and yet their persistence is still felt.

These contradictions constitute one of the most fascinating and essential aspects of Sidney's writings, and their source must be understood. Sidney finally cannot make up his mind about the central issues of his life and art: obedience and autonomy. He cannot follow his more radical impulses through to their conclusion, nor can he accept the conservative orthodoxies of conventional political thought. His uncertainty is increased by feelings of guilt and anxiety. Sidney's curiosity and intelligence were great, and he faced these issues directly; but each of these difficulties imposed severe limitations on his capacities.

65. Sir Robert Naunton, *Fragmenta Regalia,* ed. Edward Arber, p. 33.

An accurate understanding of these limitations and their sources is crucial to an assessment of Sidney's accomplishments. In this respect, the revision's third book is the most revealing thing he wrote. It comprehends all the crucial issues of his art and career—romantic passion, military strategy, political theory and statecraft, chivalric adventure, and theological speculation—and it seeks to work these into a coherent framework. The eventual failure of this enterprise does not diminish its speculative brilliance and daring. Sidney's inquiry is not constrained by the consistent orthodoxy of someone like Greville. Though the latter was more adaptive and flexible in his political career, he seems to have depended on an exaltation of obedience and a gloomy Calvinist pessimism. Sidney was more optimistic and reckless and less doggedly consistent in his thinking. His youth, temperament, and celebrated *sprezzatura* may have prevented him from glimpsing the full implications of his various undertakings, and thus he could escape Greville's disillusion and solemn resignation. Certainly, the *Arcadia*'s equivocations reveal a mind that draws back from unsettling depths of comprehension. Yet by continually begging the crucial questions of autonomy and submission, Sidney keeps them alive and engaging. Even though he could not solve all the problems he posed himself, Sidney brings an alert and restless energy to this very large task.

REFERENCES

Primary Sources

Sidney, Sir Philip. *An Apology for Poetry, or the Defence of Poetry.* Ed. Geoffrey Shepherd. 1965; rpt. Manchester: Manchester University Press, 1973.

The Correspondence of Sir Philip Sidney and Hubert Languet. Trans. Stuart A. Pears. London: William Pickering, 1845.

The Countess of Pembroke's Arcadia (The Old Arcadia). Ed. Jean Robertson. Oxford: Clarendon, 1973.

The Poems of Sir Philip Sidney. Ed. William A. Ringler, Jr. 1962; rpt. Oxford: Clarendon, 1967.

The Prose Works of Sir Philip Sidney. Ed. Albert Feuillerat. 4 vols.. 1912; rpt. Cambridge: Cambridge University Press, 1969.

Secondary Sources

Akrigg, G. P. V. *Shakespeare and the Earl of Southampton.* Cambridge, Mass.: Harvard University Press, 1968.

Allen, J. W. *A History of Political Thought in the Sixteenth Century.* 1928; rpt. London: Methuen, 1957.

Anderson, D. M. "The Trial of the Princes in the *Arcadia,* Book V." *Review of English Studies,* 8 (1957), 409–412.

Ascham, Roger. *The Scholemaster. In English Works.* Ed. William Aldis Wright. Cambridge: Cambridge University Press, 1904.

Auerbach, Erich. *Mimesis: The Representation of Reality in Western Literature.* Trans. Willard R. Trask. 1946; rpt. Princeton: Princeton University Press, 1968.

REFERENCES

Bacon, Francis. *A Selection of His Works.* Ed. Sidney Warhaft. 1965; rpt. Toronto: Macmillan of Canada, 1967.

Bindoff, S. T. *Tudor England.* 1950; rpt. New York: Penguin, 1969.

Briggs, William D. "Political Ideas in Sidney's *Arcadia.*" *Studies in Philology,* 28 (1931), 137–161.

Buckley, George T. *Atheism in the English Renaissance.* Chicago: University of Chicago Press, 1932.

Castiglione, Baldesar. *The Book of the Courtier.* Trans. Charles S. Singleton. New York: Anchor-Doubleday, 1959.

Craig, Hardin. *The Enchanted Glass: The Elizabethan Mind in Literature.* 1935; rpt. Oxford: Blackwell & Mott, 1960.

Crews, Frederick, ed. *Psychoanalysis and Literary Process.* Cambridge, Mass.: Winthrop, 1970.

Danby, John F. *Poets on Fortune's Hill: Studies in Sidney, Shakespeare, Beaumont and Fletcher.* 1952; rpt. Port Washington, N. Y.: Kennikat, 1966.

Davis, Natalie Zemon. *Society and Culture in Early Modern France.* Stanford: Stanford University Press, 1975.

Davis, Walter R. "A Map of Arcadia: Sidney's Romance in Its Tradition." In *Sidney's Arcadia.* New Haven: Yale Studies in English, 158 (1965), 1–179.

Dipple, Elizabeth. "Harmony and Pastoral in the *Old Arcadia.*" *English Literary History,* 35 (1968), 309–328.

Dipple, Elizabeth. " 'Unjust Justice' in the *Old Arcadia.*" *Studies in English Literature,* 1500–1900, 10 (1970), 83–101.

Eliot, T. S. *Selected Essays.* 1932; rpt. London: Faber & Faber, 1972.

Empson, William. *Seven Types of Ambiguity.* 3rd ed. 1930; rpt. New York: New Directions, n.d.

Empson, William. *Some Versions of Pastoral.* 1935; rpt. New York: New Directions, 1974.

Erikson, Erik H. *Young Man Luther.* 1958; rpt. New York: Norton, 1962.

Ferguson, Margaret W. "Sidney's *Defence of Poetry:* A Retrial." *Boundary* 2 (Forthcoming).

Franklin, Julian H., trans. and ed. *Constitutionalism and Resistance in the Sixteenth Century: Three Treatises by Hotman, Beza, and Mornay.* New York: Pegasus, 1969.

Freud, Sigmund. "The Economic Problem in Masochism" (1924). Trans. Joan Riviere. In *General Psychological Theory: Papers on Metapsychology.* Ed. Philip Rieff. 1963; rpt. New York: Collier-Macmillan, 1968.

Godshalk, William Leigh. "Sidney's Revision of the *Arcadia,* Books III–V." *Philological Quarterly,* 43 (1964), 171–184.

Gray, Hanna H. "Renaissance Humanism: The Pursuit of Eloquence." In

Renaissance Essays. Ed. Paul Oskar Kristeller and Philip P. Wiener. New York: Harper & Row, 1968.

Greenblatt, Stephen J. "Sidney's *Arcadia* and the Mixed Mode." *Studies in Philology,* 70 (1973), 269–278.

Greenblatt, Stephen J. *Sir Walter Ralegh: The Renaissance Man and His Roles.* New Haven: Yale University Press, 1973.

Greenlaw, Edwin. "The Captivity Episode in Sidney's *Arcadia.*" In *The Manly Anniversary Studies in Language and Literature.* Chicago: University of Chicago Press, 1923.

Greville, Sir Fulke. *The Life of the Renowned Sir Philip Sidney.* Ed. Nowell Smith. Oxford: Clarendon, 1907.

Greville, Sir Fulke. *Poems and Dramas.* Ed. Geoffrey Bullough. New York: Oxford University Press, 1945.

Guarini, Giovanni Battista. *Il Pastor Fido.* Trans. Sir Richard Fanshawe. Ed. Walter F. Staton, Jr., and William E. Simeone. Oxford: Clarendon, 1964.

Hamilton, A. C. *Sir Philip Sidney: A Study of His Life and Works.* Cambridge: Cambridge University Press, 1977.

Harvey, Gabriel. "Pierce's Supererogation." In *Elizabethan Critical Essays.* Ed. Gregory Smith. Vol. II. 1904; rpt. London: Oxford University Press, 1959.

Haydn, Hiram. *The Counter-Renaissance.* 1950; rpt. New York: Grove, 1960.

Helgerson, Richard. *The Elizabethan Prodigals.* Berkeley and Los Angeles: University of California Press, 1976.

Hill, Christopher. *The Century of Revolution,* 1603–1714. 1961; rpt. New York: Norton, 1966.

Hill, Christopher. *Intellectual Origins of the English Revolution.* 1965; rpt. London: Panther-Granada, 1972.

Hooker, Richard. *Of the Laws of Ecclesiastical Polity, Book V.* Ed. Ernest Rhys. London: Dent, 1907.

Howell, Roger. *Sir Philip Sidney: The Shepherd Knight.* Boston: Little, Brown, 1968.

Hunter, G. K. *John Lyly: The Humanist as Courtier.* Cambridge, Mass.: Harvard University Press, 1962.

Johnson, Paul. *Elizabeth I: A Study in Power and Intellect.* London: Weidenfeld & Nicolson, 1974.

Jonson, Ben. *Works.* Ed. C. H. Herford and Percy Simpson. 11 vols. Oxford: Clarendon, 1925.

Kalstone, David. *Sidney's Poetry: Contexts and Interpretations.* 1965; rpt. New York: Norton, 1970.

Kalstone, David. "Sir Philip Sidney." In *English Poetry and Prose,* 1540–1674. Ed. Christopher Ricks. London: Barrie & Jenkins, 1970.

Kimbrough, Robert. *Sir Philip Sidney*. Boston: Twayne, 1971.

Kimbrough, Robert, and Philip Murphy. "The Helmingham Hall Manuscript of Sidney's *The Lady of May:* A Commentary and Transcription." *Renaissance Drama,* NS 1(1968), 103–119.

Lacey, Robert. *Robert, Earl of Essex*. New York: Atheneum, 1971.

Lanham, Richard A. "The Old *Arcadia*." In *Sidney's Arcadia*. New Haven: Yale Studies in English, 158 (1965), 181–405.

Lanham, Richard A. "Sidney: The Ornament of His Age." *Southern Review: An Australian Journal of Literary Studies,* 2 (1967), 319–340.

Lanham, Richard A. "*Astrophil and Stella:* Pure and Impure Persuasion." *English Literary Renaissance,* 2 (1972), 100–115.

Leavis, F. R. *Revaluation*. 1947; rpt. New York: Norton, 1963.

Lever, J. W. *The Elizabethan Love Sonnet*. London: Methuen, 1956.

Levy, F. J. "Philip Sidney Reconsidered." *English Literary Renaissance,* 2 (1972), 5–18.

Lewis, C. S. *The Allegory of Love*. 1936; rpt. Oxford: Oxford University Press, 1968.

Lewis, C. S. *English Literature in the Sixteenth Century*. Oxford: Clarendon, 1954.

Lewis, Piers I. "Literary and Political Attitudes in Sidney's *Arcadia*." Diss. Harvard 1964.

Lindenbaum, Peter Alan. "The Anti-pastoral Pastoral: The Education of Fallen Man in the Renaissance." Diss. University of California at Berkeley 1970.

Lindheim, Nancy Rothwax. "The Structure of Sidney's *Arcadia*." Diss. University of California at Berkeley 1966.

Lindheim, Nancy Rothwax. "Sidney's *Arcadia*, Book II: Retrospective Narrative." *Studies in Philology,* 64 (1967), 159–186.

Lindheim, Nancy Rothwax. "Vision, Revision, and the 1593 Text of the *Arcadia*." *English Literary Renaissance,* 2 (1972), 136–147.

Machiavelli, Niccolo. *The Prince*. Trans. Luigi Ricci. Rev. E. R. P. Vincent. *Discourses on the First Ten Books of Titus Livius*. Trans. Christian E. Detmold. In *The Prince and the Discourses*. New York: Modern Library-Random House, 1940.

Marenco, Franco. "Double Plot in Sidney's Old *Arcadia*." *Modern Language Review,* 64 (1969), 248–263.

Marlowe, Christopher. *Plays and Poems*. Ed. M. R. Ridley. 1955; rpt. London: Everyman-Dent, 1967.

Miller, Perry. *The New England Mind: The Seventeenth Century*. 1939; rpt. Boston: Beacon, 1968.

Milton, John. *Complete Poems and Major Prose*. Ed. Merritt Y. Hughes. Indianapolis: Odyssey-Bobbs-Merrill, 1957.

Montgomery, Robert L. *Symmetry and Sense: The Poetry of Sir Philip Sidney*. Austin: University of Texas Press, 1961.

More, Thomas. *Utopia*. Trans. Peter K. Marshall. 1965; rpt. New York: Washington Square-Pocket Books, 1967.

Naunton, Sir Robert. *Fragmenta Regalia*. Ed. Edward Arber. London: English Reprints, IX (1870), 1–64.

Neale, J. E. *Queen Elizabeth I: A Biography*, 1934; rpt. New York: Anchor-Doubleday, 1957.

Neale, J. E. *Elizabeth I and Her Parliaments*, 1584–1601. 1958; rpt. New York: Norton, 1966.

Orgel, Stephen. *The Jonsonian Masque*. Cambridge, Mass.: Harvard University Press, 1965.

Osborn, James M. *Young Philip Sidney*, 1572–1577. New Haven: Yale University Press, 1972.

Rebholz, Ronald A. *The Life of Sir Fulke Greville*. Oxford: Clarendon, 1971.

Ribner, Irving. "Machiavelli and Sidney: The *Arcadia* of 1590." *Studies in Philology*, 47 (1950), 152–172.

Ribner, Irving. "Sir Philip Sidney on Civil Insurrection." *Journal of the History of Ideas*, 13 (1952), 257–265.

Rieff, Philip. *Freud: The Mind of the Moralist*. 1959; rpt. New York: Anchor-Doubleday, 1961.

Robertson, Jean. "Sir Philip Sidney and Lady Penelope Rich." *Review of English Studies*, 15 (1964), 296–297.

Rowse, A. L. *The England of Elizabeth: The Structure of Society*. London: Macmillan, 1951.

Rudenstine, Neil L. *Sidney's Poetic Development*. Cambridge, Mass.: Harvard University Press, 1967.

Russell, Bertrand. *A History of Western Philosophy*. 1945; rpt. New York: Simon & Schuster, n.d.

Salomon, Louis B. *The Rebellious Lover in English Poetry*. Philadelphia: University of Pennsylvania Press, 1931.

Spencer, Theodore. "The Poetry of Sir Philip Sidney." *English Literary History*, 12 (1945), 251–278.

Stillinger, Jack. "The Biographical Problem of *Astrophel and Stella*." *Journal of English and Germanic Philology*, 59 (1960), 617–639.

Stone, Lawrence. *The Crisis of the Aristocracy, 1588–1641*. Abridged ed. London: Oxford University Press, 1967.

Strathmann, Ernest A. *Sir Walter Ralegh: A Study in Elizabethan Skepticism*. New York: Columbia University Press, 1951.

Talbert, Ernest William. *The Problem of Order: Elizabethan Political Commonplaces and an Example of Shakespeare's Art*. Chapel Hill: University of North Carolina Press, 1962.

REFERENCES

Tillyard, E. M. W. *The English Epic and Its Backgrounds.* London: Chatto & Windus, 1954.

Turner, Myron. "The Heroic Ideal in Sidney's Revised *Arcadia.*" *Studies in English Literature, 1500–1900,* 10 (1970), 63–82.

Tuve, Rosemond. *Elizabethan and Metaphysical Imagery.* 1947; rpt. Chicago: University of Chicago Press, 1968.

Wallace, Malcolm William. *The Life of Sir Philip Sidney.* Cambridge: Cambridge University Press, 1915.

Walzer, Michael. *The Revolution of the Saints: A Study in the Origins of Radical Politics.* Cambridge, Mass.: Harvard University Press, 1965.

Weinberg, Bernard. *A History of Literary Criticism in the Italian Renaissance.* Chicago: University of Chicago Press, 1961.

Wyatt, Sir Thomas. *Collected Poems.* Ed. Kenneth Muir. 1949; rpt. Cambridge, Mass.: Harvard University Press, 1963.

Young, Richard B. "English Petrarke: A Study of Sidney's *Astrophel and Stella.*" In *Three Studies in the Renaissance: Sidney, Jonson, Milton.* New Haven: Yale Studies in English, 138 (1958), 1–88.

Zeeveld, W. Gordon. "The Uprising of the Commons in Sidney's *Arcadia.*" *Modern Language Notes,* 48 (1933), 209–217.

INDEX